The Quest for Revival

Experiencing Great Revivals of the Past,
Empowering You for God's Move Today!

by
Ron McIntosh

Harrison House
Tulsa, Oklahoma

Previously published as *Keep the Flame Burning: Igniting the People of God for the Next Move of the Spirit*
Previous ISBN 089274-693-9

Published by Harrison House Publishers
Shippensburg, PA 17257

ISBN 13 TP: 978-1-6675-0238-0
ISBN 13 eBook: 978-1-6675-0239-7
ISBN audio: 978-1-6675-0240-3

For Worldwide Distribution, Printed in the U.S.A.

1 2 3 4 5 6 7 8 / 27 26 25 24 23

Dedication

I want to dedicate this work to those who have been particular inspirations to me.

First, to Evangelist Mario Murillo, who initially put the seeds of revival in my life. His thoughts and influence are to be found directly and indirectly throughout this book. The thoughts and insights concerning Josiah's revival, Ezekiel's perspective on the potential of revival, the key to pursuing products and not by-products were all sown into my life years ago from his ministry and friendship. I owe him a great debt.

To Carlton Pearson, founder and pastor of Higher Dimensions Family Church, Tulsa, Oklahoma, my pastor and dear friend for many years. His encouragement, both personally and for this work, motivated me to press on when I wanted to quit.

I also dedicate this work to Tim Storey, without whose encouragement I would never have been motivated to begin or complete the task. His love of God and hunger for revival rekindled the flame in me.

Most of all, I dedicate this work to my wife and family. Without their support I would never have taken the extra hours to accomplish a task such as this. Judy's love is the greatest cornerstone of my life this side of heaven, and the very lives of my children — David, Daniel, and Jonathan — motivate me to love God more.

I thank you all.

Contents

Foreword

by Oral Roberts

Ron McIntosh, ORU graduate and former chaplain of Oral Roberts University, with a sense of history, particularly of the great revivals — past and present — has given us a valuable book to help ignite fresh revival fires and keep them burning throughout the world.

Ron is young enough to have been part — firsthand — in great revival moves, and experienced enough to recognize the signs of what is sure to come "big time" in the coming world outpouring of God's Spirit to revive God's people and to stir men's souls as mankind has not yet seen. *The Quest for Revival* is an exciting book.

I love Ron and deeply appreciate the mark he left on the thousands of ORU students as well as those of us in the administration and faculty.

This book is a winner!

Introduction:

Revival Is a Divine
Attack on Corrupt Society

The Quest for Revival is a book about the "R" word: revival!

Revival is a "dirty" word to some but a word of hope to others. The word *revival* has the connotation of being "dirty" to some because it has been flaunted and dangled in front of the people of God as a fulfillment of their most pressing needs. For many, the results have been disappointment and disillusionment. An entire generation has languished in the rubble of an unsubstantiated hope of learning the secrets of God's power.

However, the very objection of some is what makes revival a real possibility. What is revival?

- Revival is the revitalization of the Church for a divine attack on corrupt society.
- Revival is the marshalling of God's forces fatal to the kingdom of darkness.
- Revival is the drive to enlist, train, and empower believers to evangelize.
- Revival is God Almighty's military tactic to concentrate His resources for a vital blow to evil at a crucial moment.
- Revival is the divine energy that reinvigorates God's people with His truth and power.

It is the realization of the need for this revitalization that has fostered a whole new group of believers with a fervent hope and deep-seated hunger for that which is real. It is to this group of people that revival is a fulfillment of their hunger for the real power, real manifestation, and the real presence of God.

My reason for writing *The Quest for Revival* is to present an historical overview of modern revival that can serve as a catalyst to propel God's people into the next move of the Spirit. It is the heart of this work also to point out the key scriptural foundations that were at the heart of past revivals and to explain and emphasize how they offer a practical approach in our day to again ignite revival fires.

What began as my personal quest for truth became a mandate from God to share what I discovered to be the central truths that have historically promoted or postponed the moves of the Holy Spirit. By studying the revival moves of the twentieth century, I saw that there were common factors in the initiation and demise of revival.

It quickly became apparent that "history repeats itself," and that those who do not learn from past mistakes are destined to repeat them. We must learn from previous generations and not make the same mistakes they made.

It is essential to see that no revival is identical to another in form or principle involved:

God told Ezra to pray. Jonah was regurgitated by "Moby Dick." Hezekiah wrote a letter. John the Baptist dunked people in a muddy stream out in the middle of nowhere. Yet, all revivals have some common threads.

When I graduated from seminary, I served as pastor of a church in East Texas. Being very anxious to get involved with true church growth and to see a real move of God, I obtained reams of materials on that topic. One book by a California pastor could be summed up by three principles:

1. Find a good location — be in the right place at the right time.
2. Look good — have the right appearance.
3. Say good things — always compliment your people.

I thought that was good advice — until one day I read the story of John the Baptist in Luke 3. John did not operate according to the above criteria! In fact, he violated every one of those "principles."

He set up camp so far out in the wilderness, people had to know where it was to find it. There were no buses and no taxis. If an individual wanted to hear John speak, he had to walk miles.

Then there was the issue of the prophet's appearance. He probably wore "double-breasted camel's hair suits." His hair was likely matted from the honey he ate. He probably had a locust leg or two caught in his beard. As far as saying positive things, John probably qualified for the "Mr. Crassness-of-the-Year Award"!

Imagine an associate evangelist, perhaps a product of one of our great established Christian institutions, running over to the prayer tent and saying, "Brother John, you won't believe this, but there are thousands of people out there. We can build our mailing list and really get started. Go out there and say some positive things to them."

Then see John the Baptist walking out to stand before the gathered crowd, with his first words being, "You brood of vipers, *repent!*" (Matt. 3:2,7.)

John was not exactly a product of Dale Carnegie's school of *How to Win Friends and Influence People!*[1] There is little doubt that he broke all the modern rules of how to build churches. Yet revival broke out.

I am not writing this book to put anyone in a box, especially God. Instead, I want to call every reader to an understanding of the wide spectrum of principles that are at the root of revival. Some of these are broad in scope and common to every move of the Spirit. Some of them are minuscule and operate with fewer dynamics. All of them share something of the heartbeat of God.

As I studied the moves of the Holy Spirit in this century, I was startled to see the common threads interwoven in every revival. As you read this book, I believe you are embarking on a most exciting spiritual pilgrimage — the examination of some of the greatest events in the history of Christendom. At least, I have found this to be so in my experience. Also, I pray that this study will motivate you to be a part of an impending cataclysmic move of God on the earth.

I would like to begin by looking at some of the men and women God used during the past one hundred years to promote His Kingdom.

Chapter 1

ᏬᎿᎽᎤᎾ

Remember Your Leaders

The life and ministry of John Alexander Dowie (1847-1907) is a cornerstone of the healing heritage of revival.

Remember your leaders, who spoke the word of God to you. Consider the outcome of their way of life and imitate their faith.

— Hebrews 13:7

Just before he died, Smith Wigglesworth of Great Britain, one of the greatest spiritual leaders of this century, prophesied to a young evangelist concerning a vision about revival. That young man was Christian elder statesman Lester Sumrall of South Bend, Indiana, who only recently passed away in 1996 and is now with the Lord. Sumrall related the incident in these words:

I see it!

What do you see?

I see a revival coming to planet earth, as never before. There will be untold multitudes who will be saved. No man will say, "So many and so many," because no man will be able to count those who will come to Jesus Christ. *I see it!* The dead will be raised, the arthritic healed, cancer will be healed. No disease will be able to stand before God's people, and it will spread all over the world. It will be a worldwide thrust of God's power and a thrust of God's anointing. I will not see it, but you will.[1]

I find Sumrall's response to this prophecy most fascinating. He said:

> Most people are not capable of going from blessing to blessing. Most denominations and people die in the same revelation they first received from God. Many of the people who call themselves Lutherans are living in the same blessing Luther had four hundred years ago. Often, the people calling themselves Wesleyan or Methodists are living in the blessing of Wesley a couple of hundred years ago. It is difficult to get themselves out of a groove or a system.[2]

Sumrall's statement is not an indictment or criticism of denominationalism, but rather a statement about human nature.

People feel more comfortable in a known routine than in the turbulent waters of change. Many of us have the tendency to find a comfortable rut and stay in it.

Andrew, Simon Peter's brother, set a precedent for all of our lives. In a sense, Andrew was the first "Baptist." He was a convert of John the Baptist.

Then one day, as he and John were walking together with another disciple, John looked up, saw a man nearby, and exclaimed, "Look! The Lamb of God! He must increase, and I must decrease." (John 1:29-36; 3:30 NIV, KJV.)

Andrew must have been confused as he looked at the prophet, who was his mentor, then looked at Jesus. On the other hand, Andrew must have been able to accept truth when he heard it.

That day, he turned from following John to following Jesus. (John 1:37.)

When Andrew approached Jesus, however, the Lord said, "What do you want?" (John 1:38.)

Seeing the obvious hunger of Andrew and the other disciple, whose name we are not told, Jesus told them to follow Him. They spent the day with Jesus, and Andrew became so excited that he ran back home to tell his brother, Simon Peter, that he had found the Messiah. His conviction was so apparent that Simon Peter had to run to see Jesus for himself, and he too found the Messiah.

Here is a key principle of revival: Are we willing to leave the blessing we are in to receive a larger blessing? Or is it easier to call the new move one of fanaticism rather than to leave our comfort zone to flow with God's new thing? (Is. 43:18,19.)

This attitude can be best illustrated by an incident that occurred in my own life. I once asked the Lord what kind of people it will take to make a "new wineskin" into which He can pour out His Spirit in a fresh revival. While I was pondering that question, my wife and I made a trip to visit friends in Dallas.

Judy and I had been through a strenuous stretch of ministry in East Texas and had decided to take this mini-vacation in Dallas. While we were there, our friends invited us out to eat at a certain restaurant, where we found the waiters and waitresses dressed as "fictitious" characters.

A quick glance at the personnel revealed the costumes of Batman, Bugs Bunny, Indiana Jones, Wonder Woman, and many others. Guess who waited on our table. The devil!

My friend apologized and said, "Ron, if I had known the devil was going to wait on our table, I never would have brought you here!"

I calmly reassured him, saying, "That's okay, Bill. I've been looking for a face-to-face encounter with the devil all day long."

The waiter was costumed in the complete regalia. He was adorned in a red suit, with horns, a pitchfork, tail, cape, and the whole works. As he approached our table, he spoke in his vilest voice, "Hi, I'm the devil!"

To which I quickly replied, "Hi, I rebuke you in Jesus' name!"

Somewhat surprised, he said, "You what...?"

After a few halting moments, he went to get the menus, keeping a wary eye on me. When he returned, he read us the menu, and after we had ordered, he said, "Follow me to the salad bar."

"No. You follow me," I replied. "I don't follow the devil anywhere."

He finally responded, "Are you a preacher or something?"

I said, "...or something."

We all laughed and I had an opportunity to witness to the young man all night. God spoke to me as we were leaving and said, "Son, that's the same way I want you to treat the devil in real life." It's time that the Body of Christ stopped being intimidated by Satan and started being the intimidators.

Understanding God's Timing

God's people who have discernment must never be fearful of His shaking nor intimidated by the schemes of the devil. We must be like **men of Issachar, who understood the times and knew what Israel** [God's people] **should do...**(1 Chron. 12:32). Ecclesiastes 8:5 says: **...the wise heart will know** [discern] **the proper time and procedure.**

I believe that God is about to send a great wave of revival across the earth. The devil would like to confuse and intimidate us. Instead, we must understand the time and rise to God's new direction.

In Isaiah 43:18,19 the Lord says:

> **"Forget the former things; do not dwell on the past.**
>
> **"See, I am *doing a new thing!* Now it springs up; do you not perceive it?"**

Evidently, God can be doing a new thing and His people not see it. We need to understand the signs of the times. It is time "to get through what we are going through" and to "be what we want to see."

I believe the time is coming, and now is, that God is sending the fresh oil of the new wave of His Spirit. This is the season of a new generation of pure, Holy Spirit-led, committed, faith-filled, anointed believers who will rise up and take hold of their destiny.

These are men and women of God, who will believe Him and settle for nothing less than their destiny in Him. It is a time for a people who are fully informed of God's purpose and therefore will not be destroyed by a lack of knowledge. (Hos. 4:6.)

Hebrews 13:7 says, **Remember your leaders, who spoke the word of God to you. Consider the outcome of their way of life and imitate their faith.** The very next verse, Hebrews 13:8, says: **Jesus Christ is the same yesterday and today and forever.** The point is simple. We are to look back at the exploits of past leaders in order to encourage our faith that those things can happen again because Jesus never changes. What He did then, He will do now.

In "considering the outcome" of the way of life of those past leaders, we can learn what to do to align ourselves with the God of "yesterday and today and forever." That is the positive side. On the negative side, if we do not learn from the lives of past leaders, we will find ourselves repeating their mistakes and possibly aborting the next move of God.

The Church has received a legacy from the past that includes an enormous impetus from the heroes of faith who have preceded us. I want to examine some of the major figures of revival in this century in order to build a foundation of faith for a present revival.

Obviously, it is not possible to examine in depth the lives of every spiritual leader of the previous one hundred years. However, I have chosen a few prominent ones who are classic examples of those common factors I have mentioned.

Revival at the Turn of the Century

Just prior to the turn of the twentieth century, something occurred that is not well-known in today's generation of the Church. However, it was as unique and fascinating as any in the annals of church history. The life and ministry of John Alexander Dowie (1847-1907) is a cornerstone of the healing heritage of revival. Dowie's life is one of the greatest object lessons in all history.

His early years of ministry were in Australia, where his family had migrated when he was thirteen. His ministry was marked by two common partners: success and persecution. Dowie was a man of great education, eloquence, and enigma, a Scottish Presbyterian who became a member of, and a pastor in, the Congregational Church in Australia. Later, he left that denomination and formed an independent ministry.

While he was serving as pastor in a suburb of Sydney, a plague broke out that threatened to devastate the entire region. Within a few weeks, Dowie officiated at the funerals of more than forty of his church members.[3] The dead and dying were found throughout the area.

As Dowie agonized over his seeming impotence to help his people, God marvelously revealed to him the meaning of Acts 10:38:

> **"...how God anointed Jesus of Nazareth with the Holy Spirit and power, and how he went around doing good and healing all who were under the power of the devil, because God was with him."**

Suddenly, Dowie realized that Satan was the defiler and destroyer, and that Jesus was the Healer. Everything inside him cried out, "God, help me now to preach the word to all dying around...and [that] Jesus still delivers for He is just the same today."[4]

After receiving the revelation of God's healing power, Dowie saw a young girl from his congregation miraculously healed. According to the late Gordon Lindsay, founder of Christ for the Nations, Inc. in Dallas, Texas:

> The plague was stopped as far as John Alexander Dowie's congregation was concerned. Not another person from the flock died of the epidemic.[5]

In 1888, Dowie migrated to America and settled in Chicago in 1893. In that city, Dowie initiated a supernatural ministry that brought him worldwide fame, founding the Christian Catholic Church. His ministry of divine healing rocketed a small congregation to thousands of believers virtually overnight.

As quickly as the congregation grew, so did the persecution from the newspapers and a formidable list of enemies. There were ministers, doctors, tobacco and liquor vendors, and civic leaders to none of whom Dowie paid the slightest respect. *The*

Chicago Tribune printed scathing articles, branding Dowie a troublemaker, a fake, and a nuisance!

At this point of vulnerability to public criticism, Dowie started a chain of "healing homes." These houses were not advertised as hospitals, hotels, or public meeting places.[6] They were places where the sick and hopeless could go to lodge and receive faith through morning and evening praise and prayer services.

The results were astounding: the lame, halt, and blind were healed in a convincing manner, as well as the cancer-ridden. Despite the results, however, *The Chicago Dispatch* described one of them as "a private lunatic asylum where gibbering idiots were confined and from whose keeping Dowie derives a handsome revenue."[7]

He was portrayed as a huckster and a fraud. However, to the undisguised disappointment of all his opponents, it was soon discovered that their efforts had only served to act as advertisements to the healing ministry and simply drew more people to Dowie.

Undaunted, they stepped up their efforts. In 1895, he was arrested one hundred times for "practicing medicine without a license," based on a so-called "hospital ordinance."[8] As soon as a verdict of guilt was secured, however, Dowie appealed to a higher court, and in every instance, the sentence was reversed.

In 1900, in his most dramatic move, Dowie purchased six thousand acres of land north of Chicago and built a town called Zion City, his greatest venture. This was to be a community free from tobacco, drugs, liquor, brothels, dance halls, and any other forms of worldliness. Within two years ten thousand people inhabited this "paradise." While Dowie's dream of a Christian "Utopia" ultimately failed, out of its gates came great spiritual leaders such as F. F. Bosworth, John G. Lake, Raymond T. Richey, and Gordon Lindsay.

Dowie was a prolific writer and published a periodical, *Leaves of Healing*, which carried reports of the healings of celebrities such as Sadie Cody, the niece of William F. "Buffalo Bill" Cody; Amanda Hicks, the cousin of the late President Abraham Lincoln; Dr. Lillian Yeomans, among the first who wrote in defense of divine healing for today; F. A. Graves, well-known songwriter; and many others.

Dowie's was the first major ministry to bring a widespread consciousness of healing to America, and his was the forerunner of many others to come.

A Woman Who Broke New Ground

In the same era as Dowie came the remarkable ministry of Maria Woodworth-Etter. This amazing woman overcame multiple obstacles to launch one of the most supernatural ministries of the modern era.

Mrs. Woodworth-Etter was called to preach as a young girl of thirteen in Ohio. The fact that her church did not permit women preachers, coupled with a disastrous marriage to P. H. Woodworth and the rearing of six children, made her ministry even more remarkable.

After a very serious bout with illness that brought her to the point of death and the death of five of the six children, she experienced an event that would forever change her life. One day she had a glorious vision from the Lord, which she described in her own words:

> I thought I would go through a course of study and prepare for work, thinking the Lord would make my husband and

people willing in some way to let me go out and work....the dear Saviour stood by me one night in a vision and talked to me face to face....Jesus said, "You can tell the people what the Lord has done for your soul; tell of the glory of God and the love of Jesus..."[9]

Maria Woodworth-Etter c. 1900. "The dear Savior stood by me one night in a vision and talked to me face to face."

Later, she wrote that she learned more in that vision than she could have learned in ten years of study. I am a strong advocate of higher education, but the point is: Her ministry was ignited by a supernatural call of God. Once she set out fearlessly to preach, she overcame what she called a "man-fearing" spirit. God also revealed to her how He had gloriously used many women whose stories are in the Bible: Miriam, Deborah, Hulda, Anna, Tryphena, Persis, Priscilla, Junia, and others.[10]

The results of her ministry are absolutely amazing. After one of her meetings, revival swept over that country and for twenty miles round men and women were "struck down" or had "wonderful visions." Many who were involved "went into the ministry, or became evangelists."[11]

On one occasion, an eyewitness in one of her meetings said that she saw Mrs. Woodworth-Etter fall into a trance while preaching and stand in one position for three days. The power of God was so strong during the trance that non-stop miracles took place until the time of her arousal. When she awakened, she completed her sentence right where she left off.[12]

With no local church backing, she organized and preached huge campaigns in the days before women could vote. The charismatic gifts in her meetings attracted enormous support. It is reported that one camp meeting in Alexandria, Indiana, drew an estimated twenty-five thousand people.[13]

The power of God was so strong in her meetings that on one occasion a man who was "making sport of the works of God, and saying awful things about [her], and the Power" all at once "fell to the ground, a helpless man, stricken with paralysis."[14] Clearly it was a demonstration of apostolic power reminiscent of the days of Ananias and Sapphira.

This intrepid spiritual pioneer set the stage for the Pentecostal-Charismatic Revivals. *The New York Times* carried articles of her amazing campaigns in which many professional people such as lawyers and doctors were converted.

Is there any limit to what God will do for those who can believe Him again?

The Outpouring in Wales

With less than a score of intercessors when the move of God broke forth in 1904, Wales saw more than a hundred thousand people converted in less than six months.[15] The renewal in Wales lasted only about a year in its immediate form. However, its influence is still with us.

The leader of this revival was a humble young Welshman named Evan Roberts (1878-1947), a man of intense and fervent prayer. A miner-blacksmith whose genuine search after

God led him to become "a lay preacher," Roberts essentially led the revival.

After thirteen months of seeking God, Roberts said, "I had a vision of all of Wales being lifted up to heaven. We are going to see the mightiest revival Wales has ever known — the Holy Ghost is coming soon, so we must get ready."[16] In the spring of 1904, the day of visitation swept over Wales until the whole nation was shaken. Reports of the times say that Roberts was not a fiery orator. In fact, he was not much of a preacher at all. He saw his role as simply to interpret what the Holy Spirit wanted to do.

The Welsh Revival primarily was one of prayer, praise, joy, and victory — and the rediscovery of the Holy Spirit in the lives of the people. Roberts carried with him a sense of God's presence, so this revival also was a rediscovery of old truths presented in new ways for a new generation.

The Spirit of God literally swept over the land. The churches were so crowded that multitudes were unable to get in the doors. Meetings lasted from 10 a.m. until midnight with three services held daily.

This was a moral revolution which shut down bars, taverns, brothels, and anything else not of God. The Welsh Revival was a modern picture of Acts 4:21. Those like the leaders of the Sanhedrin, who saw the man crippled from birth standing healed before them, were not able to argue against it. *God vindicated His own work.*

Edward Jefferies reported miracles of healing that took place of the most amazing character. The blind recovered their sight, cripples threw away crutches, the deaf answered questions, withered and twisted arms were raised, remarkable cures of heart trouble...paralysis...and a variety of other ailments. Truly, the days of Jesus and the apostles seemed to be manifesting all over again.[17]

Stephen Jeffreys (1876-1943), perhaps the second most recognized minister of the revival, said, "I was privileged to witness no less than one hundred miracles in one week."[18]

Perhaps the most outstanding miracle, however, was that this revival was not just for Wales. Through the writings of Frank Bartleman, an observer and chronicler of the birth of the Pentecostal Movement at Azusa Street, Los Angeles, we can see that there was a definite and corresponding effect from the Welsh Revival on the outpouring of the Holy Spirit in America.

The legacy of the turn of the twentieth century was preparing for the mightiest outpouring of the Holy Spirit that the modern era has ever seen. It is to this event that we next turn our attention.

Pentecost Floods the Twentieth Century

In 1898, Charles Fox Parham (1873-1929) was determined to see if Jesus truly was the same "yesterday, and today, and forever." (Heb. 13:8 KJV.)

The simple humility of Azusa Street gives us the greatest hope of God doing it again in our time.

Now we turn our attention to another man who, at the turn of the twentieth century, led the way to the rediscovery of real power in the Church.

Charles Fox Parham: Pentecost in Topeka, Kansas

In 1898, Charles Fox Parham (1873-1929) was determined to see if Jesus truly was the same "yesterday, and today, and forever." (Heb. 13:8 KJV.) Because of his recovery from a severe bout of rheumatic fever with which he had been plagued since childhood, Parham developed a firm belief in divine healing.[1]

With his wife, he founded a "healing home" in Topeka, Kansas, in 1898. Some say it was patterned after John Alexander Dowie's "homes" around Chicago. In the summer of

1900, Parham made a tour of Holiness religious centers. He visited works such as Dowie's in Chicago, A. B. Simpson's Holiness training institute in New York, and Frank W. Sandford's Holiness commune in Shiloh, Maine, where he heard reports of people being baptized with the Holy Spirit and speaking in other tongues.[2]

Parham returned home to Topeka convinced that there remained a great outpouring of power to come for Christians who were willing to receive it. He immediately went into fasting and prayer. Then, in October of 1900, he rented an old mansion which he converted into a Bible school.

"Stone's Folly," Topeka, Kansas, c. 1901. William Parham rented this mansion in October 1900 for his Beth-El Bible School.

The prayer room at Beth-El Bible School became a vital link in what happened. Students prayed around the clock for the outpouring of God's presence. Parham was convinced that at Christ's second coming the Church would be found operating in the same power that the apostles and the early Church possessed. Parham wrote about his search this way:

> In December of 1900, we had our examination upon the subjects of repentance, conversion, consecration, sanctification, healing and the soon coming of the Lord. We had reached in our studies a problem. What about the second chapter of Acts?...I set the students at work studying out diligently what was the Bible evidence of the baptism of the Holy Ghost.[3]

To his astonishment, they all reached the same conclusion: not only was the experience for today but the initial evidence was speaking with other tongues. At a watchnight service on New Year's Eve, 1901, Parham's students set out to seek God's restoration of His divine pattern. As the midnight hour drew near and the twentieth century was about to begin, one of the students, Agnes Ozman (1870-1917) asked that hands be laid on her that she might be baptized in the Holy Spirit.[4]

Parham at first refused, not having had the experience himself. However, as she insisted, he laid his hands "humbly" on her head and prayed.

In his own words he described the experience: "The glory fell on her, a halo seemed to surround her head and face, and she began to speak Chinese. Also, for three days she could not speak English, and even when she tried to write, she wrote in Chinese. Newspapers reproduced her Chinese-language pieces."[5]

A few days later, Parham and about half his thirty-four students also received the baptism with the Holy Spirit. In Gordon Lindsay's *They Saw It Happen,* one person is quoted as saying, "At one time they spontaneously began to sing *Jesus, Lover of My Soul,* in at least six different languages, carrying different parts, but with more angelic voices than I ever listened to.[6]

Professors of languages and government interpreters put this phenomenon to a critical test. One interpreter reported finding twenty different Chinese dialects in one night.[7]

Newspaper accounts of the events at Parham's school caused the owners of the mansion to ask the school to leave the building promptly. Parham warned the owners that they were opposing the move of God and, if they persisted in this action, to expect judgment. Shortly thereafter, a mysterious fire broke out, totally destroying the facility.[8]

Along with the great gift of speaking in tongues came an outburst of the incredible power of God. Parham saw more than a thousand people healed in a three-month period.[9]

The adverse publicity and opposition by town and religious folk almost wiped out his Apostolic Faith movement, which included Bible schools and churches. All that was left was a small core of people who had truly accepted what essentially became the Pentecostal doctrine. Parham moved to Galena, Kansas, where, in 1903, his ministry reignited because of the combination of the baptism with the Holy Spirit and the teaching of divine healing.

Then later, in 1905, Parham began a ten-week Bible training school in a suburb of Houston, Texas. There a black Baptist minister, who had lost one eye from smallpox, heard about Parham and hungered to learn more about the power of God. Because segregation laws of the time decreed that blacks could not sit in the same classrooms as whites, William Seymour (1870--1922) was allowed to enroll but had to sit in the doorway outside of Parham's class and listen.[10]

William Seymour: Azusa Street Revival

Seymour was convinced that the teachings were from God, but he did not receive the baptism with the Holy Spirit in Houston nor even when he first began to preach it. Many were filled with the Spirit and were speaking in tongues before this humble black man, the instrument of their blessing, was himself filled.

At the encouragement of a young woman from the Holiness Movement, Seymour moved to Los Angeles to seek God for the coveted experience. Other men such as Frank Bartleman (1871-1936), a Holiness evangelist, and Joseph Smale (1867-1926), pastor of the First Baptist Church in Los Angeles, joined in the quest for a new move of God. Hearing of the revival in Wales, Bartleman and Smale corresponded with Evan Roberts, hoping to gain more insight for God's move in America.

Suddenly, in 1906, their hunger was fulfilled in the greatest modern-day outpouring of the Holy Spirit. Early in 1906, Seymour was invited to visit a church in Los Angeles with the possibility of becoming its pastor. Convinced that the baptism with the Holy Spirit was for modern times, he preached that message — and was promptly locked out of the church. Then Seymour held meetings in a private home. Those front-porch services quickly grew too large and another location became necessary. At the 312 Azusa Street building that had once been an African Methodist Episcopal church, and after that, a livery stable and a warehouse for a department store, God poured out His Spirit.

Azusa Street Revival actually began in his house, the Asbery family home, at 214 North Bonnie Brae Street in Los Angeles, California. c. 1906.

People were filled with the Holy Spirit, every imaginable need was met, and God's healing power was prevalent. There were no racial barriers as there had been in Houston. When the power of God fell, it drew blacks and whites alike. All races flocked to be in the presence of God. People from all over the world came to this modest facility to see the new thing God was doing.

The pews at Azusa Street were wooden planks, and the pulpit was an overturned chicken crate. Yet from this humble facility a major move of God began. For three years, day and night, God's miracle power did not stop. There were meetings three times a day, seven days a week. Some meetings ran continuously with no beginning or end. The curious, the unbelieving, and hungry believers flocked to the place.

The atmosphere was unbearable to the carnal person. Unbelievers fell to the floor in repentance. No one was honored because of his means or education but for God-given gifts. There was little form to the meetings. People prayed or sang in the Spirit and worshipped God until the Holy Spirit would give someone a prophecy, a tongue and interpretation, or a message.

Seymour oversaw the meetings, but truly the Holy Spirit was in charge. Often Seymour would sit behind two empty shoe-box crates, one on top of another. He would place his head inside the top of one during prayer, and the power of God would fall. He always remained humble, never wanting any of the attention for himself or seeking any of the credit or glory for the happenings.

No sermons were announced ahead of time; no special speakers were advertised; no human leader was depended on exclusively. Whomever God moved upon was the leader of the movement, and anyone who moved in the flesh quickly sat down in embarrassment.[11]

Many times haughty, self-appointed men came to "make their mark" at Azusa, only to find themselves on the floor repenting. Bartleman wrote, "The preachers died the hardest, they had so much to die to: so much reputation and good works."[12] He also wrote, "I would rather live six months at that time than fifty years of ordinary life."[13]

Once a preacher came from Chicago to expose the meetings as a fraud. When he walked into the mission, a thirteen-year-old girl approached him, and said, "Thus saith the Lord, 'You have come to expose the people. Yet I have brought you here for another purpose....'"[14] The man fell to his knees in humble repentance.

The overall results of these meetings were as remarkable as the individual occurrences. According to church historian Vinson Synan, from this one single revival, by 1980 more than fifty million people had been affected by the Pentecostal Movement. It also became the foundation for the Charismatic-Pentecostal outpouring. The latest statistics reveal that, by 1990, more than three hundred and seventy-two million people had been affected by this one outpouring of the Spirit.

The simple humility of Azusa Street gives us the greatest hope for God doing it again in our time.

John G. Lake: Apostle to Africa

The "roar" of the 1920s was not the sound of "flappers" or "speak-easys," but an incredible outpouring of God's Spirit. The flood that began at Azusa Street increased to a roar of the Word of God and the manifestation of the gifts of the Spirit that ran around the world.

Leaders of the "decade of the roar" included John G. Lake, Smith Wigglesworth, Aimee Semple McPherson, Charles Price, and others. Each of them had different callings and different assignments in the impending move of the Holy Spirit.

John Graham Lake (1870-1935) grew up in a home of sixteen children. An unknown disease once afflicted the family, and eight of the children died. During a period of thirty-two years, someone in the family was an invalid.[15] That situation caused Lake to develop a fervent hatred for sickness and disease. The haunting presence of sickness seemed to follow him. One of his brothers was an invalid for twenty-two years, a couple of sisters had fatal or debilitating conditions, and Lake's wife suffered from tuberculosis and heart disease.

Sometime during those years of struggle, Lake heard about John Alexander Dowie's "healing homes." He took his invalid brother to Chicago where he was instantly healed. Later, a sister with cancer was healed and, when it looked as if all hope was gone, still another sister with an issue of blood was healed instantly.

Lake also took his wife to the "healing home." Just three years after his marriage, tragedy had struck Lake's wife, Jennie. In 1896, she was pronounced incurable by several well-known physicians of the day, but on April 28, 1898, she also was instantly healed by the power of God: The news of her healing spread throughout the nation, and the Lake home became a center of constant inquiry about healing.

A new presence of God came upon Lake as he found himself in a time he called "the borderland" of a spiritual breakthrough. He discovered that he was fulfilled in the Lord but not satisfied. A hunger rose up inside of him for all God could give him. For nine months he gave himself to periodic prayer and fasting.

One day in 1907, while accompanying a friend to minister healing to a woman with inflammatory rheumatism, Lake had an unearthly experience. As he prepared to pray for the woman, it seemed as if he passed under a shower of warm rain.

When the awesome presence of God filled the room, the Holy Spirit said to him, "I have heard your prayers. I have seen your tears. You are now baptized in the Holy Spirit."[16]

Lake later wrote, "The currents of power began to rush through my being from the crown of my head to the soles of my feet."[17]

The power was so great, Lake's body began to vibrate. At that moment, his friend motioned to him to help pray for the woman. As Lake laid hands on her, a holy current seemed to go through her body. The woman was amazed at the physical sensation. The rush of the power was so intense that, when the friend touched her hand, the power of God went through him, catapulting him to the floor. He looked up at Lake with joy and surprise. Jumping to his feet, he said, "Praise God, John, Jesus has baptized you with the Holy Spirit."[18]

The baptism with the Holy Spirit launched Lake into a new dimension of the Spirit's power. A short time later, Lake received a call from God to go to South Africa, where the results of his ministry proved to be nothing less than astounding.

He left his job, distributed his funds, and set out with his wife, their seven children, and four other adults. When they arrived, a woman met them at the ship and offered to provide them with a house, saying that God had told her to do so. Unfortunately, most other people assumed that since they were Americans they were rich. As a result, the Lake party soon used up all their resources and often had insufficient food.[19]

After five years in Africa, Lake had established one hundred twenty-five white congregations and five hundred indigenous ones. According to his son-in-law, Wilford Reidt, Lake's combined work numbered seven hundred thousand members in a nation of fifteen million people. Without a doubt, the incredible miracles were the drawing card to this amazing spiritual rebirth of a nation.

Rarely a meeting passed without the demonstration of God's power in healings and supernatural incidents.

Once two young sisters came to scoff and disrupt a service. Without warning, one of the women fell down as though she were dead. The other sister quickly approached Lake, saying, "Man of God, we have sinned, but forgive us and restore my sister." Lake prayed for the woman, and she was raised to life instantly. Needless to say, both women immediately were converted.[20]

John G. Lake and wife, Jenny, c. 1902. During five years in Africa, Lake established six-hundred-and-twenty-five congregations.

As astounding as the miracles were, so was the fact that Lake's wife died of overwork and malnutrition during their early months in South Africa. Some years later, after struggling with loneliness, Lake returned to America. There he married again in 1913 and settled in Spokane, Washington, the next year. He spent some time looking over the city, then decided to set up several "healing homes." The results over the next five or six years were virtually unparalleled in Church history.

Incredibly, an estimated one hundred thousand healings took place during that time. Remarkably, that amounted to about fifty-five healings a day. Lake held services every night and twice on Sunday. Dr. Ruthlidge, a Washington, D.C., physician, declared Spokane the healthiest city in the world as a result of Lake's ministry.[21] A Better Business Bureau committee investigated the healing reports on one hundred people. After the reports had been verified, all the committee could do was commend Lake on his work. They simply commented, "We soon found out upon investigation, you did not tell the half of it!"[22]

When the Better Business Bureau declares God to be moving, that is really revival!

At one time in Lake's life he could lay hands on any man or woman and tell what organ was diseased and to what extent. He even put this ability to the test. He would go to hospitals in which physicians were unable to diagnose a case, lay his hands on the patient, and instantly discern the condition, its location and extent.[23]

There have been few ministries to rival the spectacular nature or number of healings performed by the Lord under the ministry of Dr. John G. Lake. Can we believe God to do it again?

Smith Wigglesworth: Apostle of Faith

The Englishman with two last names is unusual in that he was almost a half-century old before he was known outside of his hometown. Unlike Lake, Smith Wigglesworth (1859-1947) was born into a poor family. His wife, Polly, taught him to read after they were married in 1882, and he never read anything but the Bible.

As with numbers of other people in healing ministries, a personal healing (from a ruptured appendix) turned his attention to divine healing. Until he received the baptism with the Holy Spirit in 1907, he owned a plumbing business and assisted his wife in a mission. She was the preacher, while he was witnessing constantly to others, gaining many souls for the Kingdom.

In his later life, he was a man of such magnitude that healing evangelist Oral Roberts once said to his fellow evangelists, "We owe this man a debt beyond calculations."[24]

Smith Wigglesworth was born into a poor family. His wife, Polly, taught him to read, and he never read anything but the Bible.

During her services, Polly Wigglesworth tried to get her husband to speak, but he only embarrassed himself and others by his fear of speaking and the resulting debacle. Once the men of the congregation felt led to lay hands on him and pray. Despite their best efforts and his, he was still a dismal failure as a speaker. Finally, he declared that he would never try to speak again in public.

However, when he received the baptism with the Holy Spirit, his life was transformed. At the time, his wife did not believe in speaking in tongues, and she challenged him to preach the next Sunday, knowing his linguistic disability. The anointing fell, and he spoke with great clarity and boldness. Polly was so astonished, she kept exclaiming, "That's not my Smith....What's happened to the man?"[25]

Suddenly, a simple, uneducated plumber was transformed into a preacher of astonishing faith.

Wigglesworth's understanding of sickness and disease was that all of it was of the devil, so he became noted for his dealing with sick people with surprising, even shocking, physical demonstrations.

Evangelist Lester Sumrall recounts the first time he ever witnessed Wigglesworth in action:

While [Wigglesworth was] conducting a healing service in California, a man was brought in with cancer so near death that his physician attended with him to monitor his vital signs. In his [Wigglesworth's] gruff nature, he said to the man, "What's up?" The doctor replied, "The man's dying with cancer."

Without a moment's notice, Wigglesworth punched the man in the stomach with such force it caused the man to collapse.

The doctor quickly attended him and cried out, "He's dead, you killed him! The family will sue you!"

Wigglesworth was unmoved and simply replied, "He's healed."

Without any hesitation, he proceeded to pray for others in the service. About ten minutes later, the man came running down the aisle after Wigglesworth in his hospital gown, totally healed. It didn't impress Wigglesworth in the least — he expected it. He simply went on praying for others who needed it.[26]

No other figure in the modern era, unless it was Evangelist Jack Coe, approached people in such a physical manner. And no other figure produced such amazing miracles. Believe me, his was not a ministry you want to imitate — unless you are positive that God is speaking to you!

On another occasion at Zion College, a frail, crippled woman came up for prayer, and Wigglesworth prayed almost impatiently. As usual, he immediately commanded her to walk. Hesitatingly, she began to hobble about. Without warning, Wigglesworth walked up behind her and pushed.

As she stumbled into a run, he followed her up the aisle shouting, "Run, woman, run."

She managed just enough strength to stay out of his grasp. Eventually, she reached the exit and ran into the streets, apparently frightened as well as healed. When the evangelist began to pray for the next person, the man quickly changed his complaint from a stomach ulcer to a mild headache.[27]

Albert Hibbert, Wigglesworth's close friend, quoted the evangelist as saying, "I don't hit people, I hit the devil. If they get in the way, I can't help it....You can't deal gently with the devil, nor comfort him; he likes comfort."[28]

Wigglesworth also went through times of sorrow, because he lost a beloved wife a half-dozen years after his transformation into a greatly anointed man of faith. In 1913, his wife Polly died for no apparent reason while on her way to a speaking engagement.

When he reached home, Wigglesworth went into the room where his wife's dead body lay on the bed, *rebuked death, and commanded life to return.*[29]

Polly opened her eyes and said, "Why have you done this, Smith?"

She did not want to return to earth, and after a loving conversation, he released her to heaven.

Fourteen people were documented to have been raised from the dead in Wigglesworth's ministry, although unofficially, the record may have been as high as twenty-three. Nothing was too great for his faith. Headaches or cancers were all the same to him. Is anything too hard for God?

Aimee Semple McPherson: Woman of Destiny

The third "leader" that we want to consider from this era is Aimee Semple McPherson (1890-1944), a woman truly ahead of her time. Converted at nine years of age, Aimee Elizabeth

Kennedy was not satisfied until she had all that was available from God. To her mother's chagrin, she became involved with Pentecostals and married the young minister who brought news of the baptism with the Holy Spirit to her Canadian hometown.

She was seventeen when she was wed to Robert James Semple in an apple orchard at her parents' home by Salvation Army ministers. Aimee and Robert pioneered a church in Ontario, then moved to Chicago. From there they went as "faith" missionaries to China in 1910.[30]

She became a widow at twenty years of age when Semple died of a malarial attack in Hong Kong within weeks of their arrival and only a month before the birth of their daughter. Aimee returned to New York City that fall. Her mother joined her, and together they worked with the Salvation Army. She met Harold Stewart McPherson and remarried a little over a year after Semple's death.

The couple moved to Chicago, then Rhode Island, where their son, Rolf Potter Kennedy McPherson, was born in 1913. Not long afterwards, they moved to Canada and began to minister, with McPherson acting as advance man, but the marriage did not work out.

During the early years of her marriage, Mrs. McPherson fell prey to numerous illnesses. One such incident proved to be the turning point in her life. Hovering between life and death, as she related later, she received a visitation from the Lord, Who told her to "go preach My Word." She was healed and set out on evangelistic tours across the country in a matter of weeks.

In 1921, Mrs. McPherson arrived in Los Angeles with nothing to her name but ten dollars and a tambourine. Yet not long afterward, she had managed to erect the fifty-three-hundred-seat

Angelus Temple debt-free. At the height of God's move in the Twenties, the temple was filled five times a week. The healings that occurred there brought tremendous attention to her ministry.

The walls of Angelus Temple became lined with crutches, wheelchairs, and every conceivable apparatus formerly used by the many invalids healed under her ministry. The healing sessions caused virtual riots from the throngs of people who tried to get within reach of God's healing power.

Mrs. McPherson also published a monthly magazine, *The Bridal Call*, which she had started during the years of the Canadian ministry. This periodical went to tens of thousands of readers. However, she was perhaps most famous for her illustrated sermons.

Mrs. McPherson had thousands of costumes, props, and sets which she used to communicate messages through dramatization. One such sermon was a message on Noah and the ark, for which she brought in dozens of animals from the local zoo. Unfortunately, however, the animals did several things that were unforgivable indoors, and that marked the last time animals were used in her messages.

On another occasion, she had a volcano constructed with an eruption and lava flow. Yet another time, she dressed as a policewoman, rode a motorcycle down the center of the aisle to the podium, and preached, "Stop! You Are Breaking God's Law." She had invited all Los Angeles policemen to the service that day, and dozens of them were saved. Her productions were marvelously done. It is said that even Hollywood copied her.[31]

In the late Twenties and Thirties, the name of Aimee Semple McPherson is said to have appeared on the front pages of *The Los Angeles Times* an average of three times weekly. Mrs.

McPherson was among the first of the healing revivalists to capture the attention of the national media.

In the late 1930s, the wave of the Spirit suddenly seemed to taper off. Seymour, Mrs. Woodworth-Etter, and Parham died in the Twenties, and Mrs. McPherson, Wigglesworth, and Evangelist Charles Price were gone from the earth by the mid-Forties. Wigglesworth and Price passed away within a few days of each other in 1947.

Most of these leaders, in spite of the astounding miracles and healings of their days, looked for a time of even greater healings, miracles, and signs of God's power. They foresaw a larger "flood" of the Holy Spirit that would affect more people than the revivals in which they had participated. Some of them, such as Price and Wigglesworth, saw visions and prophesied of such a time to come.

Aimee Semple McPherson. The celebrated evangelist once dressed as a policewoman, rode a motorcycle to the podium and preached, "Stop! You Are Breaking God's Law."

I long to see that time, just as they did — and as many Christians do today — which is one reason for this book. It is my sincere hope that this reviewing of revival history can help bring about the climate and conditions for coming great revival.

Price and Wigglesworth, more than any others, overlapped the Pentecostal-Healing Revivals. Their death, along with that of others involved in this second move of the twentieth century, seemed to put revival in jeopardy.

David E. Harrell, Jr. wrote in his very important work, *All Things Are Possible:*

One minister remembers 1946 as "the year of preparation"; others, as had Charles Price, sensed a new mood of anticipation. There was a longing for a renewal in divine healing and the manifestations of the gifts of the Spirit that seemed to be disappearing from the church. People who professed to believe in healing were anxious to actually witness a miracle. A new generation was hungry for a revival in its own time.[32]

William Branham: Initiator of the Healing Revival

Out of this interlude of time emerged an unlikely champion of Christ. William Branham (1909-1965) experienced many hardships in his early life. But at seven years of age, a voice spoke to him and told him not to drink, smoke, or defile his body "for I have a work for you to do when you get older."[33]

After a personal healing as a young man, he felt called to preach, and in 1933, spoke to three thousand people in a tent revival in Jeffersonville, Indiana, where Branham Tabernacle later was built. He began as an independent Baptist minister.[34]

His first wife and a baby died in 1937, which he attributed to God's having taken them because of his refusal to become involved with Pentecostalism. His wife's family had bitterly opposed such an involvement. After her death, he did begin to move in those circles.[35]

After 1946, he operated in what was attributed to the word of knowledge and word of wisdom, though Branham himself never called it that.[36] I have seen video tapes of his services and watched him tell unknown people their names, addresses, names of doctors, dates of accidents, phone numbers, precise diseases involved, and sundry other details not possible for him to have known personally.

He said that an angel of the Lord had told him, "If you can get the people to believe," healings and miracles would happen.[37] Branham claimed he had been given two "gift signs": discerning of the secrets of a person's heart and the visible vibration of his left hand, which actually became red and swollen. The power would stop his wrist watch instantly.[38] The gifts were to raise the people's faith.

Another early Pentecostal healing evangelist and author, F. F. Bosworth (1877-1958), who worked with Branham, said:

> At these times he can say with absolute certainty, "Thus saith the Lord," and he is never wrong. He told me last week he simply *acts out* what he already has seen himself doing in a vision. The success phase of his ministry is exactly 100%.[39]

Many have declared that miracles accomplished through Branham were unsurpassed. In 1951, he brought forth one of the most famous healings in the revival's history. William D. Upshaw, a former United States congressman from Georgia, at Branham's urging, walked unaided after fifty-nine of his

William Branham and halo, 1950. Most famous photo from '47-'58 healing revivals. Many declared miracles accomplished through Branham were unsurpassed.

sixty-six years had been spent on crutches and the last seven years had been spent in bed.[40]

If William Branham was considered the movement's "initiator," another evangelist was the "innovator" of the Healing Revival. Oral Roberts was a man whose ministry kept abreast of God's moving so that he was born, converted, and grew up in the Pentecostal Movement, became the best-known leader of the Healing Revival, and ministered in and across the Charismatic Movement.

Oral Roberts: Innovator of the Healing Revival

The influence of Oral Roberts to the Healing Revival and the Church world since the period in which it flourished cannot be overestimated. This one single ministry has probably done more to cause post-World War II Christians to accept the doctrinal concepts of healing, deliverance from oppression, God's miracle-working power, and the provision of Jesus than that of any other man in the modern era.

A great communicator, Roberts was never afraid to make use of arts and music and new technology in order to get across the message of God. Perhaps his greatest impact on the nation at large came in 1955 when he initiated a weekly television program.

Through his TV series, Roberts' healing crusades reached millions of people who never would have, or could have, set foot under the large tents where he held his meetings. Therefore, Oral Roberts was the man God used to spread the healing waters from the Pentecostal subculture to the mainstream of Christianity and to the world.

Born in 1918 to Pentecostal preachers, Oral grew up in Enid, Oklahoma. I have heard Brother Roberts say many times that Jesus was very real in his home because his parents spoke to Him with such intimacy. However, at seventeen, Oral was still not committed to the Lord personally. Then he contracted tuberculosis.

At home, he waited to die, for at that time there was no medical cure. But he struggled with the concept that has plagued many down through the ages: the presence in the world of a "good God" Who is seemingly unable to touch a hurting humanity.

One day, Oral's sister, Jewel, spoke seven miraculous words to him: "Oral, God is going to heal you!"

She had heard of an evangelist who prayed for the sick with tremendous results. Oral's brother, Vaden, drove him to see Evangelist George W. Moncey, where in 1935 Oral was miraculously healed of his TB and of a stuttering problem as well.

On the way home, God spoke to him and said, "Oral, you will take My healing power to your generation."

Oral began his healing ministry around the year 1947, after a two-year evangelistic apprenticeship under his father during which he was ordained in the Pentecostal Holiness church. Afterwards he served four pastorates for that denomination.

Oral Roberts commanded the attention of an audience as few preachers could. Perhaps his greatest impact on the nation at large came in 1955 when he initiated a weekly television program.

His first city-wide campaign was in his hometown of Enid. The same year he authored his first book on healing, began a radio program, started a monthly magazine, and established his permanent headquarters in Tulsa. The next year, he launched his national ministry, traveling across America with the largest portable tent in use to that time.

Roberts could command the attention of an audience as few preachers could. His miracles held the hungry crowds spellbound. Those miraculous demonstrations included everything from the healing of headaches to the opening of deaf ears, and even a creative miracle of the formation of a hip joint.

Few spiritual leaders have had such lasting impact as Oral Roberts. His resiliency and longevity of ministry are legendary. Perhaps his greatest contribution has been the 1965 establishment of a fully accredited, Charismatic university, Oral Roberts University in Tulsa.

The ten-year period that is considered the fullness of the Healing Revival ended in 1958 about as suddenly as it began. Some of the other well-known leaders of that time are Jack Coe, A. A. Allen, W. V. Grant Sr., and Kathryn Kuhlman.

I have been able only to touch on a scattering of incidents in the lives of a few leaders representative of the first three moves of God in this century: 1) the Pentecostal Movement, 2) the Healing Revival, and 3) the Charismatic Movement. If these events I have related have been nothing more than an assimilation of some fascinating history, these chapters will have little value to you. However, if these events of the past stimulate your faith to believe that they can happen again, this book will have served its purpose. It thus behooves us to turn our attention next to discerning the seasons of the Lord.

Discerning the Seasons of God

God is going to restore to us in a greater capacity His healing power, His delivering presence, His transcendent glory, His conspicuous presence, and His mighty miracles.

Will you not revive us again, that your people may rejoice in you?
— Psalm 85:6

Recently, after I had preached at a worship service of a large institution, I was invited to eat with a group of young people from the congregation. I agreed, and as we sat down to the meal, a greater hunger quickly manifested itself.

"We've heard you speak on other occasions about the miracles of Smith Wigglesworth, Kathryn Kuhlman, and John G. Lake," the group said, "but we are hungry to see a full move of God in our day."

Suddenly I thought of my previous congregation at Oral Roberts University and began to realize that the entire constituency for whom I served as pastor was a people born between the moves of God in America. Very few of them had seen the revival Spirit of God. They are what I call a "Judges 2:10 generation."

The people served the Lord throughout the lifetime of Joshua and of the elders who outlived him and who had seen all the great things the Lord had done for Israel....

After that *whole generation* **had been gathered to their fathers, another generation grew up, who knew neither the Lord nor what he had done for Israel. Then the Israelites did evil in the eyes of the Lord....**

— Judges 2:7,10,11

It is evident from this passage of Scripture that true faith in God cannot be transmitted from one generation to another, *unless* there are new manifestations of God's power. Also, those manifestations will never transpire until the hunger the young men spoke to me about in the restaurant that day is converted to a faith that can believe it will happen again. That is why I began with the question from Psalm 85:6, "Will you not revive us again...?"

Revival is a rediscovery of an eternal truth that has been converted to new terms, interpretations, and methods for a new generation. The key to transition from possibility to reality is for a new generation "to be what they hunger to see."

The generation that followed Joshua still had all the hierarchy intact. They still had priests and leaders, but they knew nothing of the power of God. The Judges 2:10 generation had been reduced to ineptness and impotence, because each of them had been reduced to doing **...that which was right in his own eyes** (Judges 17:6 KJV).

It is easier to say that the days of miracles are past, or at least that miracles have been restricted, than to pay the price to resurrect them. That was the issue Gideon would have to face a few chapters later in the Book of Judges:

> **When the angel of the Lord appeared to Gideon, he said, "The Lord is with you, mighty warrior."**
>
> **"But sir," Gideon replied, "if the Lord is with us, why has all this happened to us? Where are all his wonders that our fathers told us about...?"**
>
> **— Judges 6:12,13**

Gideon wanted to know, "If God is for us, where are the miracles we have heard about all our lives, and why have all these bad things happened to us?"

As we continue into the next decade, we could ask the same questions. If God is with us, where are all the miracles we have heard so much about, and why have we experienced some of the things that have befallen us during the end of the last decade and the beginning of this one? Why have some of our leaders fallen? Where is God's provision? Why are so few miracles performed in our midst? Where is the zeal of God that is missing in so many of our Spirit-filled churches?

Notice that the angel of the Lord did not come to Gideon and say, "Of course, there are questions. That is because the days of miracle are past!"

Quite the contrary. He responded to Gideon's hunger by showing him a touch of the miraculous. (Judges 6:19-22,36-40.)

It is also God's intent in this hour for those who can discern the times and seasons to experience a similar touch. (1 Chron. 12:32; Eccl. 8:5.) The difficulty in such discernment comes in the period of transition, that time which comes at the closing of one era of God's move and just before the beginning of the next move.

During this period, there is a changing of the guard and new leadership is emerging upon the scene. It is also the time that the Church and the general public often see the shortcomings of powerlessness and even the sins of individual ministries. Transition periods are times of confusion and wondering what is really going on. They are "Judges 2:10 times."

When I think of those times, I am reminded of an experience my wife, Judy, and I had that seems to exemplify this principle. Before our first son was born, we took Lamaze courses to help with the delivery. We learned all the breathing techniques for the difficult times of labor. We learned techniques like what I called the "hee-hee-ho's."

We would practice simulating labor pains and I would say, "Breathe, Darling," and she would say, "Hee-hee-ho," and everything was wonderful.

Finally the fateful day arrived and we went to the hospital. As the coach, I did everything I was supposed to do. I wiped her brow, fed her ice chips, and every time she had a contraction I would say, "Breathe, Darling," and she would respond, "Hee hee ho."

Everything went great — until we hit transition. Only a woman who has had a baby can comprehend the difference in travail that comes at that moment.

I would say, "Breathe, Darling," and she would reply, "You breathe!"

Breathing was out the window. Why? The pain in "transition" had changed her perspective. Her perception of everything altered. All the surroundings were the same, but her perception of them was totally different.

It is the same way in the Church with the transitions of the Spirit. The "Judges 2:10 generation" did not have a fresh experience with God and so they grew confused and lethargic. During transition periods, people are confused, not totally cognizant of everything around them, and their perspectives change. Many times people lose hope for revival.

The Church slumbers into a survival mode.

Survival will always be the thief of revival.

As long as we are trying to survive, we will lose our perspective to revive.

Revival Is Not for Sinners

It is these periods of transition, however, that validate revival to the discerning heart. *Revival is for the Church, not for sinners.* Literally, it is a restoration or a revitalization. It is impossible to restore something that has not been lost or has never existed. In the modern Church, we have confused revival with four-day evangelistic meetings.

In reality, the Church is revived in order to reach out to the world. Revival presupposes outreach. They are part and parcel of the same thing.

In many places I go to minister, I ask the people, "How many of you want to see a revival?"

Virtually every hand in the auditorium will go up in an affirmative response.

However, on many of those occasions I might also ask those in attendance, "How would you know a revival if you had one?"

Most church members are confused about revival. Literally, to *revive* means:

- To recover from loss or death.

- To recall from a state of apathy or lethargy.
- To recall to obedience forgotten validations of God's heart.
- To reinvigorate or revitalize.
- To restore to an awareness of God's truth and power.

When this takes place, then the world is affected by the revelation of a revitalized Church.[1]

Charles Finney once said, "The fact is, Christians are more to be blamed for not being revived than sinners are for not being converted."[2]

The Church has a responsibility to recognize the times and the seasons of God to properly receive the flow of His Spirit. Revival by its nature takes place in a time of moral darkness and national discouragement. Revival occurs when a generation recognizes its impotence, sin, and apathy, and realizes that it is God's time to do something about it.

The sons of Issachar discerned the times and seasons and knew what Israel should do. (1 Chron. 12:32.) Jacob realized his sin and repented (Gen. 35:1-5), and as a result the tribe was restored. In 2 Chronicles 15, we see this principle in the life of King Asa as he responded to the words of the prophet:

"...Listen to me, Asa and all Judah and Benjamin. The Lord is with you *when you are with him*. If you seek him, he will be found by you, but if you forsake him, he will forsake you. For a long time Israel was without the true God, without a priest to teach and without the law. But in their distress they turned to the Lord, the God of Israel, and sought him, and he was found by them."

— 2 Chronicles 15:2-4

Notice, God's people had been for a long time without the Lord, but the prophet said "The Lord is with you, when you are with Him."

Asa and the people repented. They destroyed the idolatry of their day. They repaired the altar of the Lord, and in verse 9 we read that when they saw that the Lord was with Asa, the people followed him. God restored His favor to His people. The people had suddenly realized that God's glorious presence was gone from their midst and so they responded by flowing into God's new season through repentance.

Similar resurgence is found for God's people in the life of Jehoiada (2 Chron. 23,24), Hezekiah (2 Kings 18:1-7), Josiah (2 Kings 22,23), Zerubbabel (Ezra 5,6), Ezra (Ezra 10:1), Daniel (Dan. 9,10), and John the Baptist (Luke 3).

The key today is to discern the seasons of God, as these men did. What season is God leading us into? Jesus wept over the city of Jerusalem because its citizens did not recognize the season of the Lord, "the day (or time) of their visitation." (Luke 19:44 KJV.) It is entirely possible to be in the middle of God's move, the very move that we hunger for, and still miss it.

I once heard Bob Deweese, a former associate evangelist to Oral Roberts, say, "The people who most longed for the move of the Spirit in 1947 were among those who rejected it when it came."

Hosea was speaking as the mouthpiece of the Lord when he said:

> **"Come, let us return to the Lord. He has torn us to pieces but he will heal us; he has injured us but he will bind up our wounds.**
>
> **After two days he will revive us; on the third day he will restore us, that we may live in his presence.**
>
> **...he will come to us like the winter** [KJV, "former"] **rains, like the spring** [KJV, "latter"] **rains that water the earth."**
>
> **— Hosea 6:1-3**

In these verses, Hosea speaks of three days. In the first "day," God's people are humbled. Following that, Hosea speaks of a revival that will revitalize the people. Finally, in the third "day," God's people are restored to live in His abiding presence. Hosea reveals a spiritual principle governing God's dealing with His people. I believe, in our time, we are in a process of transition out of the first "day" into a revival in preparation for true restoration.

Above and beyond the meaning for the people of his day, Hosea prophesied of a revival that would be what the *King James Version* refers to as the "former" and "latter" rains combined. The former rain was an outpouring after the autumn harvest that prepared the ground for plowing and planting. The latter rain came in spring and summer to cause the crops to ripen and mature.

Hosea was saying that there is a move of God that both prepares the way and brings the harvest to full maturity. That is the move we want to see in our time.

The latter rain is said to be seven times greater than the early or former rain. If indeed, we experience the former rain with the latter rain, it will be a revival to touch the nations.

The Signs of the Times

One day while I was praying in my office, God spoke to me and said, "I am going to show you My season of time."

He took me into Ezekiel 37, to show me the raising up of a new-generation army. In that chapter Ezekiel was shown an open graveyard representing a dead people who needed reviving. In verse 1 Ezekiel had the ultimate "Star-Trek experience" as he was transported by God instantly to the middle of the valley.

The writer tells us that what he saw was "a valley of [dry] bones." (v. 1-4.) *Dry bones* in the Hebrew language is a symbol of starvation, emaciation, or leanness. In the valley, God asked Ezekiel this poignant question, **"...Son of man, can these bones live?"** (v. 3).

The typical Spirit-filled response today would be, "Yes, amen! You know, O Lord, that we have power over the devil."

Most Christians I know are lucky they never met a real demon!

Recently I saw a graphic example of this truth at a youth convention in which I was speaking. Most unexpectedly to those who were conducting the series, the power of God fell in a very unusual way. I had spoken on "The Raising Up of a New Generation."

At the close of the service, the altar was flooded with hundreds of people. Everywhere I looked, people were weeping in repentance, crying out for deliverance, giving their hearts to Christ, or hungering for more of God.

The atmosphere was charged with "we're-ready-for-anything" responses. That night I prayed for people for more than three hours as they lined up one after another. After the third hour a bizarre happening took place.

A young man, obviously demon-possessed, came running down the aisle yelling in a perverted voice, "Michael is mine, Michael is mine!"

The crowd instantly grew silent. No one seemed to know what to do. I was lost in the sea of people at the altar, and the crowd was frozen. Suddenly, a few people who had at least caught the heart of the vision of the night leaped to their feet and surrounded the young man, yelling at the top of their lungs, "In the name of Jesus, by the blood of the Lamb."

However, unlike the Israelites in 1 Samuel 4:5, their shout had no clout. Their hearts were right, but they had not yet learned how to exercise their authority.

I walked up to the young man and immediately he said in a deep, menacing voice, "Michael is mine."

Very calmly, without raising my voice, I said, "No, Michael is not yours. He belongs to God, and I'm here to claim him."

The demon almost hissed as he responded, "I'll kill him."

The people sat in stunned silence as I looked at him and answered, "No, you won't kill him. In fact, you're going to come out of him right now."

The demon blurted out, "No, I won't come out of him."

Again the people sat in shock, but in the same quiet tone of voice I said, "You already know I realize my authority, and you have to come out. I'll stay here as long as it takes, so you might as well come out now."

In a rage, the demon cried out, "I'm going to kill you."

I think demons must go to demon school or something, because every time they get to their last-ditch effort they seem to use that same threat. The auditorium was so quiet you could hear a pin drop.

I said, "No, you won't harm anyone. In fact, when I lay hands on this young man, you'll come out."

Moving closer to Michael, I very lightly laid my hands on his forehead, and he fell violently to the floor. It was so abrupt that the crowd gasped. For several minutes he lay there as if dead, but I knew that God was working. Then he stood to his feet, totally delivered. In the next few minutes I led him to Christ, and he was baptized with the Holy Spirit. Believe me when I say that great rejoicing broke out in the Lord.

The people in that place were ready for anything — until a real demon showed up. It is time for real spiritual authority to be restored to God's people.

In the valley of dry bones, Ezekiel responded to the Lord's question, "Can these bones live again?" by saying, **"...O Sovereign Lord, you alone know"** (v. 3).

Ezekiel would be kicked out of many of our churches today for making a "negative confession." Ezekiel came to God as a man in a difficult transition, decreeing his need of God. The real key here is lordship. It is not simply a matter of what you can believe for, but *what you can obey for.*

> **Then he said to me, "Prophesy to these bones and say to them, 'Dry bones, hear the word of the Lord! This is what the Sovereign Lord says to these bones: I will make breath enter you, and you will come to life. I will attach tendons to you and make flesh come upon you and cover you with skin; I will put breath in you, and you will come to life. Then you will know that I am the Lord.'"**
>
> **— Ezekiel 37:4-6**

Talk about faith! Out of pure obedience, the prophet spoke to the bones. The Bible says that there was a noise, and a rattling sound, then suddenly the bones came together and tendons and flesh appeared on them, and skin covered them. (vv. 7,8.) In verse 9, we read how God commanded Ezekiel to call for the breath of the Lord to enter the bodies that they might live. In verse 10, we are told that Ezekiel did as he was ordered and breath did indeed enter them, they stood to their feet, and became a vast army.

God said to me, "Son, you are in verse 9 at this time, about to embark into verse 10. I am preparing the soil for the latter rain."

We are living in what the psalmist referred to as a time of "leanness of soul." (Ps. 106:15 KJV.) The Body of Christ may look good on the outside, but it is a weakling on the inside. It has been puffed up by good advertising, but there is no substance. We have gone from hunger for God's presence to being content with a religious atmosphere. In the midst of all this, however, is a people of true hunger coming on the scene to claim something great in our generation.

As the Lord spoke to me about Ezekiel 37, I cried out "Lord, how can we go from the corpses in verse 9 to the army in verse 10?"

Then He brought to my remembrance Acts 3:19-21:

"Repent, then, and turn to God, so that your sins may be wiped out, that times of refreshing may come from the Lord, and that he may send the Christ, who has been appointed for you — even Jesus. He must remain in heaven until the time comes for God to restore everything, as he promised long ago through his holy prophets."

In that passage, Peter taught that just before the Lord's second coming there will be times of refreshing and restoration. Before the Lord comes again, there will be the greatest restoration of power, gifts, God's presence, and His glory that the Church has ever known.

Here is the real "kicker." As I studied this passage in the Bible, the concordance, and a Greek-English lexicon, I discovered that the word *refreshing* means revival, recovery from heat, reviving with fresh air, recovery of breath.[3] There it was — the breath of God that would make us the vast army that Ezekiel spoke about.

God is going to restore to us in a greater capacity His healing power, His delivering presence, His transcendent glory, His conspicuous presence, and His mighty miracles. He is going to restore marriages, families and homes, lost loved ones, health, authority, and a greater sense of direction than the Church has ever known. As a result, the Body of Christ will become a vast army, a force to be reckoned with on the earth.

Here is the key:

It is important to note that, when the Lord's purposes die with a generation, He never abdicates His plan. He simply waits for a new generation who will believe Him.

"For the eyes of the Lord range throughout the earth to strengthen [KJV, "to shew himself strong in the behalf of"] **those whose hearts are fully committed to him...."**

— 2 Chronicles 16:9

Second Corinthians 3:16,18 says:

But whenever anyone turns to the Lord, the veil is taken away....And we...are being transformed into his likeness with ever-increasing glory, which comes from the Lord, who is the Spirit.

The phrase "whenever anyone turns to the Lord" is the call to revival. It is the "repent" of Acts 3:19. Revival begins in a transition period when God's people begin to acknowledge that sin, lethargy, leanness, and compromise have subtly slipped into their lives so that they must repent.

Repentance means changing our thinking and our ways.

Repentance means turning from our ways to God's ways.

The initial and primary key to every revival is repentance. What can secure such outpourings of the Holy Spirit as we have discussed? If you say prayer, you are precisely right. However, there is something that must precede prayer. We must deal with the question of sin. Unless our lives are right with God, we can pray without ceasing and still see few results.

Isaiah 59:1,2 says:

Surely the arm of the Lord is not too short to save, nor his ear too dull to hear.

But your iniquities have separated you from your God; your sins have hidden his face from you, so that he will not hear.

The reason repentance is the primary key to revival is that without it, prayer is impossible. Sin prohibits God from ever hearing our petitions. There is only one real obstacle to revival: sin. Repentance is the key to unlock the door to God's unlimited light.

True repentance is not some flimsy or false change that looks good on the outside but has no real substance. Repentance is not being sorry for having been caught, but it is a God-given call to transform us from an anemic way of life to the vital life flow of a vibrant relationship with Jesus Christ.

Repentance is the call in this hour to all who are tired of mediocrity and who desire real power. Repentance is the call to those who are tired of hype without substance. It is the call away from synthetic substitutes to a viable relationship with a living God. It is a call to those who are tired of reaching into the past for their only excitement.

It is time Christians understood repentance for our time. You and I need to repent if:

- We have accepted things that violate God's will as "normative for our day."
- We can no longer differentiate between God's way and the world's way.
- We are "rapture Christians" — if we would rather escape hardship than contend for the truth.
- If we want everything instant and "microwaveable" and are unwilling to pay the price for God to move.

- If we read every verse in the Bible for what it can do for us with little regard for a hurting and dying world.
- If we as the Church of Jesus Christ are more changed by society than we are transforming society.
- If we would rather hear about exploits than pay the price to do them.
- If we have not won any lost to Jesus lately.
- If, when difficult times arise, our only response is: "I don't receive it."
- If supernatural events occur, and we remain unmoved and unimpressed.
- If the Word of the Lord is spoken, and there is no change in us.
- If we say one thing, and live another.
- If we have not forgiven everyone who has offended us.

Repentance is a call to change the limitations of simple reasoning and open ourselves to the limitless realm of God's ways.

It is those "ways" that we want to explore next. Rather than point the finger at fellow preachers, pastors, or evangelists who have made mistakes, it is time we be what we want to see. We must be like Daniel who, although innocent, repented for the sins of the nation and prayed for restoration. (Dan. 9.)

Then we must discover God's ways and pursue them in faith, believing that He has in store for us the greatest move yet for our generation. We must also understand that **...the Sovereign Lord does nothing without revealing his plan to his servants the prophets** (Amos 3:7).

In Genesis 18:17 the Lord said: **"...Shall I hide from Abraham what I am about to do?"** And Job declared, **Why, seeing times are not**

hidden from the Almighty, do they that know him not see his days? (Job 24:1 KJV).

I believe that if Jesus were again on the earth in the flesh, He would disclose that He not only wants, but expects, His people to discern the times and seasons and know what to do. We must learn from our past spiritual leaders and be inspired by their faith, but not duplicate their mistakes. Then we must hold fast to Jesus and hear what He is saying to His listening people. We must cry out with Moses, "Lord, teach me Your ways."

It is to that end that we now turn our attention.

The Battle Is Waged in Heavenly Realms

It was said of Charles Parham that "prevailing prayer solved every problem, and it is the foundation to all of his work."

I pray and obey.
— *Dr. Paul Yonggi Cho*

I will never forget my first trip to Seoul, South Korea, to visit the church of Dr. Paul Yonggi Cho located on Yoido Island. At the time I was a very young pastor in East Texas, and quite thrilled to be at a church growth conference held in the largest church on earth — today counting more than eight hundred thousand members — in the company of some of the greatest people of God in the world. I was young, hungry, and impressionable.

Also, I will never forget seeing Dr. Cho for the first time. I had read some of his writings in the early 1980s, but had never seen the man. To my surprise, a very unassuming gentleman entered the room and took the podium. He was not at all what I expected in those early years of my ministry.

Yet, I could feel the room come to attention as this spiritual giant who had accomplished a monumental task stood to address a gathering of ministers from around the globe.

He began by saying, "You may wonder how I built the largest church in the world."

Then in his heavy Korean accent, he gave us the answer with a smile, "I pray and obey — heh, heh, heh!"

I wanted to interrupt his cute little laugh and say, "That's nice, but *what is the real answer?"*

In my short ministry, I had not yet learned the central truth of prayer. I had not learned that the battle to accomplish God's work is waged in the heavenlies. Today, my deepening relationship with God, increasing experience in ministry, and broadening research into revival have brought me the understanding that every great move and every great project of the Holy Spirit is dependent on prayer.

The real battle that goes on to make way for the presence of God is not waged against the propaganda of humanists, the New Age movement, or abortion clinics. It is not waged against the halls of Congress or the seats of world governments. On the contrary, the real warfare is conducted in the heavenly realms and is directed against the devil and his hierarchy of demons. (Eph. 6:12.) It is this warfare that paves the way for manifestations in these other realms. We pray and obey our way to victory.

Every great revivalist of days gone by knew this as a valid fact. It was said of Charles Parham that "prevailing prayer solved every problem, and it is the foundation to all of his work."[1] Such prayer brought the supernatural presence of God not only in the modern era, but throughout history.

In 1745, Jonathan Edwards, son-in-law of David Brainard, prayed for revival among the American Indians until the snow melted around him and was stained by his blood.[2] Brainard recorded the results of his prayers:

> The power of God seemed to descend upon the assembly like a mighty rushing wind and with an astounding energy bore down all before it. I stood amazed at the influence that seized the audience almost universally and could compare it to nothing more aptly than the irresistible force of a mighty torrent.[3]

Charles Finney categorically stated, "A revival can be expected when Christians have the spirit of prayer for revival."[4]

Finney defined such a spirit of prayer as not simply "correct words and phrases," but a continuous desire for the redemption of mankind. He described this scene from a crusade in Antwerp, New York:

> An awful solemnity seemed to settle upon the people, the congregation began to fall from their seats in every direction and cry for mercy. If I had a sword in each hand, I could not have cut them down as fast as they fell. I was obliged to stop preaching.[5]

The real key is what Finney called "secret prayer." Believers would gather to spend hours in private prayer on behalf of their need for God. The outcry for effective prayer was astounding. In 1857, noonday prayer meetings broke out in New York, Philadelphia, Chicago, and many other cities.

The result was that the entire nation was stirred by the commitment to prayer. More than two thousand people showed up at one place in Chicago to pray. In a two-thousand-mile radius across America, the people of this country halted at mid-day for prayer. The results were nothing less than mind-boggling.

In the outbreak of the Spirit in 1857, for a period of six to eight weeks when the revival was at its height, it was estimated that fifty thousand persons were converted throughout the country, and the revivals lasted for more than a year. It became evident that the sum total reached an enormous figure. Conservative estimates placed the number of converts at five hundred thousand.[6]

Even in the frontier days of America such happenings occurred. In 1801, after prayer, Daniel Boone invited Barton Stone to hold a campaign in the isolated settlement of Cane Ridge. Astonishing for that day, twenty thousand people arrived for six days of meetings. The sparsely populated frontier was totally inundated with the presence of God. The account of one eyewitness is as follows:

The noise was like the roar of Niagara. The vast sea of human beings seemed to be agitated as if by a storm. I counted seven ministers, all preaching at one time, some on stumps, others in wagons, and one standing on a tree which had fallen against another. Some of the people were singing, others were praying, some were crying out for mercy....while witnessing these scenes, a peculiarly strange sensation such as I never felt came over me. My heart beat tumultuously, my knees trembled, my lips quivered, and I felt as though I must fall to the ground. A strange supernatural power seemed to pervade the entire mass of mankind there collected....I stepped to a log where I could get a better view....At one time I saw at least 500 swept down in a moment as if a battery of a thousand guns had opened upon them and then immediately followed by shrieks or shouts that rent the very heavens.[7]

Only the presence of God that is brought by prayer can produce such results.

In Old Testament times, Habakkuk defined revival this way:

Lord, I have heard of your fame; I stand in awe of your deeds, O Lord. Renew them in our day, in our time make them known; in wrath remember mercy.

— Habakkuk 3:2

In response to that prayer:

God came....

His glory covered the heavens and his praise filled the earth.

His splendor was like the sunrise; rays flashed from his hand, where his power was hidden.

— Habakkuk 3:3,4

Revival can be defined in two words: *God came*. And God's coming is in response to prayer. John Alexander Dowie taught that a Christian's warfare is prayer warfare. As long as he dwelled in the secret place of the most high, he said, demons gnashed their teeth in impotent rage.[8]

It was said of Maria Woodworth-Etter that, if she went into a town or city and nothing happened, she would pray all night until God's presence overcame every obstacle.

The Welsh Revival was primarily a revival of prayer. Evan Roberts prayed continually for thirteen months for the wave of revival to come. It is said of Roberts that his landlady "kicked him out" of his lodgings because she thought he

Maria Woodworth-Etter poster, Iowa, 1922. If she went into a town and nothing happened, she prayed all night until God's presence overcame every obstacle.

was possessed, or at least mad, because of his intense and loud praying.[9]

He came out of that prayer time and asked a friend, "Now do you believe God can give us a hundred thousand souls?" That vision was fulfilled in six months.

D. L. Moody's great success has been attributed to two "little old ladies" of prayer. Mrs. Sarah Cooke and a Mrs. Hawkhurst joyfully interceded on his behalf for the spiritual power he lacked. Moody resisted them at first, until he was overcome by a great new power for service.[10]

In 1905, the year before the Azusa outpouring, people throughout the South packed churches for prayer and confession. Stores and factories in the Mid-West closed to let employees go to services of dedication and intercession. Schools closed, and in Colorado, twelve thousand people attended prayer meetings in downtown theaters and halls.[11]

In Los Angeles, just before the Azusa Street revival broke out, the people were called to prayer. As I mentioned earlier, Pastor Smale of First Baptist wrote to Evan Roberts in Wales to ask him the secret of the Welsh Revival.

Roberts wrote back, "My dear brother in the faith....I am impressed of your sincerity and honesty of purpose. Congregate the people who are willing to make a total surrender. Pray and wait. Believe God's promises. Hold daily meetings. May God bless you in your earnest prayer. Yours in Christ, Evan Roberts."[12]

The advice is no different for us today. If we want to see God move in His fullness, we must make a total surrender of our lives to Him. Pray, wait, and believe God, meet regularly, and watch for Him to move.

Frank Bartleman described their application of the advice in Roberts' letter this way:

> We prayed for a spirit of revival...until the burden became well nigh unbearable. I cried out like a woman in birth pangs. The Spirit was interceding through us.[13]

In revival prayer, a person presents himself to God to give birth to the act of God in his area. Paul wrote to the Galatians: **My little children, of whom I travail in birth again until Christ be formed in you** (Gal. 4:19 KJV). Isaiah related, **At this my body is racked with pain** [my stomach constricts], **pangs seize me, like those of a woman in labor...**(Is. 21:3).

When Elijah prayed for rain, he assumed the position of a Jewish woman when she gave birth: **So Ahab went off to eat and drink, but Elijah climbed to the top of Carmel, bent down to the ground and put his face between his knees** (1 Kings 18:42).

Can children be born without pain? Yet how many of us expect in the supernatural realm what is not possible in the natural?[14]

In the entire Charismatic Movement, we have come to expect extraordinary results. We must again learn that extraordinary results require extraordinary efforts. Prevailing prayer is not easy. Only those who have wrestled with darkness know how hard that kind of prayer really is.[15]

I must warn you that this kind of praying is not some fleshly "attention-getting" ploy. This is a divine-human synergism to give birth to God's move in the hour. It is prayer directed at God's heartbeat and feeling His passion for manifestation. The first characteristic of this kind of prayer is that it is focused.[16]

Prevailing Prayer Must Be Focused

Tied to a lack of power in prayer is a lack of direction, focus, or true birthing of God's compassion in us. Daniel made this point clear as he responded to God in Daniel 9.

One day while in Babylonian captivity and desolation, he read in Jeremiah 25 that exile was to end in seventy years. Knowing that they were in the seventieth year, Daniel set himself to intercede for himself and his people:

> **So I turned to the Lord God and pleaded with him in prayer and petition, in fasting, and in sackcloth and ashes.**
>
> **— Daniel 9:3**

In verse 19 of that chapter, Daniel began to infuse his prayer with the mind, heart, and compassion of God:

> **"O Lord, listen! O Lord, forgive! O Lord, hear and act! For your sake, O my God, do not delay, because your city and your people bear your Name."**

Here we see the "divine-human synergism." God revealed Himself on one hand; and Daniel, feeling God's heart and his own grief, focused in on recourse to God in order to give birth to the deliverance of a nation.

In Evangelist Mario Murillo's must-read book on revival, *Critical Mass,* he adds a second quality to this kind of prayer. He says we must radically change our concept of when to stop in prayer. When a woman enters a hospital to give birth, she gives up her right to a time limit. She is there for a purpose. The object is to take all the time needed to bring forth a new life.[17]

That is what Parham called "prevailing prayer." It is a never-give-up spirit that perseveres in prayer until the enemy is conquered and vanquished. It is an understanding of the timing of God's seasons and a willingness to persist until it is birthed.

Here is Evan Roberts' personal experience with God, told in his own words:

One Friday night last Spring, while praying at my bedside before retiring, I was taken up to a great expanse without time or space. It was communion with God. Before this I was afar off from God. I was frightened that night, but never since. So great was my shivering that I rocked the bed, and my brother, being awakened, took hold of me, thinking I was ill.[18]

This experience then took place nightly in Evan Roberts' life for three months, occurring each evening from 10 p.m. until 5 a.m. He wrote a message to the world about this time as follows:

The revival in South Wales is not of men, but of God. He has come very close to us. There is no question of creed or of dogma in this movement. We are teaching no sectarian doctrine, only the wonder and beauty of Christ's love. I have been asked concerning my methods. I have none. I never prepare what I shall speak, but I leave that to Him. I am not the source of the revival, but only one servant among what is growing to be a multitude. I wish no personal following, but only the world for Christ. I believe the world is on the threshold of a great religious revival, and pray daily that I may be allowed to help bring this about. Wonderful things have happened in Wales in a few weeks, but these are only a beginning. The world will be swept by His Spirit as a rushing mighty wind. Many who are now silent Christians will lead the movement. They will see great light, and will reflect this light to thousands now in darkness. Thousands will do more than we have accomplished, as God gives them power.[19]

Others would say of Roberts, "Such real travail for the souls of the unsaved I have never before witnessed."[20]

Frank Bartleman describes their prayers just before the Azusa outpouring: "I spent another all-night prayer [vigil] with Brother Buehmer....one night I lay helpless for two hours under the burden for souls."[21]

Wigglesworth made prayer the key to his ministry. Someone once asked if he regularly spent long seasons of prayer. He gave his own classic answer: "I don't often spend more than a half hour in prayer at one time, but I never go more than a half hour without praying."[22]

Through prayer, Wigglesworth learned the secret of seeing things from God's perspective. That is what launched the miracles of his meetings. He kept a ready ear to the voice of God and simply obeyed Him. He fasted every Sunday and could never remember seeing fewer than fifty people saved per week.

Men like John G. Lake set aside certain hours of the day for prayer and meditation. Many who observed his extremely busy ministry would ask him, "When do you find time to be alone with God and pray?"

He simply said, "How glad I am that God has taught me to pray as I run and run as I pray."[23]

He knew that the power to pray through to victory was not something to be treated lightly. Often he would spend sleepless nights battling the spirits of unbelief. He knew that was how Jesus conducted

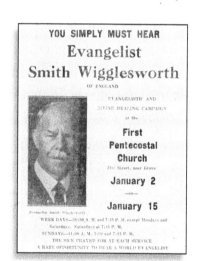

Smith Wigglesworth advertisement, 1930s. "I don't often spend more than a half hour in prayer, but I never go more than a half hour without praying."

His life, and he felt that if this was necessary for the Son of God, how much more so for his own life. He knew that wherever men have been willing to deny nights of sleep and abandon themselves to prayer, revival has followed.[24] God is looking for such intercessors today.

Revival Prayer

If you truly study revival, you will soon see that it is a cooperative effort between God's initiative and man's responsibility. Daniel saw God's timing and responded to it in prayer. (Dan. 9,10.) Zechariah said, **...Ask from the Lord rain in the seasons of latter rain...**(Zech. 10:1).[25] It is God working with us that produces true revival.

God's moves, or "rains," come in seasons. Peter said that the Lord would send seasons of refreshing, revival, and restoration. (Acts 3:19.)

Ralph Mahoney asked, "Did the people pray and fast because of His desire to revive His people, or did God send revival in readiness to the people's prayer?"[26]

Perhaps the best example of this kind of prayer is seen in the actions of the Old Testament prophet Elijah. Before we examine how he prayed, let us consider the fruit of his life, because it shows us the key of God's mantle falling from one generation to the next.

In 2 Kings 2:1,2, we find Elijah and Elisha on their way from Gilgal just before Elijah passed his mantle to Elisha:

> **Elijah said to Elisha, "Stay here; the Lord has sent me to Bethel."**
>
> **But Elisha said, "As surely as the Lord lives and as you live, I will not leave you." So they went down to Bethel.**

Why would Elisha not leave Elijah? He would not leave him because he knew that where Elijah was, the power of God was "happening." Elisha was hungry for the things of God and did not want to miss them. Others in the "school of prophets" knew as well as Elisha that Elijah was going to be taken from them that day, but they followed from a distance. (2 Kings 2:3,5,7 KJV.)

The mentality of so many Christians today is that of the "school of prophets." They want God to move, but they only want to observe from a distance. Elisha represents the kind of people upon whom God pours out His Spirit: a people who are hungry enough to do whatever it takes to see God's power in action.

Elijah challenged Elisha's fidelity four times those last days as they journeyed to four different cities. Though you will not find this in any commentary, I believe that each city was an object lesson to prepare Elisha for the passing of God's mantle of authority upon his life. For instance, Gilgal was the place where God had parted the Jordan River so the Israelites could cross on dry ground into the promised land. There, they placed twelve stones together as a monument of God's miracle on their behalf. Gilgal was a place of remembrance. (Josh. 4:1-9.)

Do you remember the first time you prayed — and it worked? How about the first time someone was healed and you were a part of that experience? You thought you were called to full-time ministry for sure. I remember the first time I thought I had received a word of knowledge from God.

I said, "Lord, if it's really You — have someone in the congregation sneeze — three times!"

To my surprise, it happened as I had asked, and out came the words from my mouth like a machine gun. Lo and behold, they were accurate! Those remembrances bring faith to us. That is what happened to Elisha. Gilgal brought remembrances of what God had done for His people. That is what this book is intended to be: a reference point for our faith to know that God is the same yesterday, today, and forever.

There were similar tests at each of the other three cities mentioned in 2 Kings 2. Finally, in verse 9, Elijah asked Elisha, "What do you want?" and Elisha replied, "I want double what you have."

That should be the heart cry of every one of us today. God is never anticlimactic. He will never be outdone by a previous move of His Spirit. He will always surpass what He has done in the past. I believe that God fully intends to finish this age with the greatest outpouring of the Spirit that the world has ever known.

Elijah stipulated that if Elisha saw him when God took him, Elisha would receive a double portion of the anointing that was upon him. In a sudden moment, a fiery chariot swept out of heaven in a whirlwind and whisked Elijah away. Elisha picked up the fallen mantle and struck the water of the Jordan with it! Why? He wanted to know if he had received what he had asked for. To his delight, the water split before his very eyes.

The Jordan River must have been schizophrenic because it was split so many times by God's men: by Joshua's priests at Gilgal, by Elijah, and now by Elisha.

I can see the fish talking to one another when prophets passed by: "Uh oh, here they come again. You guys go to the right, and we'll go to the left."

Elisha's next question, **"...Where now is the Lord, the God of Elijah?..."** (v. 14) is the same question people are asking today: "Where is the Lord God of Oral, Kathryn, and Wigglesworth?"

I submit to you, however, that the real question is not, "Where is the God of Elijah?" but "Where are the Elijahs of God?" The hour has arrived for us to be what we want to see.

John G. Lake, 1935. "The secret of Christianity is not doing.... It is being the possessor of the nature of Jesus Christ."

John G. Lake said, "...the secret of Christianity is not doing, the secret is *being*. It is being the possessor of the nature of Christ."[27]

The true secret of power is to abide in the perfect leading of Christ. It is this simple key that possessed Elijah's life. If we are to emulate and imitate such a man, if we are to "consider the ways of our leaders," we must know the fruit of their lives.

The first time we hear of Elijah is in 1 Kings 17:1 when he arrived at King Arab's palace demanding an audience. The Bible does not give us details, but Elijah pronounced a decree: "For three years there is to be no rain."

What kind of man has that sort of power from God?

During the drought, ravens fed him bread and meat. What kind of man does God send the birds of the air to supply with food? God then sent Elijah supernatural provision under a widow's care, for which Elijah raised her son from the dead. He later called down fire from heaven and singlehandedly defeated eight hundred and fifty prophets of Baal and Asherah. What kind of man commands such miracle-working power?

The answer to all these questions is that Elijah was a man of "inquiring prayer."

In the next chapter, I would like to show you that revival prayer is inquiring prayer. This kind of prayer does not "command" God, but responds to Him. That is the necessary spiritual preparation for revival to be launched.

Chapter 5

The Key to Revival Power: Inquiring Prayer

There exists a "seen" in the midst of the unseen, the temporal in the midst of the eternal.

—William Branham

..."O Lord,...let it be known today that you are God...and that I [Elijah] am your servant and have done all these things at your command."

— 1 Kings 18:36

There have been many marvelous volumes written about prayer, and it is not my intent to duplicate them. We are indeed indebted to men like Larry Lea, Paul Yonggi Cho, and Dick Eastman. However, I want to introduce you to an aspect of prayer that is birthed out of the seasons of God's heart.

About Elijah, we have asked, "What kind of man was this that he could do such great exploits for God?"

You can see the kind of man Elijah was the first time he showed up in Scriptures when he walked up to Ahab's palace and demanded an audience. The Bible does not say it exactly this way, but I am inclined to agree with Evangelist Jerry Savelle.[1]

Elijah walked up to the guard at the gate and said, "I'm Elijah the Tishbite. I want to see the king."

The guard might have said, "What's a 'tishbite'? Is that like a mosquito bite? Boys, get the healing balm! I've got a 'tishbite.'"

Elijah would have just stood his ground and reiterated his desire to see the king. I have no idea what the likelihood was of an unknown getting to see the king in those days, but I imagine it would be like me showing up at the gates of the White House and saying, "I'm Ron McIntosh, a chaplain. I want to see the President!"

The guard might respond, "Oh, great! What's a chaplain?"

Somehow I do not think my chances of being admitted would be all that great.

Ahab's guard must have finally gone in to the king's throne and said, "Sir, Elijah the Tishbite is here to see you."

Possibly the king asked, "What is a 'tishbite'?"

"I don't know, sir."

"Well, I want to see one. Send him in."

The word quickly spread that a "tishbite" was coming into the palace. The whole court would have been straining their necks to see what a "tishbite" was, when Elijah confidently strode into the throne room and declared:

"I'm Elijah the Tishbite. May I have your attention, please. *No more rain until I say so.* Thank you very much for the audience, King Ahab." — and out he walked.

James told us what kind of man Elijah was when he wrote about the principle of *inquiring prayer* in Elijah's life:

> **Elijah was man just like us. He prayed earnestly [fervently] that it would not rain, and it did not rain on the land for three and a half years. Again he prayed, and the heavens gave rain...**
>
> **— James 5:17,18**

Before Elijah could make an absolute pronouncement that there would be no rain until he said so, he had to first receive a message from God in response to his seeking of the Lord's will through inquiring prayer.

We might say, "That is okay for Elijah or Elisha or Oral, but we are just common folks."

That is the whole point of this passage. If we will learn the heart of revival prayer, it will make us the next generation of Elijahs. We will be the ones to answer when the question is asked, "Where are the Elijahs of God?"

The key to understanding Elijah's ministry is understanding that he *was* "a man just like us" — a human being. In *The Amplified Bible*, James 5:17 reads as follows:

> **Elijah was a human being with a nature such as we have — with feelings, affections and constitution as ourselves....**

First, James said that Elijah was a *human being*. So far, we are okay. We are all part of the human race. Next, he said that Elijah was a human being *with a nature*. Evidently, James was talking about the nature of our flesh. Elijah was subject to the carnal aspect of life just as we are. You might ask, "Do you mean, if he saw a woman in a two-piece camel-skin suit, he might have been tempted?" Exactly! Fortunately, Elijah learned to overcome his human tendency toward carnality.

The third thing to note in that verse is that the prophet had *feelings*. Again, we all qualify. We all have feelings. Sometimes we are up, and sometimes we do not feel so "up." There are times I do not feel like ministering to people, and there are times they do not feel like receiving ministry.

Right after Elijah finished defeating eight hundred and fifty prophets on Mount Carmel singlehandedly, one woman by the name of Jezebel said to her soldiers, "Get him!" and he fled for his life. Evidently the wrath of one woman was greater than the wrath of eight hundred and fifty prophets! The real key to understanding Elijah is the fact that after his great victory, he had an emotional "let down" and became subject to feelings — just as we do.

The Bible also says that Elijah had *affections*. He had passions that were not from God. There are times when all of us have affections that are not godly. That is why Paul wrote that Christians should set their affection on things above, not on earthly things. (Col. 3:2 KJV.)

The Greek word translated *affection* in Colossians 3:2 (KJV) does not convey the impression that we usually have of *affection* in English. We usually think of it primarily as caring for or about something. However, in the original text the Greek word is *phroneo*, which means "to *exercise* the *mind*, i.e., *entertain* or *have a sentiment or opinion;* by impl. [implication] to *be* (mentally) *disposed* (more or less earnestly in a certain direction)," or "to amuse."[2]

The concept of *to amuse* is the opposite of to muse. To muse means to think about. To *amuse* means not to think about, or to divert attention from.[3] This word *affection* is not used anywhere else in the New Testament. What Paul was conveying to his readers is that we need to set our *minds*, our thoughts, our attentions on the things of God. We need to be wholeheartedly *disposed earnestly* in His direction. We need to *muse* on Him and His desires and will for us as individuals and for the Church at large.

In America, however, we are into *amusement*. Literally, we are captivated by things that divert our attention *from* the things of God. Many of our forms of entertainment pull our thinking from things above. An overdose of MTV, heavy metal music, or movies or literature with wrong messages promote undesirable values and dilute the flow and power of God.

Elijah was a man who had affections just as we do.

Finally, we are told that he had a constitution. A *constitution* is what a person is made of. It is the quality that causes us to "press in" or "back off." Elijah had times when he grew tired of standing up for what he believed. That is where many of us are right now.

Will we settle for a "microwaveable" Christianity, or will we contend for the faith? Elijah had to face the same feelings and address the same issues in his day.

The question becomes, "How, then, did he gain such power in his life?"

The answer is found in this little phrase, he "prayed earnestly" or fervently. The word *fervently* means white hot, intense, or heartfelt.[4] The term *white hot* conveys the modern idea of two pieces of steel being heated into such a state that they can be welded into one piece. Fervent prayer makes us one with God.

In heartfelt prayer, whose heart are we feeling? We are feeling the heart of God. The word *heart* is an interesting one. In the Hebrew culture, they understood *heart* to mean soul, understanding, affections, mode of thinking, seat of emotions, or purpose.[5] To pray the heart of God is to pray from His understanding, His affections, His passion or thinking.

You might ask, how did that apply to Elijah? In 1 Kings 17:1, when Elijah pronounced a three-year drought, did he declare it by his own volition, or from the heart of God? Look at 1 Kings 18:1:

After a long time, in the third year, the word of the Lord came to Elijah: "Go and present yourself to Ahab, and I will send rain on the land."

Elijah knew it would rain again after three years, because the word of the Lord was spoken unto him. It is then equally logical that when he made his opening declaration to the king, it was at God's command as well. Similarly, when he met the prophets on Mount Carmel, the miraculous was at the word of the Lord:

> **Elijah went before the people and said: "How long will you waver between two opinions? If the Lord is God, follow him; but if Baal is God, follow him."**
>
> **— 1 Kings 18:21**

The prophet encouraged the people to construct two huge barbecue pits and then to place a prepared bull on the altar. They were then to pray, and to ask their god to display himself. The God who answered by sending fire to consume the sacrifice would be acknowledged as the One True God.

The pagan prophets cried out from morning till noon, and nothing happened. Elijah, understanding the heart of God, began taunting them. The priests of Baal began shouting to their god, even cutting themselves to get his attention.

Finally, Elijah stood again before the people and commanded them to pour water on his sacrifice until the surrounding trench was filled with water. In response to his prayer, the sacrifice was consumed by fire and even the stones, the soil, and the water in the trenches were licked up. Then the Bible says that when the people saw this, they fell prostrate before God. (1 Kings 18:39.) I expect they did! They probably thought they might be next.

The key to this great display of God's power is found in verses 36 and 37 of 1 Kings 18, when Elijah prayed to God before the consuming fire fell:

> **"...I am your servant and have done all these things at your command. Answer me, O Lord, answer me, so these people will**

know that you, O Lord, are God, and that you are turning their hearts back again."

Notice that Elijah did all these things *at God's command*. His prayer was a divinely interwoven desire of God placed in the cooperative hand of the intercessor. Elijah was in "inquiring prayer." Elijah was in *revival* prayer.

The key to revival is the heartfelt, fervent, intense prayers of God's people.

The miracle flow of God is dependent on such a divine-human synergism. This principle is not capsuled in the Old Testament alone. Jesus taught it in Matthew 18:18:

"I tell you the truth, whatever you bind on earth will be bound in heaven, and whatever you loose on earth will be loosed in heaven."

This verse is usually left in the hands of a few "Charismaniacs" who go around binding anything that is not nailed down. The verse should literally be translated this way: "What you bind on earth shall *already* have been bound in heaven, and whatever you loose on earth shall *already* have been loosed in heaven."

The initiative for spiritual warfare begins in heaven, not in the frailty of the human source. It is our job to engage in a viable, abiding relationship of God's heartbeat and passion, and then to cooperate with divine power on the earth.

This is not a popular teaching, because it demands far more than imitating a principle; it demands hearing from heaven. Jesus, Himself, operated this way in His own ministry. He said:

"...the Son can do nothing by himself; he can do only what he sees his Father doing, because whatever the Father does the Son also does....

> "By myself I can do nothing; I judge only as I hear, and my judg-
> ment is just, for I seek not to please myself but him who sent me."
> — John 5:19,30
> (see also John 7:16; 8:26-28;12:49,50;14:10)

Suddenly I am catapulted in memory back to Seoul, South Korea, and Yonggi Cho's words, "I pray and obey." It took me ten years to understand that statement, but finally I saw what he meant. It is *my* responsibility to discern the heart, timing, and passions of God, and then in conversation with Him, to implement His divine plan for the moment.

That is revival prayer.

Perhaps no one I have studied understood that principle as well as William Branham. F. F. Bosworth would say of Branham's miracle ministry:

> He sees to break through the veil of the flesh into the world of the Spirit, to be struck through and with a sense of the unseen.[6]

Branham himself said:

> There exists a "seen" in the midst of the unseen, the temporal in the midst of the eternal.[7]

Often Branham would do little more than act out that which he already had seen in a vision.

In 1 Kings 3:7,9 Solomon cried out to the Lord:

> "...I am only a little child and do not know how to carry out my
> duties....So give your servant a discerning heart to govern your
> people and to distinguish between right and wrong. For who is able
> to govern this great people of yours?"

The word *discerning* refers to "an understanding mind and a listening heart." (v. 9 AMP.) Solomon knew he must have a hearing heart to truly rule the people of God. Albert Hibbert would disclose that a "discerning heart," or "inquiring prayer," was the key to Smith Wiggleworth's ministry. He would respond to

God's instruction and then act in great confidence. His critics called it coincidence that he seemed always to be at the right place at the right time with the right word.

When Wigglesworth was asked about what methods he would use in a particular service, he would simply reply, "It all depends on what the Father has to say."[8] Once when two blind people, with very similar symptoms, came to him back to back in the prayer line, he prayed for them in two completely different fashions. With one he rebuked a demon, with the other he prayed for healing. The sight of both was miraculously restored. *Inquiring prayer is revival prayer.*

Steps to "Praying and Obeying"

Let me give you some practical steps to help you learn to hear God's voice more clearly and to discern His heart:

1. *Pray for divine desire*. Psalm 37:4 says, **Delight yourself in the Lord and he will give you the desires of your heart.** The key is in the condition, *Delight yourself*, which has the connotation of not being able to get enough of something.

It is like the bowl games at the New Year season for the "football junkie." He cannot get enough football. In my case, I cannot get enough of God. It is in such Christians that God plants His desires or gives to them the desires of their hearts.

Our ambitions mean nothing to God. He is raising up a new generation of people who will make themselves of no reputation. The way up in the Kingdom of God is down. We must be like John the Baptist when he decreed of Jesus, "He must increase, and I must decrease." (John 3:30 KJV.)

John Alexander Dowie would learn — and later in life tragically forget — that:

> Power in the church is not like power in the government of the United States, where a man climbs to the top of the pyramid of his fellows to the acme of his ambition, and there makes it fulfill his personal pride and purpose; power in the church is shown in this that a man gets lower and lower....[9]

I am not referring to some religiously ignorant ploy to kill the self-esteem of a person, but a legitimate dying of self that lets God's heart surface. How many times have we prayed to be the Ed McMahon ten-million-dollar sweepstakes winner to honor God, when that thought is nothing more than a guise to cover lust in our lives? How many people want to see God's healing power for their own reputation rather than for His Kingdom? A heart of divine desire is conditional for His voice to be manifested.

2. *Believe that you can hear God.* Most believers with whom I talk do not believe that God will really speak to them. I find that many believers are hearing from God. They just cannot believe that it is His voice. Jesus said, **"My sheep listen to my voice..."** (John 10:27). Believe it! Do it!

3. *Pray in tongues and interpret them.* I have found that almost all revivalists enjoyed a renewed fervor of tongues. Many considered it to be one of the greatest blessings from God in their lives. Tongues is the communing voice of relationship to God. It is **...groans that words cannot express** (Rom. 8:26). The *King James Version* uses the word *groanings* which refers to praying with inaudible words or from a great sense of grief or emotion and implies a painful desire to see something happen.[10]

As a pastor, I have traveled hospital corridors on many occasions, and I have heard people groaning. Most of the time, I was unaware of why they were groaning, but they knew the reason for their groans. It is the same way when spiritual groanings come through us. We may not totally understand what they mean, but the Holy Spirit is expressing a painful desire to see something happen, through one of His vessels, according to His will. (Rom. 8:27.)

First Corinthians 2:9-13,16, expresses the entire concept in this manner:

However, as it is written:

"No eye has seen,

no ear has heard,

no mind has conceived

what God has prepared for those

who love him" —

But God has revealed it to us by his Spirit.

The Spirit searches all things, even the deep things of God. For who among men knows the thoughts of a man except the man's spirit within him? In the same way no one knows the thoughts of God except the Spirit of God. We have not received the spirit of the world but the Spirit who is from God, that we may understand what God has freely given us. This is what we speak, not in words taught us by human wisdom but in words taught by the Spirit, expressing spiritual truths in spiritual words....

"For who has known the mind of the Lord

that he may instruct him?"

But *we have the mind of Christ.*

It is evident from this passage that praying in tongues (or praying in the Spirit, which is the same thing — 1 Cor. 14:13,14) is the key to the revelation of God's will for the individual to be manifested. It is the key to understanding the mind of God. Paul tells us how to do this practically in 1 Corinthians 14:13-15:

> For this reason anyone who speaks in a tongue should pray that
> he may interpret what he says. For if I pray in a tongue, my spirit
> prays, but my mind is unfruitful. So what shall I do? I will pray
> with my spirit, but I will also pray with my mind.

What Paul is telling us is this: If we pray in the Spirit, or in
tongues, or with God's passionate utterings, we can pray that we
can interpret or have an understanding of His mind. The reason
for this prayer language or praying in tongues is expressed later
in this chapter:

> For anyone who speaks [or prays, see vv. 26,14] in a tongue does
> not speak to men but to God. Indeed, no one understands him...
>
> Now, brothers, if I come to you and speak [or pray] in tongues,
> what good will I be to you, unless I bring to you some revelation or
> knowledge or prophecy or word of instruction?....
>
> For this reason anyone who speaks [or prays] in a tongue should
> pray that he may interpret what he says.
>
> — 1 Corinthians 14:2,6,13

The purpose of "tongues," or the prayer language, is to bring
the believer some revelation, knowledge, or instruction by the
supernatural act of interpretation in communion with God. A
man prays in tongues, receives the interpretation from God, and
therefore revelation (hidden truth), a prophecy (a foretelling or
forthtelling of God) or word of instruction (a verbal impartation
of supernatural knowledge, skill, or education) is given to him.
Praying in tongues is a major key to receiving the discerning
knowledge of God.

4. *Engage in scriptural screening.* No voice from God should
ever contradict the Holy Scriptures. The Holy Spirit Who authored
the Word of God would never violate it. To do so would violate the
very nature of God. In 1 John 4:1, we are exhorted to:

...test the spirits to see whether they are from God, because many false prophets have gone out into the world.

It was Charles Parham's assessment that the Azusa Street revival was brought to an end for violating this principle. It was his conviction that Azusa Street was invaded and infiltrated by witchcraft. The participants became undiscerning about "words" given there and killed the revival.[11] Parham's assessment itself is not verified by historians, but the point is well taken. A word properly discerned can initiate a move of God. A word of God improperly discerned can kill a move of God.

A word from God should:

(1) Be *directly* in tune with God's character, (2) *ultimately* disregard confusion, condemnation, or discouragement, and (3) *ultimately* create peace in the heart. (Col. 3:15.)

5. Look for *divine timing*.

In Habakkuk 2:2,3 the Lord says:

"...write down the revelation and make it plain on tablets so that a herald may run with it.

"For the revelation awaits an appointed time...."

All words from God have a season as well as a directive. It is essential to understand that every revelation has a timing. We must wait for the appointed time.

6. *Boldly obey.* Revelation has little value if it is not obeyed. There is a difference between patience and passivity. Patience is a virtue of time. Passivity is the sin of the last decade. The "yuppy sin" of our era is believing that we can no longer change our world, so we are only concerned about changing ourselves. The results have been a manifestation of lethargy. It is time to believe again.

The Quest for Revival ───────────────────────────── 🐦

The Secret of Fasting

I am including one last thought on revival prayer. Many of the great revivalists knew the secret and necessity of fasting. Most of them either fasted to launch their miracle ministries or practiced fasting as a lifestyle.

Perhaps the most noted teacher on fasting in the Healing Revival was Franklin Hall. While a great number of his doctrinal conclusions demand scrutiny, many of the major evangelists of the era followed his fasting teachings, and miracles erupted everywhere.[12] Hall was convinced that the source of the Healing Revival could be traced to 1946, when a group of Spirit-filled believers began holding all-night prayer meetings. They fasted for great lengths of time for God to manifest Himself again.

Many of the healing evangelists of this time slot acknowledged Hall as the one who planted the seed into their lives. World-renowned evangelist T. L. Osborn said that his ministry was revolutionized by fasting. He indicated that it was the turning point of his healing ministry.

Gordon Lindsay, the key organizer and chronicler of the movement, would say that many of the Voice of Healing fellowship, like himself, believed that fasting and prayer were vital keys to healing ministry.

Even Martin Luther fasted and prayed for days at a time when translating the Bible prior to the Reformation. In Jesus' life, there is no record of His ever healing the sick or performing any great miracles without having first fasted for forty days and forty nights.

Hall taught that fasting restores and amplifies prayer power — that fasting is the most potent force in the universe. It was his earnest conviction that his worldwide fasting crusades, begun in 1945, really birthed the revival that broke out in 1947.

According to Hall, many people fasted for ten to twenty-one days and with great success.[13]

Fasting is a physical hunger, the kind that reminds us of a greater spiritual hunger. Literally the word *fast* means to abstain from food, to refrain voluntarily, or to experience momentary deprivation.

Fasting is not a humanistic manipulation of God. It is instead a denial of self and the inviting of God's presence conditioned in the surrender of the will.

Fasting does not draw God to man, but man to God. It is a sensitizing of the believer to the whole spiritual realm.

The Vital Link

Inquiring prayer is the vital link which every revivalist understood opened the windows of heaven. It is what Jesus meant when He taught us to pray, **"Your kingdom come, your will be done on earth as it is in heaven"** (Matt. 6:10). It is a directive to discover what is established in heaven and to call it forth in the earth.

Inquiring prayer cannot be done in the flesh or in the frailty of our humanity, but only in accordance with the season of God. It is reminiscent of the apostles when they understood that **...the day of Pentecost was fully come...**(Acts 2:1 KJV). It is a divine-human synergism that unleashes the power of heaven. It is the divine magnetism that causes man's state to be irresistibly drawn together with God's power. It is the breaking up of the fallow ground of our hearts for the latter rain of God's presence.

Inquiring prayer is a prevailing, never-give-up prayer of victory until the gates of hell have been stormed and destroyed. This divine-human synergism is the kind of prayer that gives birth to the move of God.

Now it is imperative that we turn our attention to a key for the miraculous: a real relationship with the Holy Spirit.

The Key to the Miraculous: Communion With the Holy Spirit

Smith Wigglesworth was transformed from a bumbling, stuttering owner of a plumbing business into a vessel of faith, once he was baptized with the Holy Spirit.

The power of the baptism of the Holy Spirit cannot be overestimated.

— *Smith Wigglesworth*

One day in the Seventies I found myself sitting in the large Gothic-cathedral-type sanctuary of Tulsa's First United Methodist Church. Somehow this seemed an odd setting in which to fulfill the purpose for which we were gathered together. I — along with several thousand other people — had arrived a few hours early to hear and see the ministry of the Holy Spirit through Miss Kathryn Kuhlman.

Even though almost three hours early, my girlfriend and I had to sit several rows from the back of the church. The anticipation was incredible. Until that day, I do not believe I can remember being part of a more expectant crowd.

I had never witnessed this ministry about which I had heard so much, and I hungered to see *real* miracles. I longed with every fiber of my being to see the reality of God. The hours seemed to fly by as I eagerly anticipated the events to come that day.

Finally the preliminary part of the meeting was over and Miss Kuhlman came onto the platform. I was almost shocked to see a thin, frail-looking woman in a flowing, chiffon gown. My shock almost instantly gave way to horror, as I heard what I considered to be an overly theatrical, almost melodramatic voice.

At first, I found it impossible to get past what I considered the physical limitations of God's servant. However, suddenly, my reservations were swept away in the incredible revelation this marvelous woman began to share.

I will never forget the way she expounded on an intimacy with the Holy Spirit that I had rarely heard about. The presence of that same Holy Spirit seemed to increase with each passing moment, until it reached climactic proportions. Then she dramatically began to "shift gears."

Instead of talking about the Holy Spirit, she seemed to be taking instructions from Him. The supernatural gifts of the word of knowledge seemed to flow from her as the Holy Spirit whispered in her ear.

She would point and say, "A woman in a yellow dress in this section of the auditorium is being healed of cancer of the stomach. A middle-aged man in the back is having a cleansing of his body, and his arteries are being cleaned out."

On and on she would go. It appeared that believers and skeptics alike were being healed by the incredible power of God.
Even hearing and seeing all that, it startled me when, in her characteristic style, she pointed a long, bony finger in my direction.
My heart began to beat heavily as she continued to operate in the
supernatural anointing of the Holy Spirit.

She called out the next revelation of God, and it was in the
very back section of the church where I was sitting. The moment
was so electric I did not hear the ailment she identified. However,
almost instantly, a dialogue began behind my friend and me while
Miss Kuhlman proceeded with the service. The couple sitting
behind us began to interact in very loud whispers.

The wife said, "That's you! Go on up to the front." (It was
Miss Kuhlman's custom to bring to the platform those who had
been healed to give their testimonies.)

The husband reacted defiantly, "I'm not going anywhere. This
stuff is fake."

The entire section of the church was astir as the couple's conversation could not help but be overheard. It was all I could do
not to turn around and ask them what they were experiencing.
The service continued as if the event had never taken place, but
about ten minutes later, Miss Kuhlman again pointed to the section in which I was sitting.

She said, "I called this sickness out earlier, and you did
not respond. You have a heart condition" (she explained it in
some detail), "and you need to come forward now to receive
your healing."

Again, almost instantly, the husband and wife began to interact.

"That's you!" the wife said. "You better go forward."

Almost angrily this time, the husband responded, "I told you this stuff is fake. I'm not going anywhere."

The entire event went unnoticed by the majority of people in the auditorium, but virtually every person in the vicinity of this couple could overhear them. The conversation, however, was not unnoticed by the Holy Spirit. In five to ten minutes, Miss Kuhlman once again came back to the situation.

"This is the third time I have called out this healing," she said. "You have a heart condition." (Again she amplified upon the condition to which she was referring.) "If you do not come forward right now, you won't be healed."

With some more prodding from his wife, the man reluctantly moved to the front of the auditorium. I was now straining my neck to see what God was going to do in the life of this skeptic. In what was a short framework of time, I watched as he was interviewed by an attendant and ushered to the platform.

Miss Kuhlman finally turned to him and stretched out her hand. When she was about five feet away from him, he suddenly — and I might add, unexpectedly — was overcome by the power of God and "slain in the Spirit" (a common manifestation in Miss Kuhlman's meetings). He slumped to the floor as if dead and lay there for about fifteen minutes.

The meeting continued with numerous reports of healings, but my eyes remained riveted upon my new-found "acquaintance." When a short time had elapsed, he staggered to his feet, Miss Kuhlman approached him, and he went down again.

Almost as if it were choreographed, this happened almost identically a third time some minutes later. The man struggled to his feet the fourth time, and Miss Kuhlman again approached him. He put up his hands as if to say, "Please, lady,

I've had enough." This time, however, he did not go down, and my curiosity would be satisfied as the evangelist interviewed the man.

Miss Kuhlman looked at him and said, "My goodness, sir, it seems as if you needed something from God today."

Almost stunned, the man could only emphatically shake his head to the delight of the crowd.

She then proceeded to ask, "Sir, do you believe this is real?"

Again, all the humbled man could do was shake his head with equal emphasis. She then looked at him with eyes of compassion and asked, "What do you do for a living?"

With almost an embarrassed stance, he responded, "I'm a Baptist minister."

"Oh!" she asked, "Do you think you are ready to share this with your congregation?"

All the shocked minister could do was shake his head in a funny little manner, as the congregation howled and applauded its approval. He finally testified that he felt as if his entire body had been given an "overhaul," and he knew he had been touched by God.

That was the first time I had ever seen such a manifestation of the Holy Spirit in my young Christian life. The next year at Oral Roberts University when Kathryn Kuhlman came to Tulsa again, I sang in the choir, although I could not "carry a tune in a bucket." I joined the choir just so I could be near the power of God.

Again, the same wonderful presence of God filled the auditorium of the Mabee Center on campus. In one moment, Miss Kuhlman turned back to where the choir was sitting and simply waved her hand. The power of the Holy Spirit was so strong that several hundred of us in that section were "slain in the Spirit" at one time.

The Baptism Is More Than "Tongues"

That was a pivotal time in my Christian life, because it created an irrepressible hunger for the kind of power and relationship with the Holy Spirit that Kathryn Kuhlman experienced. It seems a foregone conclusion that any examination of Pentecostal or Charismatic revivals should have the baptism with the Holy Spirit as a "given." Yet so much of what takes place seems to have the effect of reducing Holy Spirit baptism to a believer's speaking in tongues.

While I value tongues as an inestimable gift from God, the baptism with the Holy Spirit is much more than that. It is the explosion of power in a believer's life — power for miracles and conviction.

The early revivalists saw the baptism with the Holy Spirit as far more than the subsequent experience to salvation and a new tool of communication with God. The relationship with the Holy Spirit became the launching pad for their miracle ministries. It was "the baptism with the Holy Spirit and fire" of Matthew 3:11.

John G. Lake related this relationship to an intense hunger. He said:

> When I approached this matter of the baptism [with the Holy Spirit], I did so with great care, but I approached it as a hungry soul. My heart was hungry for God.[1]

For six months after his experience with the Holy Ghost, the Spirit revealed to Lake things in his life that required repentance, confession, or restitution.[2] Not only did Lake receive tongues and power, but he received the fire of God to cleanse him and create God-given passions within him.

This was not a self-indulgent preoccupation with past wounds, but a surrender of his life to the rejuvenating revelation of the Holy Spirit. He dealt only with those things the Spirit of God brought to his attention.

Perhaps most important, however, was that after the Holy Spirit had purged his life, He created a new power in Lake, and God's healing was of a more potent order. Now there came an ability to discern and cast out demons.

The miracle power of God was so prolific that tens of thousands were drawn to Lake's meetings in Africa. One Johannesburg man was so attracted that he came to the services although everyone in the crowd knew him to be a man of "reproachable character." The power of God was so strong in the meeting that the man realized he had to make a clean slate of his secret sins.

During the meeting, which lasted until 4:00 a.m., the man ran to the altar and drew from his pockets a watch and a sum of money. Throwing these to one side, within minutes he was baptized with the Spirit and had begun speaking in tongues. Those present recognized the language as German.

Later, it was related that the money he had thrown aside was funds he had cheated out of unsuspecting rail passengers as trainmaster. He had charged them more than was required for their tickets. The watch was one that had fallen out of someone's suitcase and had not been returned by the man.

Such manifestations in Lake's ministry became commonplace after he was baptized with the Spirit.

Dr. Cyndylan Jones pointed out that the question, **...Have ye received the Holy Ghost since ye believed?**...(Acts 19:2 KJV) was at the forefront of the Welsh Revival. Gordon Lindsay wrote:

What happened in Wales would become an object lesson for the entire church in every land. If true members of Christ in every nation — be they few or many — were to *each* receive *what* God *means* by a *baptism in the Holy Ghost and fire*, signs and wonders would follow. [Emphasis mine.] It has been truly said that the world cannot be "revived," for it is dead. A worldwide revival, therefore, means the quickening of the people of God....[3]

Lindsay's words are the captivating force of recapturing miracle-working power in a prolific manner. If every member of the Body of Christ would receive what God means by a baptism with the Holy Spirit, then fire, signs, and wonders would erupt.

Smith Wigglesworth was transformed from a bumbling, stuttering owner of a plumbing business into a vessel of faith, once he was baptized with the Holy Spirit. No longer was he relegated to leading a pony through the neighborhood to take little children to Sunday school. He became a "holy rage" released upon anything that was not like God.

This relationship with the Holy Spirit also revolutionized Charles Finney. Here is his personal experience with the Spirit, which occurred before he entered the ministry, as he related it in his own words:

...The Holy Spirit descended upon me in a manner that seemed to go through my body and soul. I could feel the impression, like a wave of electricity going through and through me. It seemed like the very *breath of God*. I can recall distinctly that it seemed to fan me like immense wings. No words can express the wonderful love that was shed abroad in my heart....I literally bellowed out unutterable gushings of my heart. The waves came over me and over me, one after another until I recollect I cried out, "I shall die if the waves continue to pass over me." I said, "I cannot bear it any more." Yet I had no fear of death.[4]

The following morning after his wonderful baptism of power, there came a marvelous call to the ministry of love. All day long each encounter with the lost led to powerful convictions and conversions. His boss was the first man Finney spoke to after this experience, and the man was struck with such conviction that he was converted a few days later.

The baptism with the Holy Spirit is the inception of a relationship with God that transforms any ordinary person into the realm of the supernatural. Smith Wigglesworth would say, "We may be nothing, but in God, we can be mighty." His tapping of this spiritual secret set him apart from others who might have had greater natural ability or capacity.[5]

If anyone understood the ongoing relationship with the Holy Spirit, it was Evan Roberts. It was said of him that he was extremely sensitive to the leadings of the Spirit, and this sensitivity was to be the identifying characteristic of his entire ministry.

A London newspaper would say of him, "He seems more sensitive to the influence of the Holy Spirit than almost any Christian of our time."[6]

Roberts carried a sense of God's presence with him. He was guided and led by the Holy Spirit to Whom he was completely yielded. He was moved as God moved him.[7] Another newspaper put it this way:

...Evan Roberts, who speaks in Welsh, opens his discourse by saying that he is in *communion with the Spirit of God*. The preacher soon after launches out into a fervent, and at times, impassioned oration. His statements have had the most stirring effects upon his listeners.[8]

What we need in the Church today is a real outpouring of the Holy Spirit and fire — an outpouring of fire to purge us from anything that blocks our way to the power of God.

We Need a Real Outpouring

A real outpouring of the Holy Spirit is needed today to stir us to new heights of faith. We need a real touch from God to understand that it is not a matter of talent or mental prowess but a submission to the Godhead that will transcend our meager attempts and loose the power of heaven.

You might notice that I have used phrases such as "were each to receive what God means by a baptism in the Holy Ghost," "the baptism with the Holy Spirit is the inception of a relationship with God," and, "communion with the Spirit of God."

The reason for those phrases is that so many Spirit-filled congregations have done to this doctrine what many evangelicals have done to salvation — reduced it to a one-time culminating experience. In the Scriptures, *salvation* is referred to in three tenses:

1. "was saved" — as the experience that secures everlasting life.

2. "being saved" — as the working out of one's redemption with fear and trembling.

3. "shall be saved" — as the assurance of one's ultimate heavenly destiny.

Salvation is a one-time entrance into an ongoing growth experience. You and I were not saved simply to go to heaven, but also to destroy the works of the devil and to retrieve others from the jaws of hell and to secure their heavenly abode.

Similarly, the baptism with the Holy Spirit is a one-time entrance into an ongoing relationship of communion with the Holy Spirit. It is the secret nearly every great revivalist understood and demonstrated in the operation of miracle ministry.

I always have held that, if a person can be demon-possessed, an individual can be Holy Spirit-possessed. That was the secret to Kathryn Kuhlman's ministry. She exemplified a close personal relationship with the Holy Spirit as few people in history. She called Him "Friend," and to her He was the greatest Teacher in the whole world.

Following is a description in her own words of her close relationship with the Holy Spirit:

Four o'clock that Saturday afternoon, having come to the place in my life where I surrendered everything, I knew nothing about the fullness of the Holy Spirit. I knew nothing about speaking in an unknown tongue. I knew nothing about the deeper truths of the Word....

That afternoon Kathryn Kuhlman died....If you've never had that death to the flesh, you don't know what I'm talking about....when you're completely filled with the Holy Spirit, when you've had that experience as they had in the upper room...there will be a death to the flesh, believe me....there are a lot of professing Christians, professing to have been filled with the Holy Spirit, who have never died to the flesh.

...All He needs is somebody who will die, and when I died, He came in. I was baptized. I was filled with the Spirit I spoke in an unknown tongue as He took every part of me.[9]

This is what John the Baptist meant when he said:

"I baptize you with water for repentance. But after me will come one....He will baptize you with the Holy Spirit and *with fire*. His winnowing fork is in his hand, and he will clear his threshing floor, gathering the wheat into his barn and burning up the chaff with *unquenchable fire."*

— Matthew 3:11,12

In the gathering of wheat, a "winnowing fork" was used to toss the stalks up into the air to separate the true wheat from the chaff, which was the refuse and useless part. The chaff was to be burned up to leave that which was pure grain.

That afternoon was Kathryn's "call to death," and the Spirit would burn away the things not of God in order to give Himself freedom to be all that He could be through her. She would say of this experience:

...I surrendered unto Him all there was of me, everything! Then for the first time, I realized what it meant to have real power.[10]

This was not the end of her relationship with the Holy Spirit, but only the beginning. Simply put, more of God means less of self. On many occasions after the first time I saw her, I would hear her say that she trembled at the thought of ever grieving the Holy Spirit. She knew He was a Person, and that the only real way to be used by Him was to be sensitive to Him.

Evangelist-author Roberts Liardon describes how Miss Kuhlman warned Christians against trying to use the Holy Spirit.

"His power," she said, "is under His authority — not ours."[11]

She insisted that a Christian cannot be totally yielded to the Holy Spirit until nothing is left of self. She would describe an intimacy with the Holy Spirit few people have ever been able to comprehend:

You would have to be dead...because there cannot be two wills. There can only be one. There cannot be two personalities involved, there must be only one, and that is His....Sometimes I could go fifteen minutes and not remember one single thing [I] said.

There's a place of surrender to Him...[where] your ears aren't hearing and you're learning. You're being thrilled at what you are hearing [your own voice speak]. But it is not your mind, it is not your tongue....[12]

How does one know the woman over there in such and such a dress is being healed? I don't know. If my life depended on it, I could not tell you. I do not know, but the Holy Spirit knows.[13]

Now I understand what I witnessed in her crusade, almost twenty years ago, in that downtown Methodist church. The incredible words of knowledge that brought healing to hundreds that day, including the man who sat behind me, were the product of her intimate relationship with the Holy Spirit.

What was birthed in her by the baptism with the Holy

Kathryn Kuhlman. She lost all of herself to find all of God.

Spirit was cultivated in a communion with the Holy Spirit. Often I heard her say, "Do you want to know what it [this relationship] cost Kathryn Kuhlman? It cost me everything."

She lost all of herself to find all of God. The Holy Spirit fully desires to share Himself with His people, but in order for Him to do so, we must discover *the real truth* about Him.

The Real Truth About the Holy Spirit

The baptism with the Holy Spirit is the loosing of God's power, but that power must be cultivated for full effect.

The key is not methodology, but sensitivity.

In 1971, when I arrived at Oral Roberts University as a freshman, I had only been a Christian for a few months. In chapel services, I would hear President Roberts say, "The Holy Spirit said to me..."

I kept thinking to myself, "Why doesn't the Holy Spirit speak to me that way?"

In fact, I would see Oral on campus and would follow him at a distance in case he should get a revelation from God. I wanted to see how he did it! Some of my classmates tried to deter me from this practice, however.

They would say to me, "You can't hear God like Oral Roberts does."

"Why not?" I would ask.

The answer was always something like, "Well, because he is Oral Roberts," or, "because he has a higher call."

However, over the years, I found that God really is **...no respecter of persons** (Acts 10:34 KJV). The desire of the Holy Spirit is to share fellowship with *all* of His children, not just with certain "special ones."

The problem is not with His willingness or desire to speak to us; the problem is that we tend to reduce our relationships with Him to one-time experiences, such as when someone helped us to speak in tongues.

Kathryn Kuhlman used to say that many people believe they are baptized in the Holy Spirit when, in fact, they have not been truly and continuously filled with God's Holy, life-giving Spirit.

I would never minimize the one-time experience of Holy Spirit baptism, but it is the start of something, not the ending. The evidence of the baptism with the Holy Spirit is not simply "tongues," but a different relationship with Him.

"Tongues" did not cause Peter and the apostles to suddenly become different men on the Day of Pentecost. The difference came as a result of a new level of relationship, a fellowship of being able to have a new level of communication with God. (For verification, see verses such as Acts 8:29, 10:19, 11:12,28, 16:16.) "Tongues" simply was the evidence that this on-going relationship had come into existence.

We can readily see this truth in the Bible. When Jesus was ready to leave the disciples and return to heaven, He made them this promise:

> **"I am going to send you what my Father has promised; but stay in the city until you have been clothed with power from on high."**
> **— Luke 24:49**

The word *clothe* means to put on, to hide in, to be furnished with what is necessary, or to be armed.[1]

I do not get up in the morning, shower, towel off, then call out to my wife, "I'm off to work now, honey!"

People get arrested for going out on the street unclothed, or not dressed in what is considered acceptable attire for modern society. In the same way, we should not attempt to walk out in the Spirit realm in ministry — particularly "miracle" ministry — without being dressed in our spiritual clothes. In the above verse in Luke, Jesus actually was calling the baptism with the Holy Spirit our *clothing*.

The *real truth* of the Holy Spirit is that He clothes us with power. We are to "be clothed with," "furnished with," or "armed with" the power of the Holy Spirit. A gun will do no good in battle if it is not loaded. When Christians are "loaded," it is with the power of the Holy Spirit.

In Acts 1:1,2, Luke stated, **In my former book** [the book of Luke]**...I wrote about all that Jesus began to do and to teach, until the day he was taken up to heaven....** Jesus' life, as recorded in the Gospels, was about what He *began* to do and teach while on earth. The book of Acts is all about what Jesus will continue to do and teach until His second coming to earth.

The baptism with the Holy Spirit marked the transition of Jesus from the limitations of time and space that were there in His earthly ministry. He is no longer limited to the physical constraints of a human body. Now He has limitless access in His Body of all who name the name of Jesus as Savior and Lord and submit to Him as Baptizer with the Holy Ghost.

This knowledge was the secret to Kathryn Kuhlman's ministry.

Understanding of this truth is what motivated Smith Wigglesworth to say, "You cannot overestimate the value of the baptism with the Holy Spirit."

It is why Charles Parham was moved so strongly to study this aspect of the Word at the turn of the twentieth century, and why William Seymour sought God until he finally received the baptism with the Holy Spirit long after he had been preaching it at Azusa Street.

The key to this understanding is found in Acts 2:1-4:

When the day of Pentecost came [KJV, "was fully come"], **they were all together in one place. Suddenly a sound like the blowing of a violent wind came from heaven and filled the whole house where they were sitting. They saw what seemed to be tongues of fire that separated and came to rest on each of them. All of them were filled with the Holy Spirit and began to speak in other tongues as the Spirit enabled them.**

Verse four of this passage uses the Greek tense called an ingressive aorist. That means that the event described was a one-time entry into an ongoing experience.

In Ephesians 5:18 the Apostle Paul urges all believers: **Do not get drunk on wine, which leads to debauchery. Instead, be filled with the Spirit.** Literally this verse could be translated: "Do not get drunk on wine, which leads to debauchery. Instead, *continue being filled* with the Holy Spirit."

The idea is that the presence and power of God are released in the baptism with the Holy Spirit, but as the cleansing fire of the Holy Spirit is cultivated, the power of the Spirit increases. That is why so many Spirit-filled leaders can be baptized with the Holy Spirit, yet seem powerless to overcome their own sin — let alone see miracles.

The baptism with the Holy Spirit is the loosing of God's power, but that power must be cultivated for full effect. We must continue to be filled with the Spirit in order to grow into communion with Him.

Communion Is Necessary for Fellowship

Paul wrote in 2 Corinthians 13:14 (KJV), **The grace of the Lord Jesus Christ, and the love of God, and** *the communion of the Holy Ghost*, **be with you all....**

The outgrowing relationship with the Holy Spirit is communion with Him. That is the key to all the power of the great revivalists. *Communion* means a sharing together, an association, a partnership with another in doing something, joint participation, partaking of the same mind, communication with, fellowship, a shared presence.[2] Every aspect of this definition contributes a key to the restoration of miracle power.

This communion produces the partaking of the same mind — if we truly yield to Him. Many problems that develop in ministries do so because God's servants are not sensitive to the working, operations, and administrations of the Holy Spirit.

We should always be ready to be obedient to the leading of the Holy Spirit when we have a witness that the voice we hear is that of God. A communion, or close personal fellowship with the Holy Spirit, will guarantee that we have this "witness" or awareness of the mind of God and how He is moving.

I cannot tell you how many times I have been in Spirit-filled congregations when a holy hush would come over the place. However, the pastor would panic, because it did not seem as if anything was happening. He would begin to try "to raise the emotional peak of the people," and unwittingly would end up quenching the movement of the Spirit.

Communion with the Holy Spirit is not a *method;* it is *relationship*. About the time we think we have Him figured out, He will move in a different way. If we remain sensitive to Him, however, the result will be great manifestations of power. Some examples of such obedience come to my mind.

Not long ago, on a Trinity Broadcasting Network program, I saw some footage of Evangelist Reinhard Bonnke's services in Africa.

Bonnke felt as if the Holy Spirit said, "Step to the front of the platform, and give a wave of your hand."

Instantly, he obeyed, and about fifteen thousand people out of the audience of a hundred thousand were simultaneously "slain in the Spirit."

One of my precious friends in the Lord, Tim Storey, now ministering in California, came to ORU to conduct a series of meetings while I was serving as chaplain there. Tim has an outstanding healing ministry and is very sensitive to the leading of the Holy Spirit.

On this particular occasion, Tim issued an altar call and felt the Holy Spirit say to "blow" on the people. That is not exactly a common request, although it happens in some other ministries. Sitting behind him on the platform, I thought he had "flipped his lid" when he began to be obedient to the voice of the Lord! I wanted to say something profoundly religious like, "Thou art nuts!" However, people were "slain in the Spirit" all over the auditorium, and dozens of healings and/or miracles took place.

A friend told me of a service he attended in which a minister suddenly took up a glass of water and threw it on the congregation! Amazingly, everyone the water touched was healed.

As I mentioned previously, Smith Wigglesworth was noted for his bold — and sometimes bizarre — acts of obedience to the Holy Spirit. A number of examples from his ministry could be recounted that were truly unique. One particular incident occurred when a totally incapacitated woman was brought up to his healing line by two friends.

Wigglesworth commanded the friends to "let her go," and when they did, she slumped to the floor. Undaunted, the evangelist told them to "pick her up." When they did, he again said, "Let her go and stand by herself."

Smith Wigglesworth and daughter Alice Salter, September 15, 1924. He was noted for bold, sometimes bizarre, acts of obedience to the Holy Spirit.

By this time, the congregation was feeling hostile toward Wigglesworth and sorry for the woman, but he paid no attention to them. She fell, and again he said, "Pick her up" and "Now, let her go."

"You callous brute!" some man called out, and Wigglesworth looked directly at him, and said, "You mind your own business. I know my business."

Again, turning to the two women who supported the invalid, he repeated his command, "Let her go and stand by herself. Now do as I say!"

Infuriated by this time, but in awe of him, the two friends released her again. This time, she did not fall. As everyone could see, there on the platform was a cancer that had been dispelled from her body. What sensitivity to the presence of the Holy Spirit Wigglesworth displayed![3]

Every summer at ORU, as campus pastor, I commissioned several hundred students to the foreign mission field. One of them, Rolph Youngless, was at an altar ministering overseas when he was confronted by a young man with no cornea or pupil in his eye.

Youngless felt the Holy Spirit say to him, "Spit in the man's eye," which is one of those "words" that certainly calls for confirmation before being obeyed.

However, when the Spirit again said, "Spit in his eye," Youngless submitted, spit on his fingers, and placed them in the man's eye. To his amazement, a creative miracle transpired right before his own eyes. God created a cornea and pupil instantaneously.

I once related this story in a service I was conducting and said, "I would do anything the Spirit of God told me to do — including spitting on people."

I must say that fewer people than normal responded to the altar call in that particular service!

The point is not that bizarre behavior brings miracles. The point is that simple obedience to the presence and flow of the Holy Spirit brings miracles. Jesus Himself once spat on a man's eyes. (Mark 8:22-25.) But there is no scriptural evidence that He made this a standard practice or a prerequisite for healing.

What happens in the Church is that, when something works, we want to make a "method" or a "formula" out of it, instead of understanding that the *key* is simple obedience. The Spirit may not do anything the same way twice in a row. Many people seeing that incident with Youngless might have wanted to start a new denomination, "The First Church of the Spitters."

The key is not *methodology,* but *sensitivity.*

One of the definitions of *communion* listed above is "fellowship." How many of us truly fellowship with the Holy Spirit? In common language, how many of us "hang out" with Him?

Every day, I fellowship with my wife. As a result, I know her voice. Even in a large crowd of people, I could pick out her voice calling, "Ronald." Why? I could do that because I *know* her. I have had a continuing fellowship with her for years. I have an intimate relationship with her.

Do we fellowship with the Holy Spirit enough to pick His voice out of a crowd of voices? Many voices will vie for our attention: the voice of the body or soul, the voice of the devil, the voice of the world. All are seeking our attention, but only one voice is important to hear.

Many people whom I meet while traveling to minister say to me, "Oh, I know Oral Roberts," when they discover my position at ORU. Always interested in learning how such a relationship began, I will usually ask them how they met him.

Generally, they will say, "He prayed for me at a crusade," or, He writes me every month." Without a doubt, they have a "relationship" of sorts with Brother Roberts. There is a difference, however, in that kind of relationship and that of an individual who truly *fellowships* with Oral Roberts.

Those of us who have watched him preach, talked to him personally and privately after services, and dreamed and prayed together with him have a different relationship. His wife, Evelyn, and members of his immediate family have a still different, deeper relationship because of a more intimate fellowship. Friends and family relationships produce an intimacy that allows the anticipation of the moods and actions of one another.

The question we must deal with is, "How can we move in the kind of presence and power that characterized the great revivalists?" I would like to close this chapter with five keys I have isolated from their lives.

How To Cultivate Communion With the Spirit

1. We must be willing to *die to self*. Kathryn Kuhlman said it best: "His power is under His authority....you have to be dead, because there cannot be two wills. There can only be one...His." We must deny ourselves, take up our cross daily, and follow Him. (Luke 9:23.)

God is not the least bit interested in our ambitions. They pale in comparison to His anyway. We must be willing to make ourselves of "no reputation" in the pattern of Jesus (Phil. 2:7 KJV) in order to exalt His reputation.

I have seen on many occasions that the Holy Spirit was about to move, only to be quenched by some fleshly manifestation. If He is grieved or quenched, the Spirit of God will depart.

2. *We must not quench the Holy Spirit.* (1 Thess. 5:19 KJV.) The word *quench* means to extinguish, to go out, or to suppress a divine influence.[4]

I have found three major factors that contribute to quenching the Spirit: sin, doubt, and resistance to Him. (Acts 7:51.) I will elaborate more on these in the chapter on character. Suffice it to say here that resisting the Holy Spirit will dispel the presence of God.

3. *We must learn to commune with the Holy Spirit.* We need to learn to talk with the Holy Spirit. The second time I went to

South Korea, I heard Dr. Cho acknowledge that he never goes into his pulpit without saying, "Let's go, Holy Spirit. Together we can help the people."

I often talk with the Holy Spirit out loud as if another human being were in the room with me. That creates an atmosphere for His "abiding presence." To *abide* simply means "to maintain unbroken fellowship with" Him.[5] If we will practice the presence of God, He will become more real to us.

4. *We must learn to yield to Him.* This is another subject that will be discussed more completely in a later chapter, but I will say this here: We need to learn to slow down (ease the pace of our lifestyle), stop doing anything that grieves Him, and give Him the right of way. If we grieve a person, he will not stay in our presence long — neither will the Holy Spirit.

5. *We must learn to develop our conscience.* First Thessalonians 5:23 says: **May God himself, the God of peace, sanctify you through and through. May your whole spirit, soul and body be kept blameless....**

We must purify our souls — our minds (thinking faculties), wills, emotions, and consciences. The reason is that one of the ways the Holy Spirit communicates with us is through our conscience. In Romans 9:1 Paul says, **...my conscience confirms it in the Holy Spirit....**

The word *conscience* has a literal meaning. It means "coperception."[6] Our conscience serves as a coperceptor of God's will in our life. That is why it is essential that we understand how to protect it. First Timothy 4:2 warns us against those who have their conscience seared. The word *sear* suggests a withering, shriveling, or a rendering insensitive.[7] Repeated sin will burden our conscience. We must break bondages to free the presence of God to flow through us.

Every great revival has been accompanied by a true revelation of the Holy Spirit. This one principle of relationship is the key to restoring the flow of miracles to the Church in a prolific manner.

Holy Spirit, we submit ourselves to You.

Once we truly do that, we again will come to the place where we can "expect a miracle."

Chapter 8

Expect a Miracle

Smith Wigglesworth was a man who expected God to move when His servants acted in faith and obedience to the commands of His Holy Spirit.

Expect a miracle...
— *Oral Roberts*

My early Christian life was formed on the campus of Oral Roberts University in the 1970s. As students of the era, we were constantly inundated with the key phrases of Oral Roberts' ministry.

We continually heard such expressions as, "God is a good God," "Seed faith," "Go into every man's world," and "Expect a miracle." No phrase was more captivating than "Expect a miracle." It adorned prominent places on campus and even outlined the arena floor of our then nationally ranked basketball team.

That phrase was a constant theme in Oral Roberts' ministry and would one day form a cornerstone to my own life.

Recently, I sat in a worship service of one of the largest Spirit-filled congregations in America. The pastor did an absolutely masterful job of laying out the doctrine of healing. He shared that healing was in the atonement as much as salvation, and he quoted such Scriptures as:

But he [Christ] **was wounded for our transgressions, he was bruised for our iniquities: the chastisement of our peace was upon him; and with his stripes we are healed.**

— Isaiah 53:5 KJV

...I am the Lord that healeth thee.

— Exodus 15:26 KJV

Many are the afflictions of the righteous: but the Lord delivereth him out of them all.

— Psalm 34:19 KJV

For fifteen minutes he continued to weave a montage of biblical truth drawn from Deuteronomy 28, Matthew 8:17, James 5:17, 1 Peter 2:24, and other pertinent verses on the subject of divine healing. He exhorted the people to believe that Jesus purchased healing for body and soul. He pointedly and categorically emphasized that to deny divine healing was to deny the very atonement itself.

It was a motivating portion of the service as he called the sick to stand to their feet for prayer. As many as two hundred and fifty people stood, and believers began laying their hands on them and praying intensely. In a few minutes the prayer was concluded, and the pastor asked for those who knew they had been healed to come forward and testify.

What took place in the next few moments brought an overwhelming ache to my heart. About half a dozen people came forward. Two of them claimed to have been healed of headaches. (I do not mean to minimize such a healing; it is important to the person who is suffering from that kind of painful malady). Another person told of being healed of a cold. (Ditto.) Three testified of healings that had taken place in their lives years earlier.

I began to weep openly. My wife, Judy, reached over, took my hand sympathetically, and asked if everything was okay. All I could do was to nod affirmatively and continue to weep. I wept for most of the remainder of the service.

Later, I explained to my wife that I had been overwhelmed to see, after such a greatly anointed exhortation, that so few touches from God actually had taken place. In a congregation that large, there was so little expectancy for God to do anything.

I was so hungry for God to do something! The next day I cried out to the Lord, "Why is there so little expectancy among Your people in America? People want to see You move and, yet, so little is being manifested."

After some agonizing moments in prayer, I heard the Holy Spirit say to me, "Son, many of My people are defeated, wounded, and most of all, disappointed."

I began to see that a *genuine expectancy* for healings and miracles denotes the presence of real *faith*. The decades of the Eighties and Nineties — and even today — have brought much disappointment to the Body of Christ. We saw leaders fall, open displays of miracles were not prominent, we were victimized by scandals, and many promises seemed to lie in the rubble of unfulfillment. The result for many people was disillusionment and a loss of faith; therefore, they have little expectancy for God to really do anything in their day.

My reaction to all these events has been exactly the opposite. If we understand God's season, it becomes apparent that He was cleaning His own house in order to revive His people. Not only did all of the happenings — and lack of happenings — not disappoint or disillusion me, but my expectancy was heightened. That is why I have written about the importance of understanding God's times and seasons.

God was creating a "new wineskin" into which to pour out His Spirit.

We must learn to be like Kathryn Kuhlman. In the 1940s, Miss Kuhlman began to attend services of certain healing evangelists, including Oral Roberts, to judge their validity. Intrigued by this phenomena, she searched the Scriptures for verification.

Once she saw the miraculous in the Scriptures, she would say:

> I knew that if I lived and died and never saw a single healing miracle like the apostles experienced in the book of Acts it would not change God's Word....God said it. He made provision for it in our redemption at Calvary. And whether I ever saw it with my earthly eyes did not change the fact that it was so.[1]

From that day forward her face was set like flint toward God's miracle-working power. She knew that God was a miracle worker. In an unexpected occurrence in 1947, a woman testified that she had been healed of a cancerous tumor during one of Miss Kuhlman's services the night before, the first of many thousands of healings to follow. Miss Kuhlman had been teaching on the Holy Spirit that night and had not had a healing line or even prayer for healing.[2]

The Healing Revival, which filled the era of 1947-1958, was a revival of signs, gifts, healings, salvation, deliverance, and miracles. All of the gifts of the Spirit were manifested, including speaking in tongues, prophesying, and the expressions of joy that were common in the Pentecostal Revival — but those three events were not the central theme. The common heartbeat of every service was the miracles — the time when the Holy Spirit moved to heal the sick and raise the dead.[3]

Why Is the Miraculous Important to Revival?

Gordon Lindsay once said of John Alexander Dowie:

Disappointment followed disappointment as long as Dr. Dowie attempted to reach the masses with human methods. It was when he made up his own mind he would sink or swim in God's miraculous flow that success came to his ministry. Up until that time the world turned a deaf ear to him, but once his ministry was inundated with the miraculous, they beat a path to his door.[4]

While Dowie was still in Melbourne, Australia, before the turn of the twentieth century, a woman named Lucy Parker came to one of his services. She had been totally blind for almost three years because of a cancerous tumor. She was about to give birth to a child, but the doctors told her husband that she would die while the child was being delivered, if not before. Her greatest desire was not simply to live, but to be used in God's Kingdom. This is what happened the night she attended Dowie's meeting:

About this time she heard some of the remarkable healings that had taken place in the Melbourne Tabernacle, and she came to Dr. Dowie *expecting* healing. He laid hands on her and prayed. The miracle happened at once. The cancer burst and discharged into two handkerchiefs. The swelling of the eye disappeared and the opening closed. When she opened that eye, she was immediately able to see perfectly.[5]

It was the demonstration of miracles of this nature that allowed Dr. Dowie's work to receive rapid prominence in Australia.

On another occasion, a sixteen-year-old boy lay in an Australian hospital suffering from tuberculosis of the bones. He was emaciated and had to be carried from place to place. He was given one of Dowie's tracts, and, having read it, would give his parents no rest until they agreed to take him to the tabernacle. They told Dowie that their son *expected* to be healed that night. Dowie promptly led the young man to Christ and then told him to stamp his feet on the floor. The young man let out a shriek as he was totally healed.[6]

The young man returned to the hospital and testified of what God had done in his life. Soon many of the other patients in the hospital, suffering from every imaginable disease, raced to Dowie's meetings and were wonderfully converted and healed.

It was Dowie's undaunted conviction that a great revival of the magnitude of that of the Early Church could only come through the ministry of healing and miracles, such as had launched his great ministry. Miracles draw the lost, hungry, and needy to God.

On August 7,1890, Dowie came to Chicago to minister. He was requested to pray for Mrs. Jennie Paddock, a woman dying from a fibroid tumor. The doctors had given up hope because of "mortification" (gangrene), which had already set in. Dowie took this challenge as a test of whether he should begin a work in Chicago. He prayed for the woman, and she was instantly healed. The healing was so remarkable that the entire account of it was carried in several Chicago newspapers.[7]

The miraculous is the invitation of God to His Kingdom.

Miracles validate God's existence to the skeptic.

Robert Ingersoll, the famed atheist and skeptic, gave an address in Chicago during Dowie's initial years there. The talk was entitled "God Must Perish, Because He Is Useless and Never Answers Prayer."

Dowie took this speech as a personal affront to God and as a challenge to prove that God does indeed answer prayer. He assembled a large array of testimonials of people who had been miraculously healed and documented the proof of their healings. That was the only time that Ingersoll had been effectively challenged for his assertion, because up until that time the Church had been impotent to respond.

Ingersoll was well aware of biblical claims to the miraculous, for he used them as proof that the Bible could not fulfill its promises. Then one man, who displayed the power of God through his life, called Ingersoll's bluff and challenged him to debate.

After hearing Dowie's remarkable collection of documented miracles, Ingersoll decided to leave town steeped in his own prejudice. Soon afterward, this atheist, who predicted that the Bible would not last, died crying out to God for mercy. Later, his home was converted into the national headquarters of the Geneva Bible Society.

A miracle settles the issue. Either an individual submits to God as a result of seeing it, or stammers in his own intellectual stupor, but he cannot disprove it.

One group of skeptics set out to do just that, however, in the ministry of the great healing evangelist of the 1920s, Dr. Charles Price. In Vancouver, British Columbia, Price rented a great arena which could hold about twelve thousand people. At first the services were only modestly attended, but soon miracle after miracle began to occur.

Suddenly, there was an "explosion." Thousands of people seemed to "come out of the woodwork." Diseases of every kind were healed. The crowd swelled in attendance so much that one night ten thousand people were turned away from the entrance to the building.[8]

Like the Pharisees of old, some theologians sought to justify their own positions and attempted to discredit Price rather than to submit to the joy of God's wonderful touch. They interviewed dozens of people said to have been healed in the crusade. Each one was thoroughly examined and, to the theologians' surprise, found to be well.

Undaunted by their findings, they continued to pursue their own ends, asking each person which doctor had diagnosed them with whatever the problem had been. Then this group of skeptics followed up their investigations by interviewing the doctors in question. In each case, they found that the doctors had given thorough diagnoses and had reached their conclusions justifiably.

These skeptics were set so adamantly against the operation of the power of God today that they asked each of the doctors:

"But, Doctor, this person is well now. Don't you know that the days of miracles have passed? Don't you think it is far more likely that you made a mistake in your diagnosis than that this individual was really cured of disease by prayer?"

When many of the doctors recanted their original diagnoses, because of "peer pressure" and because miracles did not fit their intellectual frameworks, Price's crusade was written off as fakery.[9]

I have seen the books of modernists today who refer to this report without ever knowing the facts of what actually transpired. As in Jesus' days, prejudice and distortion of facts sufficed to satisfy a few religious intellectuals. However, the mass of common people were drawn to the Kingdom through the miracles. So were they through the ministries of Charles Price and other great revivalists.

There have always been "Pharisees" (religious leaders) and "Sadducees" (liberal thinkers and intellectuals) who seek to disprove what happens among God's people. Even in the days of the apostles, such men sought to discourage belief in miracles. In Acts 4, Peter and John were brought before the Sanhedrin for preaching the Word "with signs following." (Mark 16:20 KJV.) This is the report of that occurrence:

When they [the Sanhedrin] **saw the courage of Peter and John and realized that they were unschooled, ordinary men, they were astonished and they took note that these men had been with Jesus. But since they could see the man who had been healed standing there with them, there was nothing they could say...."What are we going to do with these men?" they asked. "Everybody living in Jerusalem knows they have done an outstanding miracle, and we cannot deny it."**

After further threats they let them go. They could not decide how to punish them, because all the people were praising God for what had happened. For the man who was miraculously healed was over forty years old.

— Acts 4:13,14,16,21,22

A miracle settles the issue. It can be denied, but it cannot be disproved. Multitudes are attracted to the restoring nature of God's power.

Miracles: The Drawing Card of the Spirit

The "apostle of faith," Smith Wigglesworth, would say, "Only believe," and, "Fear looks, faith jumps."[10]

What a simple but profound theology. Once during one of his crusades, a deformed child was brought to Wigglesworth. He looked at the mother and in his gruff fashion said to her, "Lay the child on the stage."

After she had done as she was told, he turned around and kicked the child across the platform. As you might imagine, the entire crowd gasped at such an action. When the child landed on the other side of the stage, however, every limb was normal and the youngster was completely healed. Needless to say, Smith Wigglesworth was a man who expected God to move when His servants acted in faith and obedience to the commands of His Holy Spirit.[11]

It was this same Smith Wigglesworth who said:

> I can see the days when the ministry of healing is going to be more difficult. There are already too many remedies in which people can trust....I can see that it will get worse, until it will be hard to get people to believe at all. It is what has happened to many today.[12]

It is the miraculous, however, that draws the countless skeptics to see if there really is a God — a God Who is more than fancy words, a God Who will not only lay out principles, but actually get involved in people's lives. Too long we have used substitutes for His power to draw people to church, until worship in many congregations is carried out on a human level with the element of the supernatural almost completely gone.

It was this principle of the power of the miraculous that was demonstrated in William Branham's life. Where true miracles are in evidence, skepticism and unbelief are put to flight. Who can argue when a man can discern unknowable truths, spiritually perceive the origin of a disease, and bring deliverance to the most hopeless medical case?

Oral Roberts is the one who told me, "Miracles are the drawing card of the Holy Spirit."

A good example is Nathaniel who was resting in the shade of a fig tree before Philip came to get him to bring him to meet Jesus. To Nathaniel's astonishment, the Lord described his personal character to him before they were ever introduced.

Nathaniel asked, "How do You know me? I never met You before."

...Jesus answered, "I saw you while you were still under the fig tree before Philip called you" (John 1:48).

Then Nathaniel declared, "Teacher, You must truly be the Messiah and the rightful King of Israel." (v. 49.)

As this same supernatural revelation of Jesus operated in Woodworth-Etter, Lake, McPherson, and others, miracles occurred among the multitudes.

Once a woman from Greece, who had no opening in her throat by which to swallow, entered the prayer line at a Branham crusade. When he prayed for her, she was able instantly to drink a glass of water and eat a candy bar. A night or two later, nine deaf mutes came into the prayer line, and all nine were healed. On other occasions, those born blind received their sight. In a meeting in Jonesboro, Arkansas, a woman was raised from the dead.[13]

Perhaps best of all, these miracles were an entree that brought the lost under conviction. In Romans 15:18,19, Paul wrote of calling the **...Gentiles to obey God by what I have said and done — by the power of signs and miracles, through the power of the Spirit. So from Jerusalem all the way around to Illyricum, I have fully proclaimed the gospel of Christ.**

To Paul, "fully proclaim(ing) the gospel of Christ" meant having signs and wonders following the ministry. The effect was absolutely amazing upon those in entire regions who had not previously known Christ or even heard about Him.

The role of miracles in the Scriptures was threefold:

1. To draw people to God. (Acts 2:16; 5:15; 9:35.)

2. To destroy the work of the devil in people's lives. (Acts 10:38; 1 John 3:8.)

3. To give credence to the Kingdom of God. (Matt. 10:1,7.)

However, there was a "common denominator" in the miracles of Jesus and the disciples: the people *expected* something to happen. A great sense of expectancy followed the ministry of the Lord and those in the Early Church. We need to regain that "sense of expectancy" for today, if we truly want revival to come in our time.

Expect a miracle is not just a slogan or a catch phrase. It is a profound truth.

It Is Time To Restore Expectancy

Smith Wigglesworth used to say, "I would rather die trusting God than live in unbelief."

"...Jesus of Nazareth was a man accredited by God to you by miracles, wonders and signs...."

— Acts 2:22

If anyone understands the need for a miracle, I do! Some time back, I was almost killed in a head-on collision. I was going home to Tulsa, from Broken Arrow, Oklahoma, about twenty miles away, on a snowy day. A young teenager lost control of his car, which shot across the highway hitting me head on. My car ricocheted off another vehicle and ended up some fifty feet from the highway.

I was knocked unconscious by the impact. When I awakened, my car was in the middle of a snow-covered field, and I was surrounded by blood and glass. At my window was a precious woman who had seen the collision and run over to help. As a witness to me of God's ongoing protection, she was a Spirit-filled nurse. When I opened my eyes, she was monitoring my vital signs and praying in the Spirit over me.

Soon after I regained consciousness, I realized that I was in a great deal of pain and that I could not move the left side of my body. A short while later the ambulance arrived and the paramedics began to assist me. My car was completely destroyed, and they could only evacuate me by cutting through the door with a chain saw. I remember then, clearly, the attendants reaching through the rubble and debris to place me on a hard stretcher and take me to the hospital.

While I was in the ambulance approaching the hospital, I had no idea how badly I was injured, but I remember calling out to the God of miracles, for what only He could do. I was greeted in the emergency room by my wife, family, and some friends. Shortly thereafter, a set of X-rays was made of me in the emergency room. After a little while, the attending doctor returned with the diagnosis.

She looked at me and said, "Mr. McIntosh, you have a broken neck. That is exhibited right here in your X-ray."

The peace of God seemed somehow to pervade and sustain me, and very calmly I asked her, "What exactly does that mean for me?"

At that point, the doctor stepped back a little to be out of my peripheral vision and mouthed the words to my wife, "It's not good."

The hospital staff did the best they could to clean me up (later a plastic surgeon would work on my face for over two hours, putting some fifty stitches in it), and some time later took me upstairs for a full battery of X-rays.

By that time, many of my minister friends from around the city had arrived to stand with me and pray on my behalf. Oral Roberts was joined by Carlton Pearson, the pastor-evangelist of Higher Dimensions Evangelistic Center. My brother, who is the co-pastor there, also arrived. Billy Joe Daugherty, founder and senior pastor of Victory Christian Center, came to my aid.

En route to the hospital were Richard and Lindsay Roberts. While on their way Lindsay received a word of wisdom from the Lord.

"Richard," she said, "I feel as if we should pray 'reverse the diagnosis.'"

Soon they were all standing at my bedside as I got ready to go into the lab for my second set of X-rays. All of these concerned people gathered around me to pray. I will never forget lying there in pain with the entire left side of my body numb. Yet a peace from God filled the room.

I was surrounded by men and women of God in whom I had great confidence, and now I came face to face with what it really meant to "expect a miracle." Still, no one knew the extent of the damage to my body, or what the full ramifications of my injuries might be. All I knew in that one single moment was that God was fully able to do what man was limited to perform.

Those great men and women of God laid hands on me, and Oral started to pray a brief, but intense, prayer for my healing. I felt nothing take place at the time, only an inner cry of my spirit to expect a miracle. After the X-rays were completed, those who had gathered to support me surrounded me with much love and encouragement. My face was jagged and torn, but my spirit was high.

A short time later another doctor came into the room with a surprised look on his face.

"I can't explain it," he said, "but, on this set of X-rays, we can't find any break in the neck."

That prayer between X-rays had "reversed the diagnosis." I was miraculously healed. That *sense of expectancy* has not left me since that time. Without a doubt I knew that what God had done for me, He could and would do for anyone. I was indeed a miracle — but not an exception!

Miracles Are Not Always Received Rightly

Miracles were an evident desire of Jesus' heart.

In John 6, we find a passage that shows us this truth. Jesus had just supernaturally fed five thousand men and countless women and children with five loaves and two fish.

Verses 14 and 15 say:

After the people saw the miraculous sign that Jesus did, they began to say, "Surely this is the Prophet who is to come into the world." Jesus, knowing that they intended to come and make him king by force, withdrew again into the hills by himself.

So although miracles always are drawing cards, they are not always properly understood.

It is easy to misunderstand the event, and thus, hunger for what is not intended. In our human nature, it is easier to pursue our own agendas than to follow the heartbeat of God. Most Christians would rather be around the "wonder worker," than to understand the wonder.

At that point, Jesus sent His disciples in a boat to cross the lake, while He stayed behind to pray. After they had rowed some miles, Jesus followed, walking on the water. Evidently, Jesus did not need normal modes of transportation. He was obviously light years ahead of "Beam me up, Scotty."

His arrival at the disciples' boat, not surprisingly, provoked an immediate reaction: **When...they saw Jesus approaching the boat,**

walking on the water...they were terrified (v. 19). Their response is quite understandable: after all, you would not want just anyone walking on the water to get in your boat!

Once Jesus identified Himself, the disciples took Him into the boat, **...and immediately the boat reached the shore where they were heading** (v. 21). We are not talking about your basic means of transportation. "Star Trek, the Next Generation" is way behind this group.

The next verses described the reaction of the public to this event:

The next day the crowd that had stayed on the opposite shore of the lake realized that only one boat had been there, and that Jesus had not entered it with his disciples, but that they had gone away alone....

When they found him on the other side of the lake, they asked him, "Rabbi, when did you get here?"

— John 6:22,25

That was a logical question, but I find Jesus' response far more fascinating. He never answered their query, but instead answered the question they should have asked. The important thing was not when (or how) He had got there, but *why they were there*, as we see in His response:

"...I tell you the truth, you are looking for me, not because you saw miraculous signs but because you ate the loaves and had your fill."

— John 6:26

What did that answer have to do with their query?

Jesus was saying to them, "You are not asking the right question. The point is that your appetite for being here is wrong. You are not here for the right reason. You are hungry for the wrong thing."[1]

I have heard many ministers explain this passage by saying things such as, "The people didn't come because they loved Jesus. They came because of something supernatural," and thus try to discredit the miraculous. That is not the context of this passage.

Jesus was saying the opposite: "People, the problem is, you didn't come because of the miracles and because those miracles proved the power of God. You are not seeking after the power of My Father. You are seeking to have your fleshly needs met."

Jesus wanted them to hunger for what was real. The loaves and fishes were not the miracle, the Provider was!

I understand liberal theology. I spent my first year of seminary in a liberal institution on the East Coast. These people were so liberal they did not believe in anything — they did not even believe in gravity!

They were always challenging the miraculous. They constantly expressed their discomfort at "supposed" supernatural occurrences, suggesting that kind of thing kept Christians immature.

Finally, to one fellow student, I said, "Brother, you've got it all wrong. It is miracles that promote a real awareness of God."

Jesus did not rebuke the people for wanting miracles. The miraculous never keeps people immature.

On the contrary, in the Bible every time the lame were made to walk, the blind to see, the deaf to hear, the crippled to be restored, there was always an open display of praise among the people, and they were drawn to God.

In John 6:2, we read that the people followed Jesus **...because they saw the miraculous signs he had performed on the sick.** In Acts 2:22 Peter told the leaders of his day:

"...Jesus of Nazareth was a man accredited by God to you by miracles, wonders and signs, which God did among you through him, as you yourselves know."

The same was true even of the followers of Jesus who preached the Gospel among the common people:

When the crowds heard Philip and saw the miraculous signs he did, they all paid close attention to what he said....

Simon himself [a man of sorcery] **believed and was baptized. And he followed Philip everywhere, astonished by the great signs and miracles he saw.**

— Acts 8:6,13

If miracles are the drawing card of God, what will bring the sense of the miraculous back to the Church in our day? What will revive miracles again?

Following are some things that we must do in order to provide a climate for miracles to be revived in our lives and in the life of our churches, as well as in the Church at large.

A Climate for Miracles

1. *We must come to the same understanding that captivated Kathryn Kuhlman.* She said, "I knew that if I lived and died and never saw a single miracle like the apostles experienced in the book of Acts, it would not change God's Word...God said it!"[2]

Miracles are a part of God's plan. No matter what disappointment we may have experienced in the past, it does not change the Word of God.

Smith Wigglesworth used to say, "I would rather die trusting God than live in unbelief."[3]

Categorically, God will use the realm of the miraculous to defeat the devil and to draw the lost. Transition times only serve to purify a vessel for a greater outpouring.

2. *We must hunger for that which is real.* I will deal with this subject more extensively in the next chapter. Suffice it to say here, when an American goes to a foreign country for a long period of time, he will begin to hunger for food that looks and tastes familiar. By the time he gets back on home soil he would pay twenty dollars for a McDonald's hamburger. Similarly, the absence of miracles should create hunger, not disappointment.

3. *We must choose a life of holiness.* Smith Wigglesworth would say, "The child of God was in a position of power to deal with the devil. . . providing that child of God was living right. He was absolutely sold out to the principle of holiness."[4]

There is little doubt that many skeptics and people in sin received miraculous healings in Kathryn Kuhlman's services, but purity is still the gateway to God's heart.

There is a lot of confusion about what holiness actually is. In most churches we have reduced the whole concept of holiness to telling people what being unholy is and why it is wrong. The real key is understanding why being holy is right. Holiness is an honor given to us by God, not a meaningless requirement of skirt or hair lengths. Holiness is the most exciting lifestyle that has ever been developed.

Holiness in its simplicity can be defined as "doing things God's way." Why is that so important?

Hebrews 12:14 says, **...without holiness no one will see the Lord.** In other words, if we do not do things God's way, it will be impossible for us to discern what God is doing or saying. That situation grieves the Holy Spirit. Just as when we grieve someone at our home, they are likely to leave, so does the Holy Spirit. That is why holiness is the cornerstone of the miraculous. (2 Chron. 16:9.)

4. *We must be moved with compassion.* The one common bond which linked every great revivalist's miracle ministry was compassion for the hurting. John Alexander Dowie witnessed firsthand the misery and sorrow of life. The result was a revulsion toward evil, and a heartfelt desire to see the masses delivered. Maria Woodworth-Etter grew up with such tragedy in her early life that her heart was moved toward those in misery and pain. John G. Lake saw half of his family members die and, as a result, was a man filled with love and concern for suffering humanity.

Smith Wigglesworth was a man who sincerely loved others. Albert Hibbert would write, "Often people would ask me what I considered to be the secret of Wigglesworth's power. There were several aspects. One of them was his love and compassion for people."[5]

Compassion is a powerful spiritual force that unlocks the miraculous. Often I find that people want to see miracles for ill-conceived motives. Frequently it is for little more than personal gratification and recognition. In reality, miracles are the manifestation of God's love. Love is always the nature and expression of God, and compassion is its motivation.

Smith Wigglesworth at Angelus Temple, Los Angeles, California, c. 1929. One secret of his power was his love and compassion for people.

Nine times in the *King James Version* of the Scriptures the word *compassion* is used of the Lord in describing His motive in action. In all nine of the occurrences of the word *compassion* as related to Jesus, a miracle followed: In Matthew 9:36-38, moved with compassion, He sent the twelve to heal the multitudes; in Matthew 14:14, moved with compassion for a multitude, He healed the sick among them; in Matthew 15:32-38 and Mark 8:2-9, because He had compassion on them, He miraculously fed four thousand people; in Matthew 20:30-34, because He had compassion on them, He restored the sight to two blind men; in Mark 1:40-42, moved with compassion, He healed a man of leprosy; in Mark 5:2-19, expressing the compassion of God the Father, He healed a demon-possessed man; in Mark 6:34-44, moved with compassion, He miraculously fed — both spiritually and physically — five thousand hungry men; and in Luke 7:11-15, because He had compassion on her, He raised from the dead the son of a poor grieving widow. Finally, in Mark 9:17-27, He healed a boy with an evil spirit after the boy's father asked Him for "compassion" (v. 22).

Compassion is the key that unlocks the door to the miraculous. Quite simply, **Love never fails...**(1 Cor. 13:8).

In the Old Testament, particularly in the *King James Version*, that phrase is expressed by the phrase "His mercy endureth forever." *Mercy* means love or compassion.[6] In fact, the *New International Version* often translates *mercy* as "love." (See 2 Chronicles 20:21 as an example.)

Similarly to the New Testament, when that phrase is used in the Old Testament, the miraculous follows. In 2 Chronicles 7:1,3 we read of Solomon's dedication of the newly constructed temple:

When Solomon finished praying, fire came down from heaven and consumed the burnt offering and the sacrifices, and the glory of the Lord filled the temple....When all the Israelites saw the fire coming down and the glory of the Lord above the temple, they knelt on the pavement with their faces to the ground, and they worshiped and gave thanks to the Lord, saying,

"He is good; his love [KJV, "mercy"] **endures forever."**

Similarly, when God set ambushes for Jehoshaphat's enemies, He turned them upon themselves and they destroyed each other. (2 Chron. 20:1-29.) Jehoshaphat, King of Judah, had appointed men to precede his army into battle and who sang before them, **"...Give thanks to the Lord, for his love** [KJV, "mercy"] **endures forever"** (2 Chron. 20:21).

God moved when His people learned to operate in supernatural love rather than by military might. Operating in God's love and compassion is operating in God's motivation. When you and I perceive God's motive (His mercy, His love) and then provide the proper corresponding action (James 2:17), we have discovered the key to the supernatural. In fact, the word *compassion* comes from two words: *com* (a prefix) meaning together with, and *passion*, meaning overpowering emotion or outreaching affection.[7]

To operate in the compassion of the Lord is to work together with His outreaching affection or emotion. The natural outgrowth of such love never fails, but brings what is necessary to those in need. We do not pray for people to be healed in order to attract attention or to draw crowds, but because we love them with the love of the Lord. That motive in God will never fail.

5. *We must hear a clear word from God.* Perhaps this is the most important factor in restoring the expectancy of faith.

Faith is the key that unlocks the door to revival. In fact, it is an indispensable prerequisite for revival. Listen to the words of Oswald T. Smith:

A man who is used by God will hear from Heaven. God will give him a promise, not the general promises that apply to any of His children, but a definite unmistakable message direct to his heart. Some familiar promise...will suddenly grip him in such a way that he will know God has spoken. Hence if I would attempt a new work for God, let me ask myself first of all these questions: "Have I a promise? Has God spoken?"[8]

The major prerequisite for expectancy is the clear word of God to the revivalist. Nothing is more important as an igniter of God's move.

That is why understanding the times is listed as a spiritual weapon in 1 Chronicles 12:32. Ecclesiastes tells us that everything has a time and that there is **...a season for every activity under heaven...**(3:1). It also tells us that a wise individual discerns both **...the proper time and procedure** (8:5). Proverbs tells us of the power of **...a word spoken in due season...**(15:23 KJV). Isaiah claimed that he knew how to speak a **...word in season...**(50:4 KJV.) Nothing will ignite a person or a people to expectancy more than God's Word at the right moment.

I pray that you can say, "Now, I can expect a miracle. Lord, let me hunger for a new dimension of Your loving miracles."

There still is a missing ingredient, however, and I want to show you what that vital ingredient is in the next chapter.

Chapter 10

The Missing
Ingredient

Wigglesworth was a
man hungry for all
that God had.

"Blessed are those who hunger and thirst for righteousness, for they will be filled."

— Matthew 5:6

In 1986, my wife and I went with some friends on a mission
trip to Mexico. We ministered in several places, but primarily on
the outskirts of Guadalajara in rural cities.

We traveled through town after town, and our host would say,
"A town of twenty-five thousand people, no gospel work. A
town of fifteen thousand, no gospel work. A town of fifty thousand, no gospel work."

I remember my heart breaking at the thought of city after city
with no knowledge of Jesus Christ. Finally, we arrived at the
place where we were to minister. Truly, it was a town of abject
poverty and few modern conveniences. We ministered daily,
and God began to pour out His Spirit in an amazing way.
Conservatively, ninety percent of those we prayed for were
instantly healed. The people came from all over the little town
to attend the church services.

The church itself was only three unfinished walls with a can-
vas canopy pitched over it, essentially a tent. One evening we
ministered in a torrential downpour. The tent leaked like a sieve,

but the people stayed for more than four hours as we ministered the Gospel and prayed for the sick.

One night I was asked to minister on marriage and sex, because this portion of Mexico was notorious for extramarital affairs among its men. Somehow the male population in that area believed that such extracurricular activity was an extension of their masculinity, even in the Church. That was not the most exciting prospect to me, but nevertheless, I acquiesced. I was warned ahead of time, however, that the men would not receive such a message no matter what I said.

I was delivering a non-controversial message when I decided to launch out into the deep. I started to preach about marital fidelity, God's plan for the home, and the elevated role God saw for womankind. No sooner had I begun my discourse than I noticed a man in the front row vehemently shaking his head no! I decided not to be discouraged by this open display of rejection, and I intensified my speech. However, it seemed that the louder I spoke, the more vigorously he shook his head.

Boldly, I leaped off the platform into the midst of the people, with my interpreter following me. I got right down into the man's face, but he continued to defiantly shake his head no! Finally, I gave up and ignored him but continued to preach my message. God did some wonderful things, including restoring some marriages and calling into marital union a couple who had been living together for ten years.

After the service was over, our American team assembled together, and everyone commented on how this man had sat in open defiance in the meeting, shaking his head no!

Still later, the host pastor came by and I said to him, "You told me there would be men who would disagree with me, but I was surprised that one would openly defy me in the meeting — especially since God has done so many wonderful things this week."

The pastor looked at me and said, "Who was the man who defied you?"

I looked over the crowd, spotted the man, and pointed him out. Suddenly the pastor began to laugh.

"Oh, that's Julio," he said. "He has a nervous condition, and his head always goes like that."

Everyone had a good laugh at my expense. Later that evening the Spirit of the Lord spoke to me about that incident and said, "Things are not always as they seem."

I chuckled to myself as I relived those moments, but I also got His point. Things are not always as they seem, and how we interpret them largely determines the outcome of our life. In moments of confusion, we often find ourselves making key decisions. These can be decisions of discouragement and defeat, or of hunger and thirst for God, the source of every good and perfect gift. (James 1:17.)

A few years ago I was confronted with such a decision. My spirit was crying out for more of God, but I felt the sting of the moment: fallen ministers, impotence in the Church, and a lethargic spirit that seemed to pervade the entire Body of Christ. That summer I locked myself away to pray and seek God.

After days of travail in my spirit, I heard the Spirit of the Lord speak to me, "Son, I am going to show you the missing ingredient to revival." Everything in my body rose with excitement. Then in a very simple voice the Lord continued, "The missing ingredient to revival is momentum."

I was almost disappointed at what I heard. "Momentum," I thought to myself. That is not even a biblical term. How could that be the key to what is missing in revival?

I was vacationing in Ohio at the time in the home of my wife's parents. I scrambled to find a dictionary to see if I could get any clarification on the term. This is the way it defined *momentum*: "A property of a moving body that determines the length of time to bring it to rest when under the action of a constant force. . ."[1]

Suddenly, I understood what God was saying: The impact of a continued force of an entity, as the Church, is in direct correlation to the action against it.

Let me say it another way:

The devil is unconcerned about individual victories against his action as long as they do not become continuous. Such actions will develop momentum. Anything in motion creates friction. A church in motion will be confronted by Satan. Momentum is the quality that overcomes the opposition of the enemy.

Mario Murillo says it this way, "Satan does not fear revival nearly as [much as] he fears our discovery of the fact that revival can be permanent."[2]

I like to express it this way, "Momentum is the ongoing force of the Spirit that transforms momentary victory into a perpetual move of the Spirit."

This is why the devil fights this progression so vehemently. The number one weapon of the devil to halt momentum is discouragement. If he can preoccupy the Church with momentary defeat, hurdles, or problems, he can reduce God's move to sporadic victories interspersed with devastating defeats.

That is how the momentum of the Lord is halted. That is why the Church goes from victory to defeat, often taking three steps forward and two backward. The devil is never discouraged by momentary defeat. He simply waits for "a more opportune time" in his long-range plan.

It should be the same way in the Church. We should never be discouraged by a temporary setback. We should simply draw closer to God, reload, and continue forward in greater momentum. Momentum takes the Church from defeating the devil's works to destroying the devil's work.

As I continued to pray over the weeks of that summer vacation, I cried out to God, "If momentum is the missing ingredient to revival, what is the key to momentum?"

In a flash the Holy Spirit led me to Matthew 5:6: **"...those who hunger and thirst for righteousness...will be filled."** Hunger is the true missing link. The word *hunger* is defined this way: to have an appetite, to crave, to demand, to yearn, to be famished, or to be starved for.[3]

Hunger is not a mental craving to see the spectacular. That is merely a "soulish" desire.[4] True hunger is an appetite for God that becomes a driving force. It is a divine yearning for what is missing in life. It becomes a driving force to see anything that is not like God touched by His hand and transformed. It is this hunger that is one of the prime prerequisites to revival.

When you and I become aware of what is missing in our spiritual life, it should never be an opportunity for discouragement. "Missing links" are instead a divine call to hunger to see them restored.

Hunger is the greatest driving force on the face of the earth. If you do not believe it, look at reports of the actions of starving men.

Some time ago, a newspaper article included an item about a man caught stealing from a grocery store. This was an individual whose character made such an act of dishonesty highly unlikely.

When asked why he had stolen, he responded, "My family is starving, and I am out of work. What else could I do?"

Desperate people will do desperate things.

Hunger in the Great Revivalists

Hunger is the one dominating characteristic I saw emerge from accounts of all the great revivalists. They were desperate for God to do something. They were hungry for God to be what they knew Him to be. They were divinely starved for the lost to be saved, the sick to be healed, and the oppressed to be set free. They longed for the joy of the Lord. They felt a burden that only a manifestation of the heart of God could relieve.

Look at the words of Kathryn Kuhlman:

> I can only tell you with my conversion there came this terrific burden for souls. When you think of Kathryn Kuhlman, think only of someone who loves your soul, not somebody who is trying to build something — only for the kingdom of God, that's all — souls, souls, souls. Remember! I gave my life for the sole vision of lost souls. Nothing, nothing in the whole world is more important than that, lost souls.[5]

Miss Kuhlman hungered for lost humanity to come to the reconciling, saving knowledge of Jesus.

Men like John Alexander Dowie hungered for God's touch in humanity. In 1877, Dowie left the organized church, because he felt it was misdirected. Dowie "felt an increasing burden for the ignorant, uncared for, perishing masses" of lost souls. He dreamed of the formation of a church which would work day and night for the reclamation of the perishing.[6]

It is this hunger that formulated his passion for ministry. Just before he left Australia to come to America, Dowie recorded these words concerning a vision he had from God:

...Then suddenly, the earth seemed to be vocal. I could hear the wave of pain and the cries of the dying, rising from all continents, swelling up from all cities and hamlets, villages and solitudes, from ten thousand times ten thousand homes where babes in mothers' arms, and children lay dying, breaking loving hearts. Oh, how can I tell it? I could hear the cry of the suffering coming up from all the earth, from millions of beds in weary pain crying, "Oh, Lord, how long, how long?" and my heart was broken. I wept bitterly and threw myself down in agony. Was there no help?[7]

It was his passion to be a vessel in the hands of God to help that became the motivating force in Dowie's life.

Other men, such as Smith Wigglesworth, demonstrated an insatiable hunger for God. Wigglesworth was far from being discontented, but the more he had of God, the more he wanted. There is an adage that says:

All of self, none of God.

Less of self, more of God.

None of self, all of God.[8]

That little saying summed up Wigglesworth's perspective on Christianity for his friend, Albert Hibbert. Wigglesworth was a man hungry for all that God had. He was conscious that God's plan for mankind involved power, and he was unrelenting in his pursuit of everything of God. He so longed for this power, that when the concept of the baptism with the Holy Spirit did not meet his doctrinal criteria, he laid down his pride to receive the truth. Real hunger will always crucify pride, so that which is real can manifest itself.

When the multitudes pursued Jesus in John 6, after He had miraculously fed the five thousand men (perhaps as many as twenty thousand people in all, if we include the women and children), He rebuked the crowd. He did *not* rebuke them, however, for following a miracle as we saw in the last chapter. He rebuked them *because their appetites were wrong*. They hungered for the easy way, instead of for God Himself. They hungered for the by-product and not the product.

Many people will substitute fellowship with men for fellowship with Jesus. Lots of churches are content with the atmosphere of the music program instead of the presence of the Holy Spirit. Churches will fill their calendars with social events rather than filling their hearts with the love of God.

Wigglesworth was never willing to settle for a substitute, he wanted the authentic — even if it meant reevaluating his set of truths. He was hungry! He wanted nothing but God, and would settle for nothing less.

Wigglesworth once wrote a letter to W. Hacking. The opening read as follows, "Pleased to receive the news of much blessing in your ministry, especially in souls being saved and God keeping you in a very hungry and needy place."[9]

Hacking himself would say of Wigglesworth, "Wisdom, brokenness, purity, and spiritual hunger characterized his ministry."[10]

Wigglesworth was always burdened in his heart for the sick, the afflicted, and the oppressed.

John G. Lake was another revivalist who demonstrated an intense hunger for God. He so longed for the power of the baptism with the Holy Spirit that he described it this way:

When I approached this matter of the baptism [with the Holy Spirit], I did so with great care, but I approached it as a hungry soul; my heart was hungry for God.[11]

Lake, himself, was not only personally motivated by his hunger for God, but also ministered in accordance to the hunger he saw in other people. Once, while in South Africa, he began small open-air meetings in Doornfuntein. He described a segment of people there as "hungry for God's best at any price." He would minister with these people in the harmony of the Lord.

Often when Lake was preaching, one of his associates would step forward and intimate, "I believe I could amplify on that point."

In this way, frequently each one of these brothers would speak five or six times in the course of a meeting, and no one could tell where one message ended and the other one began. The results were astounding. Those meetings became a launching pad for seven hundred thousand people to be converted in South Africa. Hunger for God's best at any price will lead to an irrefutable momentum that will be enduring.

The Momentum of Spiritual Hunger

Spiritual hunger proved to be not only an initiating catalyst for revival, but also its sustaining force. Every revival was initiated through people who hungered for all of God at any price. The revivals were birthed by men and women who longed to see suffering humanity reconciled to God. Revivals have been indelibly etched with the hunger pangs of those sensing that God was about to do something great and who decided they would settle for nothing less than God's fullest and best.

That is why it is essential to understand the spiritual concept of hunger. Hunger for God, like physical hunger, is one of the most powerful instincts. In the Spirit realm, it motivates us to seek fulfillment. Spiritual hunger makes three important contributions:

1. It produces a desire to see a hurting humanity helped, which serves to identify the need of the hour.

2. It motivates people to move toward God and all that is right.

3. It promotes the recognition that a signal is being given by the Holy Spirit for a new season of God to begin. It causes us to long for the things of God that are not present in our lives to fulfill that hunger.

These principles are what Jesus was alluding to in Matthew 5:6:

"Blessed are those who hunger and thirst for righteousness, for they will be filled."

The word *blessed* is a divine invocation of God's care, spiritual prosperity, and happiness in God's favor. The beatitude in which this principle is found is God's invitation to the fulfillment of His lifestyle.

The Lord's use of the word *hunger* in that passage indicates that there is a missing ingredient that appetite alone brings to the surface. Without a doubt, hunger is one of the greatest motivating factors on the earth. Spiritual hunger is a continuing desire for more of what is right in God's eyes.

Every revivalist understood this principle.

While on that mission trip to Mexico, I saw this principle in action in a simple way. Every morning before we left our lodging, we would fill our pockets with bubble gum. As we walked down the sidewalks of the villages, the neighborhood children would make a "beeline" to us to acquire the gum.

As a result of poverty, they usually had few, if any, treats. Once we displayed the gum, we were surrounded by scores of children. They hungered for what was absent in their lives. Spiritual hunger longs for what God has for us that is missing in our lives. The children would have followed us for miles to get a single piece of bubble gum. Real spiritual hunger also does not give up until it is satisfied.

Maria Woodworth-Etter understood what it meant not to give up because of the driving hunger in her heart. Once she was converted and filled with the Holy Spirit, there arose within her an insatiable desire to see the Gospel manifested in the world. She was denied ministry opportunities because she was a woman. She had to overcome her fear of man. Death and disease devastated her family (she lost five children, and almost died herself), but she could not deny the urging of the Holy Spirit within her.

Many times she would come to a town and nothing would happen in her meetings. Rather than quit, she would stay up all night praying until there was a breakthrough in the Spirit realm. Hunger never gives up until it is fulfilled.

There is a further revelation in Matthew 5:6 of what spiritual hunger really means. The word hunger in the Greek is written in what is called a present durative tense. What that means is that *the hungering continues even after it is fulfilled.* When we experience this kind of hunger, we can be fulfilled but never permanently satisfied. Once we see the operation of God's power in action, we become hungry for more.

Once we see the oppressed set free, we want to see more. Once we see a person converted, we long to witness others being saved.

Once the captive is released, we want to see everyone set free. This then, is the driving force that builds momentum, that makes revival permanent, *a hunger that is fulfilled but divinely never satisfied.*

I do not know about you, but I am hungry to see God do some things. I am hungry to see the delivering hand of God.

One night I was ministering in a service and had given an altar call, asking all those who wanted to be set free from oppression to come forward. The altar area quickly filled, and each aisle was crammed with people all the way to the back of the room.

I began ministering to the people, but it soon became evident that I could not possibly touch everyone who had a need. I assigned altar workers to assist me, asking them to bring all the difficult cases forward. At the close of the service, about half a dozen people were ushered to the platform. I was going to simply pray for them and dismiss the service, because it was late. I prayed for the first five, and they were immediately "slain in the Spirit."

I came to the last young woman, who was about nineteen or twenty years old. As I laid my hands on her, I felt led of the Lord to say, "In the Name of Jesus, loose this young woman."

Suddenly, a deep male-sounding voice came out of this girl and said, "No! I won't come out."

Trust me when I say that got everyone's attention! The voice continued now in a rage, "I'm going to kill her." Everyone in the auditorium was straining to see what was taking place. I immediately took authority over the demon and commanded it to come out. The demon cried out in a shrieking voice, "No!"

We battled back and forth for some time, then the demon decided to try the typical way demons intimidate by saying, "I'm not only going to kill her, but I'm going to kill *you!*"

I tried to maintain my composure, because when the threat was made an obvious new strength and power came into this young woman. I found myself battling her physically as well as spiritually. I knew my authority in Christ, however, and I would not be denied. I prevailed in prayer for almost an hour. When the power of God broke through, she went totally limp, and deliverance took place.

Later, we found out that she had been involved in witchcraft and heavy metal music. (I have found many young people's bondage tied back to this source.) She had been prayed for on numerous occasions but never really set free. After a series of counseling and prayer services, and dealing with some root causes, this young woman was totally free for the first time in ten years. I am hungry to see people delivered.

I am tired of healing services where evangelists pray for every unseen disease and yet walk by the wheelchair section. I am hungry to see miracles that bring lasting changes and motivate people toward righteousness. It is the single greatest motivating factor in the life of revivalists of the past.

It is not enough to be hungry, however, *we must be hungry for "righteousness,"* as Matthew 5:6 says. Sometimes we take Bible words and make them complicated. *Righteousness* simply means what is right in God's eyes.[12] The result of hungering and thirsting after righteousness is simple: Those who do so will be "filled." Filled with what? They will be filled with "what is right in God's eyes."

This whole verse is fascinating when it is all brought together. It can be translated this way, "God invokes a divine favor in increasing proportion upon those who hunger and crave continually for those things that are totally right in His eyes. The result is they shall be filled and fulfilled with those right things."

God's people then will see a hurting humanity, but also see a God Who is right to meet that humanity's needs. The result is a hunger that is fulfilled but yearns to see more. The consequence will be the birth of a new season of God's flow of the Spirit.

How Can This Hunger Be Cultivated?

There are four keys to cultivating this kind of hunger:

1. *Fasting*. Fasting is God's way of using physical hunger to remind us of our need to remain spiritually hungry for more of Him. It is God's way of drawing people to hunger after Him.

2. *Feasting*. At first, that may sound like a contradiction, but it is a complement instead, something that is not opposite but "goes along with." Feasting complements fasting. "You are what you eat" is a phrase that applies to the spiritual realm as well as the physical realm. Feasting on Jesus creates a hunger for what is right. In John 6:32-35 our Lord told the people of His day:

"...I tell you the truth, it is not Moses who has given you the bread from heaven, but it is my Father who gives you the true bread from heaven. For the bread of God is he who comes down from heaven and gives life to the world."

"Sir," they said, "from now on give us this bread."

Then Jesus declared, "I am the bread of life. He who comes to me will never go hungry, and he who believes in me will never be thirsty."

How can Jesus call us to hunger and thirst on one hand and then on the other hand tell us that we will never hunger and thirst?

The answer is simple: feasting on Jesus causes us never to hunger for the world again. It wipes out any hunger pangs for that which is artificial, synthetic, incomplete, or of the world.

Eating the true product, the bread of life, alleviates the need for the by-product. The bread that Jesus offers to us eliminates any hunger for **...the lust of the flesh, and the lust of the eyes, and the pride of life...**(1 John 2:16 KJV).

The only hunger that can remain is the hunger for righteousness.

3. *Becoming a desperate person.* Hungry people do desperate things. We must be a people desperate for the things of God. Perhaps a more practical way to explain this concept is the saying: "If you want to see something you have never seen before, you have to do something you have never done before."

Without a doubt, this is an overstatement, but it communicates a key thought. If you and I want to see God move in revival again, we cannot remain in the "status quo." Hunger for God cannot be "business as usual," but demands that we be willing to take new risks for Him. True hunger will not be denied until it is satisfied.

4. *Being where the hurting are!* Nothing will create hunger in a person more than seeing the need of a hurting society. That experience motivated virtually every revivalist. Certainly their primary motivation was seeing God, but seeing people helped was certainly the secondary one. Every time I look at an altar full of people, I am filled with compassion to see God move on their behalf.

Spiritual hunger is what initiated and sustained the moves of God. It is hunger that leads an individual to seek fulfillment in His presence.

Even so, Lord, let Your presence be established in the earth.

Chapter 11

Revival: When All Heaven Breaks Loose

Allen was among the most dramatic and daring of all the healing evangelists. His meetings were lively and filled with remarkable miracles.

...O thou [God] that inhabitest the praises of Israel.
— **Psalm 22:3 KJV**

On February 3, 1970, without warning, all heaven broke loose during a 10 a.m. chapel service on the campus of an evangelical institution, Asbury College in Wilmore, Kentucky. The almost shocking move of God transpired when members of the administration, faculty, and student body showed up for one of the college's three regularly scheduled weekly chapel services.

The service that morning was expected to be little more than an ordinary fifty-minute chapel assembly. Instead, it lasted one hundred and eighty-five hours and was a non-stop, twenty-four-hour-a-day, visitation of God in the midst of His people. Intermittently, the revival continued for weeks until ultimately it spread throughout pockets of the United States and even to other parts of the world.

Dr. David Hunt, a former student, recalls the incident this way, "When you walked into the back of Hughes Auditorium...there was kind of an aura, kind of a glow about the chapel."[1]

The academic dean, Custer Reynolds, was scheduled to preach that morning. For some reason unknown to him (but obviously known to the Holy Spirit), he decided to give his testimony instead. After he had finished, he issued an impromptu invitation to students to come forward to share what God had done in their lives.

One student responded, then another...then another...then another. Suddenly, spontaneously, students from all over the room began pouring down to the altar. The "ordinary" chapel service broke open under the presence of God. Gradually, inexplicably, students and faculty members alike found themselves repenting, praying, weeping, and worshipping.

Those first affected sought out others whom they had wronged and asked forgiveness and reconciliation. The chapel service went on and on. Asbury, like most Christian campuses held scheduled "revivals" booked in advance, but this was not the same. This was not the plan of man, and certainly no man was leading it. No one could put a halt to what God had begun.

The word spread like wildfire, "God is on the scene."

Other faculty members, students, and even people from the community who had not been present at that historic chapel service, came racing to see what was happening.

One faculty member, Dr. J. T. Seamands, was skeptical, but once he witnessed what was transpiring, he felt as if he was baptized in an unaccountable spirit of love, and his skepticism vanished: Without a doubt this phenomenon was not of man, it was of God.

The school president, Dennis Kinlaw, described the visitation this way:

You may not understand this...but the only way I know to account for this is that about twenty minutes before 11 a.m. that day, the Lord Jesus walked into Hughes Auditorium, and He's been there ever since. The whole community is *paying tribute to His presence.*[2]

Earlier, I gave a simplistic definition of revival: "God came." When God's presence fills the Church, revival always comes. Every revival of history is simply the restoration of God's presence among His people.

There is little doubt that man cannot plan it, organize it, or set its date. The key responsibility for God's people is to prepare their hearts for God's move. Nothing is more central to cultivating the presence of God than a heart of worship among His people.

Many of the great revivalists knew the supreme value of the atmosphere of worship, which cultivates a communion between God's people and the Holy Spirit.

Kathryn Kuhlman knew the value of music to bring a crowd into the unity of the Spirit. She would gather the best musicians and singers available and encourage them to submit to the anointing of the Holy Spirit.

Jimmy Miller, Charles Beebee, Dr. Arthur Metcalfe, Dino Kartzonakis, and Jimmie McDonald were assembled for such a task. They were never simply to exhibit their talents or to entertain. Miss Kuhlman abhorred that kind of self-centered activity. Instead, they were to lead people into the throne room of God, where His presence was evident.

Kathryn Kuhlman hated any manifestation of the flesh. Everything that transpired in her meetings was totally dependent upon the presence of God. She understood that praise and worship was the key to ushering His presence into her meetings.[3]

The Healing Revival of the late-1940s and the early-1950s was infiltrated by a renewed call of God's people to worship. Perhaps no one more exemplified this heartbeat than A. A. Allen.

Allen was among the most dramatic and daring of all the healing evangelists. His meetings were lively and filled with remarkable miracles. Being a musician, he knew the captivating power that came from the atmosphere of praise and worship. He was among the very first to add "gospel rock" to his services, and he emphasized old-time Pentecostal worship. The music was often pulsating, but it was directed toward God and had an amazing effect upon people's faith.

Look magazine described one of Allen's later meetings:

> The music so activates the air that, in an open space between the platforms and the 4,000 metal folding chairs, two dozen or so of the swelling congregation spin, flail, twitch, and boogie in a frantic spiritual ecstasy.[4]

A. A. Allen, c. 1960. Contagious joy in his ministry found expression for the God of miracles.

That is a secular description of people dancing and expressing joy before the Lord. The people would dance, hop, "buck" (a Pentecostal phrase for a religious dance form), and leap before the Lord. The people clapped and shouted in the presence of the Lord. Theirs was a contagious joy, finding expression for the God of miracles, Who is the same yesterday, today, and forever.

A Revival of Singing

Similarly, the 1904 revival in Wales was primarily a move of praise and worship, along with prayer. Gordon Lindsay described the sound of these meetings this way: "...The singing — Oh, the singing!" It was a revival of singing.

One newspaper reporter wrote:

The fact is, unless heard, it is unimaginable, and when heard it is indescribable. No human (song)books are used. Once a song is started, it seemed to be motivated by a simultaneous unity; the melody and song were caught up by the whole congregation, merging into a myriad-headed personality of song in a perfect blending of mood, purpose, and unity which is only possible through the Spirit of God. Three-fourths of the meeting consisted of this "singing in the Spirit."[5]

Evan Roberts wrote about the November 14, 1905, meeting:

We had a mighty downpouring of the Holy Spirit last Saturday night. This was preceded by the correcting of the people's view of true worship: (1) To give unto God, not to receive. (2) To please God, not to please ourselves. Therefore, looking to God, and forgetting the enemy, and also the fear of men, we prayed and the Spirit descended.[6]

Notwithstanding my minor disagreement with Roberts on the reciprocal relationship of giving and receiving from God in worship, the correction brought the focus directly to God in worship. Undoubtedly, the people came to the meeting in great expectancy to receive from God, but had forgotten the One Who was the giver of "every good gift and every perfect gift." (James 1:17 KJV.) Worship leaves man in a submitted state to God acknowledging His unparalleled character and power.

During the same era in India, the spontaneous composition of hymns was a key feature in some of the meetings there. In some places where the people were in worship and prayer, pictures would appear on the walls depicting the life of Christ. They were in color and the figures moved in detailed depictions. They had a tremendous effect in breaking up the hardness of heart of the non-believers and bringing them to a saving knowledge of Jesus Christ.[7]

The Azusa Street revival was dominated by prayer and worship as well. An eyewitness described the meetings this way:

We were on holy ground. The atmosphere was unbearable to the carnal spirit....on Friday, June 15, at Azusa, the Spirit dropped the "heavenly chorus" in my soul....it was indeed a "new song" in the Spirit....it was a gift from God of big order, and appeared among us soon after the "Azusa" work began. No one had preached it. The Lord had sovereignly bestowed it, with the outpouring of the residue of oil, the latter rain baptism of the Spirit....it was sometimes without words, other times in "tongues." The effect was wonderful on the people. It brought a heavenly atmosphere, as though the angels themselves were present and joining with us. And possibly they were. It seemed to still criticism and opposition, and it was hard for even wicked men to gossip or ridicule....must we necessarily follow some man's composition before us, always? We are too much worshippers of tradition....why not a gift of song?...yet, some of the old hymns are very good to sing, also. We need not despise them or treat lightly of them. Someone has said, "Every fresh revival brings its own hymnology," and surely this one did.[8]

In the beginning at Azusa Street, there were no musical instruments. The whole move was spontaneously inspired by God. Hymns were sung by memory as the Holy Spirit would lead. The "new song" of the Lord came down not from human composition, but under the anointing of the Holy Spirit. It was truly "singing in the Spirit." Seymour was the man in charge but, without a doubt, God Himself was leading. The worship served as a cornerstone for the miracle-working power of God.

There were other revivalists who understood the primacy of praise and worship. John G. Lake, for instance, did not believe in a rigid form of worship. He always remained flexible, so that the Holy Spirit could truly govern the meetings.[9] Smith Wigglesworth said that his communion with the Lord was founded in worship.

Worship and music were a central theme for Aimee Semple McPherson as well. Her services were filled with worship. In the 1930s, she published her own hymnal with sixty-four of her own compositions. She wrote more than one hundred and eighty songs and composed seven full-length sacred operas. The music of worship filled Angelus Temple during the services.[10]

It is safe to say that worship has been a vital and viable key to revival in history. Worship helped break up "fallow ground," bring the people into submission to God, and promote the presence of His Spirit. This is an old truth that we must rediscover again in new proportions if we desire to see the next wave of God's move.

Only Worship Brings His Presence

I sit in large numbers of churches with Spirit-filled congregations that have magnificent music programs. The choirs are outstanding, the musicians are talented, and the singers are harmonious. None of these, however, constitutes worship. It is easier to rely upon talent and atmosphere than it is to rely upon the presence of Almighty God. Talent and atmosphere may bring "goose bumps," but only the presence of the Lord can change a life. Music can develop an atmosphere, but only worship can bring the presence of the Lord.

Worship is not simply the "first part of the service" before the Word is preached. Worship is a ministry unto the Lord, an expression of love that cultivates His presence. Psalm 22:3 (KJV) says, **But thou art holy, O thou that inhabitest the praises of Israel.** In other words, God dwells in the praises of His people. As I have shared this concept some people have challenged me with statements like, "God is omniscient; therefore, He is always present." I am not disputing that fact; what I am saying is that praise and worship invite the conspicuous, full presence of God.

Worship is the call that manifests the glory of God. The glory of God is the heavy, copious, conspicuous manifestation of His presence. It is this presence that the revivalists were so dependent upon for God's miracle-working power.

The word *dwell* or *inhabitest* in this passage also means enthroned.[11] Worship places God upon His throne as an all-powerful Master to Whom we have both submitted and have access as Lord of the universe. Praise and worship create a heavenly atmosphere for "Thy kingdom come, Thy will be done in this place as it is in heaven." Hallowing, venerating, or revering the Lord in praise always preceded the act of manifesting His Kingdom (see the "Lord's prayer," Matt. 6:9-13). The principle is simple: praise, then power.

Churches today — Charismatic, Spirit-filled, Pentecostal, or otherwise — are filled with traditions that can drain spiritual vitality. Religious routine can replace real adoration. Worship is not simply a style, but a relationship. New songs versus old songs is not the question; it is the spirit out of which we sing them that really counts. It is the Lord we sing them to that really matters.

In the next chapter, I would like for us to take an overall look at why we are to worship God and what results we are to expect.

⚬⚬⚬

Chapter 12

Why Do We Worship?

If God dwells in the praises of His people, then worship is obviously a necessary ingredient for His miracle presence.

Praise ye the Lord: for it is good to sing praises unto our God; for it is pleasant; and praise is comely....

Let every thing that hath breath praise the Lord....

— Psalm 147:1,150:6 KJV

One day at the chapel service at Oral Roberts University, we had a very fine speaker, Bishop O. T. Jones of the Church of God in Christ (COGIC). That evening he was speaking to a group of that denomination's pastors in one of our university facilities. I was asked to come to the meeting to deliver a greeting on behalf of the university.

When I arrived at the service, I felt right at home, although I was one of only two white faces in the entire crowd. The worship was lively but not exceptionally so, and the people seemed to wait in anticipation, virtually ready to explode. I was asked at the end of the music portion of the service to come to the podium and bring the greeting.

For whatever reason, I was feeling spiritually rambunctious.

I got before the crowd and said, "I might be white on the out-side, but I'm black on the inside; I like this style."

The crowd immediately began to prod me on.

I continued, "On the outside, I might be doing *this* [a two-step dance often done in Charismatic services], but on the inside I am doing *this* [a "buck," or lively dance step, often seen in COGIC church services].

Immediately the organ player hit a chord, and the whole crowd began to join in. The place went wild. I had enough rhythm to keep going for about sixty seconds, and that was all. I tried to shut the enthusiasm down to hide my ineptness, but I could not. The aroused crowd kept going for almost another twenty minutes in an incredible expression of joy. Afterwards, everyone had a warm feeling and a good laugh at my initiation, but limitation, of that expression of worship. It was a wonderful experience.

The point is simple: *The style is not nearly as important as the heart.*

I can summarize *why we worship* in three basic principles. I precede these principles with the presupposition that we worship first and foremost because we love God. Our expressions of worship are simply an outgrowth of that love.

1. *Worship reminds us of God's power.* Does God need our worship? This may surprise some people, but the answer is no! Worship is not a massaging of God's heavenly ego. Praise is not a pampering of God's insecurities. Worship is unto God, but for man's benefit.

All my life I have heard people say that God created man for fellowship. The only problem with that concept is that it's not primary in Scripture. God enjoys fellowship with man, but He made him for rulership (Gen. 1:6-29), to be steward over God's handiwork. Worship allows man to remain in a position of submission, and thereby enhances his authority.

2. *Worship opens the door for incredible events in the heavenly realm.* If God dwells in the praises of His people, then worship is obviously a necessary ingredient for His miracle presence.

3. *Worship confounds the powers of darkness.* Recently, I had the privilege of seeing the deliverance and the restoration of a young woman who was an ex-satanist. We met together for several months in securing her freedom. During that time I would ask about the strategies of this demonic organization.

She told me that Halloween marks the beginning of the religious year for the satanic church. It is at this time that the leaders, among many other abominable practices, train followers to invade key churches in America. Their sole intent is to divide and destroy these churches.

Her next bit of information is what really fascinated me since it concerns the principle of praise and worship. "These infiltrators have the most difficulty weaving the destructive web in churches where they speak in tongues and where there is true worship," she said.

"Why?" I asked, and she responded, "Because praying in the Spirit, or true worship, throws the kingdom of darkness into confusion."

I got up out of my office chair and immediately began worshipping and praying in tongues. What a phenomenal revelation if we can just get hold of it.

Praise and Worship Defeat the Enemy

Let me exemplify these principles by citing some key examples in the Bible.

First, let's look again at the story of King Jehoshaphat in 2 Chronicles 20. This passage begins by telling us that God's people in Judah were about to come under attack by other nations. In verse 3 we read that Jehoshaphat responded in fear.

I love the honesty of the Bible. First, I respect Jehoshaphat, because he had a good grasp of numbers. Being outnumbered three-to-one is enough to get anyone's attention. Then the Bible says that fear overtook him. That is a natural response to being greatly outnumbered!

However, I can almost hear someone echoing in the background, "A faith person should not have any fear!"

Initial fear in a crisis does not negate or disqualify us from faith or victory. The key is *what we do with fear.* Second Chronicles 20:3 says:

Alarmed [in fear], **Jehoshaphat resolved to inquire of the Lord, and he proclaimed a fast for all Judah.**

Jehoshaphat knew the first great principle of revival, *inquiring prayer.* Together all the people of Judah inquired of the Lord. (v. 4.) The whole prayer is fascinating, but it ends with these words:

"O our God, will you not judge them? [good inquiry] **For we have no power to face this vast army that is attacking us. We do not know what to do, but our eyes are upon you."**

— 2 Chronicles 20:12

What a phenomenal actualization of a principle. A whole nation fixes their eyes upon the God of their deliverance and inquires of Him what to do. Then the Lord answers them with this magnificent response:

> **"...This is what the Lord says to you: 'Do not be afraid or discouraged because of this vast army. For the battle is not yours, but God's....You will not have to fight this battle. Take up your positions; stand firm and see the deliverance the Lord will give you...Go out to face them tomorrow, and the Lord will be with you.'"**
>
> **— 2 Chronicles 20:15,17**

Fear is never dispelled by mental gymnastics, but by the Word of the Lord. God told His people that He was going to be with them and deliver them. The manner and power of deliverance is the unfolding of this incredible power of praise and worship.

The story of Jehoshaphat continues in verse 21:

> **After consulting the people** [this king was not insensitive to the needs of his people; he wanted them to know what he had now come to understand], **Jehoshaphat appointed men to sing to the Lord and to praise him for the splendor of His holiness as they went out at the head of the army saying:**
>
> **"Give thanks to the Lord, for His love endures forever."**

That phrase "for his love endures forever" is an expression of the compassion of God for His people, which is a key to the manifestation of miracles. Also, notice that it was the leader who called the men to praise.

First, they were to sing *to the Lord*. God never called us to sing *songs,* but to *sing unto Him*. Why? It is not because He needs praise and worship, but because we need it. It is unto God, but it is for us. I can see the peoples' faith soar, as they worship the omnipotent God.

Second, He called them to *praise Him for the splendor of His holiness*. Their worship was to elevate His character, not simply

His exploits. True worship acknowledges God for Who He is, not simply for what He can do. His doing is an expression of His being. His actions on their behalf are an extension of His relationship with His people.

How would you feel if the only time one of your children sat on your lap and told you he loved you was when he wanted something from you?

I do not think God is excited about that attitude either. True worship of God centers on Who He is, not on what He can do for us.

Now suppose that same child sits on your lap and tells you he loves you — for no particular reason at all except to express the genuine affection of his heart.

That kind of endearing expression opens the floodgate of a parent's heart. It also opens the passion of our heavenly Father.

Notice what takes place with Jehoshaphat and Judah in 2 Chronicles 20:22,23:

> **As they began to sing and praise, the Lord set ambushes against the men of Ammon and Moab and Mount Seir who were invading Judah, and they were defeated. The men of Ammon and Moab rose up against the men from Mount Seir to destroy and annihilate them. After they finished slaughtering the men from Seir, they helped to destroy one another.**

Two things transpired as a result of the praises of the men of Judah:

(1) God came to dwell in their midst, and it was He Who set the ambushes against their enemies, and (2) the attacking armies became confused and turned on each other.

Now notice how the people of Judah reacted to this turn of events:

> So Jehoshaphat and his men went to carry off their plunder, and they found among them a great amount of equipment and clothing and also articles of value — more than they could take away. There was so much plunder that it took three days to collect it. On the fourth day they assembled in the Valley of Beracah, where they praised the Lord. That is why it is called the Valley of Beracah to this day.
>
> — 2 Chronicles 20:25,26

I find it fascinating that the people of Judah named the valley *Beracah*, which interestingly means "praise."[1] There was no doubt in the mind of anyone in Judah that praise had brought them deliverance on this day. If we will rediscover it, I am just as sure that praise will bring us deliverance in our day.

Acts 16 gives us another graphic example of the power of praise and worship. Here in this passage, Paul and Silas are thrown into jail for casting out a spirit of a fortune teller. Let me amplify the description offered by a black preacher who graphically and imaginatively elaborates on verses 25 and 26:

> Paul and Silas were probably beaten, thrown into a cell, and chained to a wall. It was undoubtedly darker than a thousand midnights in that cell; they likely couldn't see their hand in front of their face. Maybe they could hear rats scurrying across the stone floors, but couldn't see them.
>
> About midnight, Paul says to Silas, "Silas, are you there?"
>
> Silas responds, "Yes, Paul, I'm here."
>
> "Silas," Paul adds, "you know what?"
>
> "What, Paul?"
>
> "I can feel a...hallelujah coming on!"
>
> Silas says, "Paul, you start and I'll join in."

The Bible says that at midnight they began praying and singing hymns. I can imagine their praise, going up through the atmosphere, up through the stratosphere, and up through the ionosphere, until it reaches heaven.

Suddenly, God stands up and says, "Hey! What's that I hear?"

One of the angels says to Him, "Oh Lord, that's just music!"

God responds and says, "No, that's not just music; that's My kind of music — praise and worship."

Just as suddenly, God starts tapping His foot to the music. That tapping travels down through the ionosphere, down through the stratosphere, and down through the atmosphere, until the Bible says that there was an earthquake that set the prisoners free.

I'm telling you, praise and worship will set the captive free, if we will allow it to do so. True praise and worship creates an undeniable presence of Almighty God.

Similarly, Joshua's conquering of Jericho (Josh. 6) was a victory of praise, as the nation of Israel entered Canaan. That is a common Sunday school story for most of us, but we must never miss the full impact of its meaning.

Joshua and Israel entered the promised land and faced their first obstacle — the massive walled city of Jericho. It is said that the walls of Jericho were so wide that chariot races were run on top of them. They were impenetrable to an invading army.

Everyone knows the story of the victory at Jericho. The Israelites were told to march around Jericho once every day for six days. On the seventh day, they were to march around the city six times, then on the seventh time around they were to blow the trumpets and shout. Not exactly the kind of advice we might expect to find in "General Patton's Military Tactics for Conquering Cities."

The reason it is important to understand this undertaking are the secrets of praise and worship revealed in this crucial incident. In Joshua 6:4 when God gave the instructions for the military exploit, He told the children of Israel, "Have seven priests carry trumpets of rams' horns in front of the ark."

The trumpets made of rams' horns were "jubilee trumpets." (Num. 10:1-10.) These trumpets were instruments of praise. The conquest of Jericho was not a military undertaking, but a spiritual one. The trumpets declared that the Lord of heaven and earth was weaving His invisible presence around a doomed city.

In Joshua 6:5, after the people had marched around the city and blown the trumpets, they were to give a shout. The shout is used twelve times in Scripture as an act of praise. Again, as with Jehoshaphat later, God fashioned a victory by His presence in praise and worship.

The conclusion of the story is well-known. The trumpets sounded, the shouts of the people rang out, and **...the wall collapsed...**(Josh. 6:20) so that the Israelites charged straight in and took the city in God's name.

The word *collapsed* used here of the wall literally means "fell down in its place."[2] I am told that the walls did not crumble as a normal wall would, but were pushed straight down as if they were a venetian blind. Truly, praise and worship bring the power as well as the presence of God for revival.

As I have examined the Scriptures, I have discovered that there are multiplicities of ways to worship. We can worship God with singing, with instruments, by speaking (that is why the whole service is a worship service), with the shout, with clapping, with dancing, with offerings, by kneeling, by bowing, by falling down prostrate, with spiritual songs, by lifting up holy hands, and by waving.

Worship is *emotional, rational, physical,* and *spiritual.*

Read Romans 12:1,2 as a worship passage, and you will find all four expressions viable. People try to elevate one kind of expression over another. Each expression is valid within scriptural boundaries.

The key is not to encourage one at the expense of another, but to incorporate everything God has for the Body of Christ.

King David understood worship perhaps better than any man in history. He initiated most of our Old Testament standards. David appointed worshippers to praise God twenty-four hours a day. (1 Chron. 15:16-22;16:6.) Then he appointed hundreds of people in various types of worship to perform before the Lord continually. (1 Chron. 25.)

Why did he do that? David understood that Israel's success was unlike that of other nations but was directly dependent upon the presence of God. He knew he had to do whatever was necessary to create that presence. It is no less necessary for us today.

Six Elements of Praise and Worship

Psalm 149 (KJV) serves as a standard and guideline for our praise and worship. Here David outlines several keys to promote such a presence:

1. **Praise *ye* the Lord...**(v. 1a). There is a responsibility in worship. I know people who say things like, "I would worship if everyone else would worship." That is a completely unbiblical response. We are responsible for ourselves and no one else.

Also, who knows whether our response to God might be contagious to others?

We might be tempted to say, "I'd do it if everyone else did." We need to stop worrying about Frieda Frigidaire and obey God. We might find out Frieda's following our lead.

2. **...Sing *unto the Lord*...**(v. 1b). Nowhere are we exhorted just to sing songs, instead we are exhorted to sing unto the Lord. Churches are filled with people who sing meaningless songs, and coast through a service on the atmosphere of music. Singing to the Lord in pure devotion is what brings His true presence into a place.

3. **..a new song...**(v. 1c). A *new song* in the Hebrew culture was an expression of spontaneity and freshness. It is the kind of spontaneous expression we have seen in modern moves, such as the Welsh and Azusa Street revivals.

Paul exhorted the Church to sing **...psalms and hymns and spiritual songs...**(Eph. 5:19 KJV).

A *psalm* is a composition based on Scripture. A *hymn* is simply a song to or about God, but of human composition.[3] It includes not only what are considered to be traditional anthems, but new choruses as well. I agree with Frank Bartleman that every generation gives way to its own hymnology. There is, however, a precious depth of tradition that is held onto by past compositions. A *spiritual song* is a spontaneous song of the Lord given at a particular moment.[4] All of these expressions are proper in worship.

4. **Let Israel *rejoice*...**(v. 2). The word *rejoice* used in this passage means "to brighten up" or to change one's countenance.[5] Rejoicing is not simply a matter of emotions, but also a matter of

will. Rejoicing does not depend on circumstances, but on acknowledging God in the midst of life.

5. **Let them praise his name in the *dance*...**(v. 3). In this context, to *dance* means to twirl or spin. If God truly restores dance to His people, it will shut down every dance club in America. Young people will no longer have to "get down" with the latest rock star as much as "get up" through their expression of love to Jesus Christ.

I used to be inhibited about any expression of dance in the church, because I had limited rhythm. One day, while I was serving a pastorate in East Texas, Terry Law came to speak at my church and brought his own praise and worship team. A great spirit of freedom entered the auditorium, and I was doing my normal expression of freedom — shuffling my right foot. Suddenly, Terry began to dance in the Spirit. He took me by the right arm and swung me in a circle with him. I was so shaken up I did not know what to do. I stumbled and bumbled around for a while, but my pride kept me from totally entering into the joyful activity.

About a year later, God broke pride from my life in a far greater way. A man who came into my church falsely accused me of sin and sent a letter to the entire county. I was shocked and horrified. I wondered what people might think. I had labored in as much integrity as I knew how for three years. I could not help but wonder if all my work would go up in smoke.

The following Saturday night, I was in my office praying and considering what I might say to the people the next day in services. My stomach was filled with anxiety as I speculated on what the ramifications of this situation would be on my young ministry. I prayed earnestly that night.

As was my custom in those days, I moved from behind my desk to sit on the other side of it as a physical demonstration of my submission to Jesus as the true Head of that church. When I came around to the far side of the desk, I caught a glimpse of my most prized possession, a portrait of Jesus laughing.

Almost in anger, I cried out, "What are You laughing at?"

In an immediate response, I heard the Lord say to me, "I'm laughing at you!"

"But You don't understand what I'm up against!" I replied in anguish.

The Lord responded to me with words that have forever changed my life, "The reason I'm laughing is that *you* don't understand what this man [coming] against you is up against!"

Suddenly, the revelation of God flooded over my spirit. The truth will always outlive a lie. If God be for us, who could be against us? I broke out in a belly laugh for about thirty minutes straight. The presence of the Lord filled the room. I went home that night and slept like a baby.

The next morning I awakened with some anxiety, but it soon gave way to my new-found revelation. I went to church not knowing what the reaction of the people would be, but I already knew God's reaction. I did not know if anyone would even show up for the service. Quite the contrary, however, people who had not been to church for years were present. There was an overflow crowd all waiting to see my reaction to the allegations.

As the worship began, I felt a freedom I had never known before and broke forth in a dance for the first time in my life. The effects were liberating. I had never felt more free. The results equally freed up the congregation. I had assumed that any worship that day would only be a formality, but instead, the presence of the Lord flooded the place.

Finally, I stepped up to the microphone and said, "Folks, I love you. I have led my life as an open book before you for three years. Therefore, I make no defense of myself."

(The letter had been completely ambiguous, leaving the door open for a person to think the worst. I really did not even know of what I was being accused, since the man would not return my calls.)

"In fact," I continued, "I want to urge you to love this man in hopes it will bring him back to Christ."

The congregation broke forth in spontaneous applause. I did not lose a member or a dollar over that incident. God was the preserver of my integrity. That morning, the freedom in me affected the congregation and, from that day forward, a new dimension of the presence of the Lord was upon them.

Expressions of worship bring God's presence.

6. **Let the *high praises* of God be in their mouth...(v. 6).** *High praise* is the embracing of anything lofty and exalted. There is a praise that is involved in a more momentous purpose than our own. It is all of God's people on earth joining with all of God's people in heaven in the ultimate celebration of the presence of God. It is the ultimate joy in the Lord. It is the intoxicating, captivating release of God's presence that was experienced by the believers on the Day of Pentecost. It dominated the Welsh Revival and must again pervade the Body of Christ.

True praise and worship is motivated, marked and manifested by joy — as we will see in the following chapter.

John Alexander Dowie, c. 1900. Dowie was a prolific writer. His periodical, *Leaves of Healing,* carried reports of healings of many celebrities.

John Alexander Dowie, c. 1900. His ministry of divine healing rocketed a small congregation in Chicago to thousands of believers virtually overnight.

John Alexander Dowie and wife, Jane, at their booth at 1894 Chicago World's Fair. His ministry introduced a widespread knowledge of divine healing to America.

John Alexander Dowie in his later years.

John G. Lake, 1930s. In Spokane, Washington. From 1914 to about 1920, Lake's ministry saw an estimated 100,000 healings.

John G. Lake. "How glad I am that God has taught me to pray as I run, and run, as I pray."

John G. Lake (left) and Cyrus Fockler, c. 1910s. The anointing of God through Lake resulted in one hundred thousand healings in five years.

John G. Lake (front, center), Milwaukee, Wisconsin, 1913. (From right: Rex Andrews, Hugo Ulrich and Florence M. Lake.)

John G. Lake (center) at tent meeting, Milwaukee, Wisconsin, 1913. (From left: Rex Andrews, Hugo Ulrich and George Finnern.)

Maria Woodworth-Etter (hand raised) near Indianapolis, Indiana, with August Feick (right). A supernatural call of God ignited her ministry.

Maria Woodworth-Etter with Indian Evangelist Watt Walker. An intrepid spiritual pioneer, Mrs. Woodworth-Etter set the stage for the Pentecostal-Charismatic revivals.

Meeting in Maria Woodworth-Etter Tabernacle, Indianapolis, Indiana, c. 1920. One camp meeting drew an estimated twenty-five thousand people.

Maria Woodworth-Etter, 1922. *The New York Times* carried articles of her amazing campaigns in which many lawyers and doctors were converted.

Aimee Semple McPherson. The Lord told her to "go preach my Word."

Advertisement for **Aimee Semple McPherson** revival, July 1922. McPherson was perhaps most famous for her illustrated sermons.

Aimee Semple McPherson arrived in Los Angeles in 1921 with ten dollars and a tambourine. Before long, the 5,300-seat Angelus Temple had been built debt-free.

Aimee Semple McPherson (with tambourine) and followers, Victoria Hall Mission, Los Angeles, California, 1919. To her mother's chagrin, Aimee got involved with Pentecostals.

Aimee Semple McPherson (seventh from right) at tent meeting, Philadelphia, Pa., 1918. Among others pictured is her second husband, Harold McPherson (sixth from right).

Aimee Semple McPherson, Stretcher Day at revival, municipal auditorium, Denver, Colorado, 1927.

312 Azusa Street, c. 1910. William J. Seymour standing in front. Wooden planks served as pews. The pulpit was an overturned chicken crate.

William J. Seymour, c. 1912.

William J. Seymour with his wife, Jennie, 1912. Seymour always remained humble, never wanting any attention or seeking any credit or glory.

Azusa Street revival leaders, 1907. No sermons were announced ahead of time; no special speakers were advertised; no human leader was depended on exclusively.

Azusa Street leaders c. 1915: (from left, front) William Seymour and John G. Lake; (back) Mr. Adams, F. F. Bosworth and Tom Hezmalhalch.

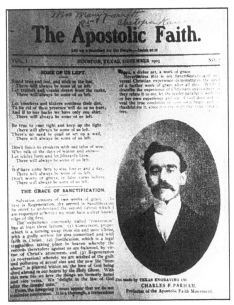

Charles F. Parham Advertisement. To Parham's astonishment, his students all reached the conclusion that the Baptism in the Holy Ghost was for today and its initial evidence was speaking with other tongues.

A page from a periodical published by **Charles Fox Parham**. Minutes into 1901, Parham laid hands on a student and she started speaking Chinese.

Charles F. Parham (front) and followers, Carthage, Mo., courthouse, 1905. A small core of people truly accepted what essentially became the Pentecostal doctrine.

Charles F. Parham. In 1903, the combination of the Baptism with the Holy Spirit and the teaching of divine healing reignited his ministry.

Charles F. Parham (seated center) and followers, Bryan Hall, Houston Texas, 1905. That year, Parham began a ten-week Bible training school near Houston.

Evan Roberts. The 1904 Welsh revival led by Roberts saw more than a hundred thousand people converted in less than six months.

Evan Roberts, in latter years. A miner-blacksmith whose genuine search after God led him to become "a lay preacher," Roberts led the 1904 Welsh revival.

Smith Wigglesworth. Until he was baptized in the Holy Spirit in 1907, Wigglesworth owned a plumbing business and helped his wife in a mission.

Jack Coe, c. 1951.

William Branham tent crusade, September 1950, Kansas City, Kansas, Gordon Lindsay at microphone. Lindsay said of Branham, "Without the anointing he is helpless."

The Explosion of Joy

It was said of Smith Wigglesworth that he was so full of joy he was always smiling and never without a Bible.

...in thy presence is fulness of joy....

— **Psalm 16:11 KJV**

A while back, I was in a worship service listening to a pastor I respected as a man of God. That morning he boldly preached a prophetic message titled, "There Is a Revival of God in the Birth Canal."

His message immediately bore witness to my spirit, and I knew that what he said was true. God is getting ready to pour out a higher dimension of His Spirit. I believe God is getting ready to move with the greatest outpouring of His Spirit that the world has ever known.

I found myself during the next week asking God what a revival in the birth canal meant to the Body of Christ. The Lord led me to Isaiah 37:3:

> **"...This is what Hezekiah says: This day is a day of distress and rebuke and disgrace, as when children come to the point of birth and there is no strength to deliver them."**

Suddenly my eyes were opened, and I began to realize that the revival was in the birth canal, but there was no strength to give birth to it. Every generation that goes through a "transition period" is sapped of its strength to birth God's will. It is perennially a time of distress, rebuke, and disgrace. This is true of every era. Virtually every generation goes through a similar period of discouragement prior to revival.

The terms Isaiah used are illuminating.

Distress — trouble, adversity, anguish, intense pain, sorrow, or great strain.[1]

Rebuke — chastisement, refutation, reasoning.[2]

Disgrace — blasphemy, contempt.[3]

Events at the end of the Eighties up through today have brought distress, rebuke, and disgrace. A large segment of the Church fell into sin, excesses, and lethargy. We saw exposed the hidden sins of some of our key leaders. In many cases, prosperity eroded into materialism and greed. In many corridors, a self-indulgent attitude began to pervade the Church.

The result was strain and worry, and our rationale of ministry was questioned. A feeling of shame overshadowed part of the Body of Christ. The corresponding result was the sapping of energy to release God's presence through the earth. There was no strength to give birth.

My mind again flashed back to when my wife, Judy, and I gave birth to our first child, as I related in Chapter 3. We took all the right courses. We prepared diligently, and most of all, we learned how to breathe. Only a woman can understand what it takes to give birth to a child, but a husband can understand the agony of watching his wife go through it.

I labored diligently to care for Judy in every way. However, when transition comes, the pain intensifies as only a woman can know. Instructions from coaches come to mean very little in that time. I tried to comfort her by holding her hand or helping her breathe. Trust me, there is little the husband can do in a situation like that, except to urge his wife to hold on and "push."

In those days, my wife had long, beautiful fingernails. As a contraction would "hit" her, she would go into contortions. During transition the pain would intensify and she would let out a scream, then take those long, beautiful fingernails and forcibly embed them into my stomach. She would scream — and then I would scream. We both learned about labor pain in that experience!

There comes a time in labor, however, when a woman no longer determines whether she will "push" or not. It is no longer her choice. Another force takes over, and all she can do is cooperate with it. It is the same way with revival. We labor through the distress, rebuke, and disgrace. We breathe, we push, and we work until another power takes over. We cannot promote it, we can only cooperate with it.

As this revelation unfolded before me, I cried out to God for the key of how we could come to the point where His resurrection power is released so that we would regain the strength to simply cooperate with Him in the birth of revival.

I pored over the Scriptures, searching for the answer. In Romans 8:11 (KJV), I found where Paul wrote:

> **But if the Spirit of him that raised up Jesus from the dead dwell in you, he that raised up Christ from the dead shall also quicken your mortal bodies by his Spirit that dwelleth in you.**

That is an incredible promise: The same power that raised Jesus to life again is available to revive us as well. Then I made an amazing discovery, the Greek word translated *quicken* as used by Paul in this passage means to make alive (or revive), to vitalize or revitalize, to cause to live, to bring forth, to give life to, to bear living young, or to give birth to.[4] This same power that gave birth to a miracle of resurrection is available in us to give birth to revival.

The question is: How?

Look at Hebrews 12:2:

> **Let us fix our eyes on Jesus, the author and perfecter of our faith, who for the joy set before him endured the cross, scorning its *shame,* and sat down at the right hand of the throne of God.**

There it is. The key to resurrection power to overcome shame or distress, rebuke, and disgrace is joy that must precede resurrection power. Jesus overcame the agony of the cross and endured to the resurrection because of the joy set before Him.

If we put the pieces all together we see that worship creates the presence of God in which He dwells.

From that presence Psalm 16:11 (KJV) says of the Lord, **...in thy presence is fulness of joy....**

Nehemiah 8:10 exhorts us, **"...Do not grieve, for the joy of the Lord is your strength."**

Psalm 30:5 (KJV) encourages us, **...weeping may endure for a night, but joy cometh in the morning.**

Psalm 126:5 promises, **Those who sow in tears will reap with songs of joy.**

First Thessalonians 5:16-18 brings it all together in a marvelous three-step approach to an explosion of joy:

> **Be joyful always; pray continually; give thanks in all circumstances, for this is God's will for you in Christ Jesus.**

Joy is the enduring quality that sustains a person through difficult times to the birthing of God's power.

Joy is a characteristic far different from happiness. Happiness depends on happenings, while joy depends on the presence of God (in happenings). This is why Paul could be in a prison cell and begin to sing to the Lord...in the middle of the night...in the midst of his misery. That is why Shadrach, Meshach, and Abednego could remain calm in the fiery furnace.

Joy is the ability Jesus had to endure the cross.

Joy is not simply a characteristic; it is a powerful spiritual force of the Kingdom.

It is a force that invaded revivals throughout the ages. The Welsh Revival was dominated by the spirit of joy. As I previously noted, the dominant feature of the revival was prayer and praise, but another striking element was the unabashed joy of Evan Roberts and the people.

Roberts himself would say, "Ah, it is a grand life....I'm so happy I could walk on air. Tired? Never! God has made me strong."[5] The joy of the Lord was his strength.

It was said of Smith Wigglesworth that he was so full of joy he was always smiling and never without a Bible. He saw almost every kind of miracle in his ministry, including the raising of the dead.[6] The meetings of healing revivalists

Smith Wigglesworth witnessed almost every kind of miracle in his ministry. Fourteen people were documented to have been raised from the dead through his ministry.

also were filled with the joy common in Pentecostal worship. Joy was an open floodgate that granted the revivalists the overflow to freedom and the sustaining qualities necessary to give birth to the realm of the miraculous.

A Joy for Today

I have rarely noted a time historically in which the world was more discouraged than it is today. In America one million teenagers run away from home every year. Suicide is the second leading cause of death among college students. AIDS is reaching epidemic proportions, and it has been projected that it will reach plague status by the turn of the twenty-first century. The divorce rate for new marriages hovers near the fifty percent mark, and the American home is in an emotional shambles. Words like anorexia and bulimia were not even known fifteen or twenty years ago, but are now common household words.

I once heard Mario Murillo say that there are ten thousand "crack" houses in Detroit alone. One out of every four Americans is addicted to some drug. Twenty-five to thirty percent of all youth in this country are physically or sexually abused. East Los Angeles has a higher murder rate than Vietnam. When coupled with the scandal and impotence of the Church, these conditions have left a dark cloud hanging over America.

The Middle East conflicts complicate our sense of security, and the "land of the free" and "the home of the brave" has become subject to a fatalistic mentality that has spawned a feeling of doubt as to whether or not the Church can really exert an impact upon the world. As a result, many believers have adopted the attitude that since we cannot change others we should only be concerned about changing ourselves.

The entire youth culture is responding to a wrong set of heroes.

It is time for men and women of God to again assume their rightful roles as heroes of this age. It is time for the Church of Jesus Christ to shake off the shackles of distress, rebuke, and disgrace, and let the joy of the Lord return to and revive the house of God. That is why James wrote:

> **Consider it pure joy, my brothers, whenever you face trials of many kinds** [why?], **because you know that the testing of your faith develops perseverance** [or patience].
>
> **— James 1:2,3**

I often ask congregations how many of them have prayed for patience.

Then I add, "How many of you will never do it again?"

The reason I do so is because I have learned by experience that about the time we pray for patience, God will send circumstances to help develop it. Trust me when I say that enough "patience building" comes our way without our asking for more! Perseverance, however, is the enduring quality that helps us through difficult times. It is the ability to turn neither to the right nor to the left, but to stay on course with God in hard times.

James continues in verse four:

> **Perseverance must finish its work so that you may be mature and complete, not lacking anything.**

If we want to be something, we must go through something, and perseverance is the quality necessary to do it. I have ministered on a college campus where students studied all the time. They would not have known whether they really knew the answers, however, until they were put to the test. That is why there are exams. That is why there are also tests in the Christian life — to see if we know the answers.

I have heard countless pastors read this passage in James and say that we are to rejoice because trials test our faith and develop perseverance. The trying of our faith does not produce perseverance. I know a lot of people who have tried and quit. It is *joy in the midst of trial* that produces perseverance, and that is what sustains God's people. That is why James wrote, "Count it all (trials and tribulations) joy."

Joy is the key to sustaining power to give birth to revival in our cities. Look at John 16 to see how this principle works. Jesus told His disciples:

> **These things I have spoken unto you, that in me ye might have peace. In the world ye shall have tribulation: but be of good cheer; I have overcome the world.**
>
> **— John 16:33 KJV**

His indication was: **In the world ye shall have tribulation....** That pretty much includes all of us. We are all in this world. It is utter nonsense for anyone to claim that because we are Christians, we will not have any trouble. If we live in this world for very long, sooner or later we definitely will have to face tribulation — just like everyone else. The only difference is that we will have the "Tribulation-buster" on our side!

Therefore Jesus said, **...be of good cheer....** This term *good cheer* means to be encouraged, to have comfort, or joy, to have a good spirit, to shout or incite.[7] About the only cheer some Christians know is, "Give me a D-E-F-E-A-T."

Jesus says, however, "Shout V-I-C-T-O-R-Y, that's the Christian battle cry! And the joy of the Lord will be your strength."

Seven Principles for Appropriating Joy

I once heard a man say that he had seen a commercial on a laundry detergent called *Shout*. A little boy is shown falling down in the mud. The announcer says to his mother, "What are you going to do?" and the woman responds, "Shout it out!"

The scene changes to a little girl with spots on her pretty party dress. The announcer says to the child's mother, "What are you going to do?" Again the response is, "Shout it out."[8]

That is what the Spirit of God is saying to you and me in the midst of our tribulation: "What are you going to do when your back is against the wall?"

Our reply should be, "I'm going to shout it out!"

Why is that important? It is important because the shout is an instrument of cheerful praise. God dwells in the praises of His people. In that presence is fullness of joy. The joy of the Lord is our strength, and strength is the ability of God to give birth to revival. Joy is the force of God in revival to release heaven in our midst.

Paul gives us a three-tiered approach to appropriating joy in our lives. **Be joyful always; pray continually; give thanks in all circumstances...**(1 Thess. 5:16-18).

We previously examined joy and earlier discussed prayer without ceasing. Now let's look at the principle of thanksgiving. Many people wonder what the difference is between joy and thanksgiving. Quite simply, thanksgiving is the manifestation, the expression, of joy. It is a powerful spiritual force. For instance, it is the force that led the city of Nineveh to God. Most Christians are familiar with the story of Jonah, but few have seen it as a key for revival.

When God called Jonah as an evangelist to Nineveh, Jonah decided to take a fishing expedition to Tarshish instead. Little did he realize that he would be the bait. After boarding a ship to escape his call, a major storm arose jeopardizing the ship's safety. The crew cast lots to determine who was responsible for the calamity. The lot fell on Jonah as the guilty party. He encouraged the frightened crew to throw him overboard to calm the sea. They were reluctant at first, but the severity of the storm compelled them to comply. (Jonah 1.)

Immediately the water was calm, and Jonah was swallowed by a big fish. He remained in the belly of the whale for three days and three nights. After three days, Jonah realized that his life was ebbing away and repented of his sin. (Jonah 2.) It is amazing how three days in the belly of a fish, with all its decaying debris, sea weed, and gastric juices, will cause a man to repent.

Toward the end of Jonah's prayer of confession, he said to the Lord:

> **"But I, with a song of *thanksgiving*,**
>
> **will sacrifice to you.**
>
> **What I have vowed I will make good.**
>
> **Salvation comes from the Lord."**
>
> **And the Lord commanded the fish, and it vomited Jonah onto dry land.**
>
> **— Jonah 2:9,10**

Please do not let your recollection of this oft-repeated Sunday school story rob you of a dynamic truth of God's Word. Suddenly, in the belly of the fish, Jonah came to himself. He repented and with thanksgiving — the manifestation of joy —

he responded to God's call. This powerful force of joy was released, and Jonah was set free.

The Bible does not say it exactly this way, but imagine two old Ninevites sitting on a dock fishing. Suddenly out of the water emerges a huge fish, who vomits something upon the shore. Out of the vomit emerges a man whose clothes are torn to shreds. He is covered with seaweed, and the gastric juices of the fish have bleached his skin white. As he rises up out of the fish's vomit, he yells, "Repent!"

What would you do? Well, that is exactly what the entire city of approximately four hundred thousand people did — they repented! Thanksgiving was the dynamic force that caused the conversion of an entire city.

I have found seven key principles in Scripture that promise joy to those who follow them. Quite briefly they are:

1. *Meditation on the Word brings joy.* Psalm 19:8 says, **The precepts of the Lord are right, giving joy to the heart....** If we meditate on the Word of God until revelation is birthed, and then obey it, the result is joy.

2. *Prayer brings joy.* I am not talking about repeating little formal prayers, but about entering into the throne room of God in viable relationship. Larry Lea and others have shown practical steps in daily prayer to lead the believer into God's presence.

3. *Sowing brings joy.* In Galatians 6:7 the Apostle Paul says, **Do not be deceived: God cannot be mocked. A man reaps what he sows.** Each sower decides what his harvest will be. If a man sows to the flesh, he will reap to the flesh. If a man sows love, he will reap love. If a man sows joy, he will reap joy. This is what Oral Roberts calls "Seed Faith."

When I attended ORU, we learned to live by this principle. I saw many downtrodden students catapulted to joy by being involved in Christian Service Council (CSC). CSC was our local outreach into the Tulsa community. Our students would extend themselves to hundreds of people in the Tulsa community. The result was not only magnificent transformations among the Tulsa people in need, but an explosion of love and joy in the hearts of the students.

Peter said it this way:

> **Do not repay evil with evil or insult with insult, but with blessing, because to this you were called so that you may inherit a blessing.**
>
> **— 1 Peter 3:9**

Giving a blessing brings a blessing.

4. *Emotional healing brings joy.* Psalm 126:5 adds, **Those who sow in tears will reap with songs of joy.**

I have ministered to hundreds of people who, when emotional scars were healed, experienced an explosion of joy in their lives. The devil will try to convince people there is no hope or try to accentuate a disappointment, but it is God's nature to be a Redeemer. With the redemption of a negative situation always comes joy.

5. *Vision brings joy.* Jesus endured the cross **...for the joy set before him...**(Heb. 12:2). That verse reveals that Jesus understood that the resurrection was on the other side of the cross and, as a result, joy was birthed in Him. Joy is the product of seeing the end of the Lord's plan.

6. *Praise brings joy.* Approximately one hundred and seven times in the Book of Psalms, the psalmists refer to thanksgiving and joy. Elsewhere, Isaiah the prophet said that the Spirit of the

Lord was upon him and had anointed him to minister to the needs of God's people...

...and provide for those who grieve in Zion — to bestow on them a crown of beauty instead of ashes, the oil of gladness instead of mourning, and a garment of praise instead of a spirit of despair. They will be called oaks of righteousness, a planting of the Lord for the display of his splendor.

— Isaiah 61:3

The garment of praise will destroy the spirit of despair and heaviness.

7. *Salvation brings joy.* In Isaiah 12:3 the prophet assures us, **With joy you will draw water from the wells of salvation.**

After his sin and failure, David cried to the Lord, **Restore to me the joy of your salvation...**(Ps. 51:12).

The New Birth causes the joy of the Lord to flow out of our belly like living water. If for any reason we have fallen out of fellowship with God, He does not want us to wallow in self-pity, but instead, to get back into fellowship and be restored to Him.

I will never forget Jerry Savelle sharing an illustration in a service at the ORU Mabee Center. He related how he and Kenneth Copeland were shopping at a mall. As they were walking toward an escalator, they saw a large black man walking ahead of them. The man was really "decked out" in an array of white. He had on white shoes, white socks, white pants, a white vest, a white shirt, a white coat, a white, wide-brimmed hat, and white-rimmed sunglasses.

When the man reached the top of the escalator, he tripped and fell. He did not just stumble, but tumbled head over heels down the escalator. Copeland and Savelle raced to the top of the escalator to see if they could help. They arrived just in time to see the man somersaulting off the foot of the escalator.

When he hit the bottom, amazingly, he landed on his feet and caught his sunglasses flying off his head in midair.

He paused for a moment, squared his shoulders, and exclaimed, "Well, all right!"— and kept right on walking.

That is precisely the way God wants us to respond to life. God said to Jeremiah, "...'**When men fall down, do they not get up?'**..." (Jer. 8:4). It does no good to wallow in defeat. We must learn to repent, dust ourselves off, and let God restore to us the joy of our salvation.

That is why revival brings such great joy to the Church. When a person is shaken to a new awareness of Christ, distress, rebuke, and disgrace give way to joy. It is that joy that provides the strength to give birth to revival. It is in the atmosphere of a joy-filled congregation that the anointing of the Spirit works best.

And the anointing with "fresh oil" is what we are desiring and seeking for the Church in our day.

Chapter 14

Fresh Oil for Revival

It was only because of the anointing that Maria Woodworth-Etter, Charles Parham, and William Seymour were able to perform miracles.

...I shall be anointed with fresh oil.
— Psalm 92:10 KJV

I began my graduate studies in a liberal seminary on the East Coast. To say they did not believe in miracles is an understatement. They were so liberal they didn't believe in gravity. They offered a required course of religious graduate study called "supervised ministry." Each student in the class was assigned to some institution in the city.

My assignment was to serve as an acting chaplain in the cardiac intensive care unit of a large hospital. I must admit that, in those days, my duties really intimidated me. I almost felt that if I prayed for someone who died, I would be asked to resign from the pastoral care team, and my ministry would be over. Obviously, I was a "real man of faith" back in those days.

One day as I was making my rounds, exhausted from a grueling schedule, I thought, "I only have one room left, why don't I just slip out five minutes early?"

As I was walking down the corridor on my way out of the hospital, I was intercepted by a "a Holy-Ghost guilt trip." I knew I had to go back and finish my ministry. I had one last person on my agenda to see, a Mr. Pugh. I wandered down the end of the corridor to Mr. Pugh's room. When I got there, I was surprised to find him asleep.

I started to leave, but somehow felt led to stop at the other curtained-off room in the area. The compassion of the Lord overcame me as I began to visit with an elderly black couple, both of whom were in the intensive care unit. However, I had no sooner begun to minister to them, than we were interrupted by some visitors. I was confused, because I felt the Lord had led me back to that room.

However, I had excused myself and again started to leave when I noticed that Mr. Pugh had awakened. So I paused to visit with him. I rarely have seen a man so depressed. He began to rehearse for me the events of the previous day. He had just had another heart attack (the latest in a recent series), and the doctors had told him to restrict himself from all activity and to lie still in bed. Any aggressive activity might initiate another coronary reaction. Discouragement rolled over him in waves.

I remembered that Mr. Pugh attended church, and I felt that a bit of conversation on a topic of personal interest might help to get his mind off his physical state. So I started asking him about his church. Immediately his whole disposition changed. Joy and encouragement seemed to invade his being as he related story after story to me about his blessed Savior and his dynamic church.

In a matter of minutes, his entire countenance had undergone a radical transformation. His darkness had suddenly given way to brightness, and I thought to myself, "I have done what I came to do."

I gently took hold of his hands and began to pray very softly for him so as not to disturb the others in the room.

"Father," I prayed quietly, "thank You for joy in Mr. Pugh's life. Now I ask You to heal him in Jesus' name."

Suddenly, in a very loud voice, Mr. Pugh yelled, "Hallelujah!"

Mr. Pugh was a Pentecostal! He yelled it again, "Hallelujah!"

I jumped back in shock at his sudden burst of faith, and the whole room turned to see what the "hallelujahs" were all about.

"Young man," he bellowed, "I feel pretty good!"

He started to sit up in bed, and being the man of God that I was, I thought to myself, "Oh, no, this is it!" Hurriedly, I began to plead with him, "Mr. Pugh, lie back down. Please don't die on me."

"Nah, I'm doin' great," he assured me. "Give me a little room!"

Now I could hear the "pitter-patter, pitter-patter" of the nurses running down the hallway to see what all the commotion was about. The head nurse quickly pushed me aside and started attending to Mr. Pugh, trying to get him to settle down.

All I could think about was sneaking out of the room, hoping that no one would remember I had been there. As I was leaving I heard the old couple call out to me, "Chaplain!"

I thought to myself, "Oh great, they probably want to add insult to injury."

"Chaplain," I heard again, "will you pray for us too?"

Do you know I prayed for them and led them to Christ right there in that room — with Mr. Pugh crying out "Hallelujah!" in the background all the while. That was on Friday. The next Monday, I raced to the hospital to check on Mr. Pugh. I walked down the corridor, arrived at his room, and quickly glanced into his area. His bed was empty!

I thought, "Oh, dear Lord, what happened to Mr. Pugh?"

Quickly I made my way to the nurses' station and asked in a quivering voice, "Excuse me, can you tell me what happened to Mr. Pugh?"

"You know, that is the funniest thing I have ever seen," answered the nurse on duty. "He had a heart attack on Thursday. We ran another full set of tests on him on Friday and then again on Saturday. We could not find one thing wrong with him. We observed him for a couple of days, and he was doing so well, we finally had to dismiss him a few hours ago. He was so cantankerous; it was like he was healed...."

My spirit leaped inside. I knew that was exactly what had taken place. Somehow, amazingly, God had supernaturally and miraculously healed Mr. Pugh. I rejoiced in that occurrence for a week.

One day, while I was praying, I heard the Holy Spirit speak to me, "Son, I healed that man in spite of you, not because of you."

You know, that will hurt a guy's feelings, but inside, I cried out, "Lord, I don't ever want that to happen again. I want You to be able to use me, not heal in spite of me."

I wanted to be part of a divine-human synergism that brings healing to suffering humanity. God began to pour His Word into me. Over a period of time He started teaching me about faith and the anointing. That is what catapulted me into a study of revivalists. I wanted to know the secrets of the dynamics of their ministry — not for history's sake, but to see God do it again.

I saw that it was with the anointing that John Alexander Dowie healed the sick. It was only because of the anointing that Maria Woodworth-Etter, Charles Parham, and William Seymour were able to perform miracles. It was the enabling power of God that we call the anointing that resulted in one hundred thousand healings through John G. Lake in just five years.

It was the anointing at Azusa Street and Angelus Temple that wrought signs and wonders. It was said of Aimee Semple McPherson that at times when the anointing was the greatest, a blue haze would fill the temple like a cloud. Everyone who was touched by it was "slain in the Spirit" or healed.

For three solid months I locked myself away in study for six to eight hours per day, and by the end of that time I had concluded that it was only

Aimee Semple McPherson, c. 1930. It was said that when the anointing on her ministry was greatest, a blue haze would fill her Angelus Temple.

by the anointing that men like Smith Wigglesworth and Oral Roberts could delve into the realm of the miraculous.

The Healing Revival of the 1940s and 1950s was primarily an age of the anointing. Some of its leaders were great preachers. Some of them were not. But they all understood the anointing of the Holy Spirit. Some of these men and women of God were naturally gifted, some were not so intellectually or linguistically endowed. But none of them saw miracles without the anointing of the Spirit.

Gordon Lindsay would say of William Branham, "Without the anointing he is helpless. He does not have natural talents that he can fall back upon if that all important element should be missing."[1]

No matter what limitations the leaders might have had, the anointing of the Holy Spirit was able to more than make up for them. For three months I fed myself with little more than this information about the revivalists. At the end of that time I felt as if I had gone into a phone booth and had emerged as Faithman! I was ready for anything!

One day, I cried out to God, "Lord, open the door for me to prove that You can do these things again."

Prepare, and the Lord Opens the Door

No sooner had I got the words out of my mouth than the phone rang. A representative of a certain church was calling, and the person said, "We have heard about your ministry. I know it is very short notice, but could you come in the next few weeks and substitute for our pastor?" I immediately jumped at the opportunity.

When I arrived, to my great surprise, the church was almost completely dead to anything spiritual. The people had never seen a gift of the Spirit in operation. They had never seen a miracle or any manifestation of God. Of all things, the Lord had led me to preach that morning on "The Baptism with the Holy Spirit."

The only thing I can tell you about this church is that it was a dead church. Let me tell you how dead it was. Bela Lugosi was the pastor. Boris Karloff led the choir. There was embalming fluid rolling down the aisle. This was a dead church.

As I began to minister, I truly wanted to be in the faith movement. I did not want to "be moved by what I saw." When I began to preach, people were yawning, stretching, scratching, and doing just about anything but paying attention. As I came to the end of my message, I quietly deliberated whether I should give an altar call or try to sneak off the platform.

Finally, a "holy boldness" came over me and I gave the altar call. To my shock, the entire altar area was soon filled with people. Now I was really confused. I said, "Lord, what do I do now?"

Lovingly, He responded, "Pray for them, Dummy." I laughed and began to pray for the people. The first person I began to pray for was a proper-looking young woman in her middle twenties. When I laid my hands on her, she was almost violently slain in the Spirit.

Trust me when I say, now I had the attention of everyone. There had never been such a manifestation of God in that church. It was like the wind of the Spirit blew into the crowd. People started dropping over everywhere. God began to touch, heal, and deliver the people.

After the service was over, the first woman I had prayed for and who had been "slain in the Spirit" grabbed me.

"What happened to me?" she asked excitedly.

When I briefly explained the phenomenon, she broke out in a smile and said, "Let's do it again!"

Evidently she loved it. She was not alone in this respect. The anointing of the Spirit entered that congregation and left an indelible impression upon its people.

A few weeks later I was scheduled to speak at a youth convention in a nearby state. I arrived with one of my associates to share at the initial service.

I looked out over the young people and thought this must be a Kellogg's convention. There were "fruits, nuts and flakes." I realized that there was not a single normal-looking person in the crowd. One young man was dressed all in black with a pentagram (a Satanic symbol) on his shirt. His head was half-shaved on one side, and on the other, the hair hung down to his shoulder. There was an earring in his right ear.

I thought to myself, "This should be an interesting meeting!" However, very little happened that night.

The next morning we were joined by some other more ordinary appearing people, and my associate ministered effectively with a bit more success. That evening, as we were heading for the evening service, he said to me, "Ron, what are you going to preach on tonight?"

I replied, "Brother, I don't think it matters as much what I say as much as what I do! These people don't need to hear another message, they need to see God."

That evening I preached a short message, and the Holy Spirit was present to minister. The Lord began to give me several "words of knowledge." One was so specific that a young woman thought someone had talked to me about her situation and so she ran out of the service. Later, when she realized that no one had spoken to me about her personal affairs, she gave her heart to Christ. Soon I opened the altar for prayer and deliverance.

What took place next completely took me by surprise. The altar filled with people, but many of them began to shake uncontrollably. I did not know what to make of it at first, but it became evident that God was ministering at a very deep emotional level. I began to personally minister and touch the people. God began to heal some and deliver others. Many were "slain in the Spirit" and others were ministered to very profoundly.

Then the Spirit of the Lord spoke to me and said, "Now, call the people for salvation."

When I did, guess who was the first person to come forward. Mr. Pentagram himself. Why? When he saw Jesus alive in their midst, he knew he had to meet Him. Truly the yoke is destroyed because of the anointing. (Is. 10:27 KJV.)

I sought to gain greater understanding of the anointing of God. I once heard Oral Roberts say, "The anointing is divine energy that empties you of yourself and fills you with the presence of God, so much so that when you speak, it is like God speaking and when you act it is like God acting."

What an astounding truth about God's miracle-working power. The anointing of God causes us to empty ourselves and elevates the presence of God in such a way that Jesus Himself speaks and moves through us. More of God means less of self.

The psalmist said, **...I shall be anointed with fresh oil** (Ps. 92:10 KJV).

David declared the anointing to be like a fresh oil smeared on an object for consecration. What a profound thought. How many times have we sat through services of a stale rehash of old material? I have been in healing services, and there was no oil. I have seen men pray for deliverance, and there was no oil. I have watched people attempt miracles, and there was no fresh oil from God.

There must be the divine energy that empties us of ourselves. It is easier for a servant to be emptied of himself if he is already dead to self. An empty servant is a candidate for the infilling of the presence of God. The anointing was the key to the ministry of Jesus.

Look how the Bible describes it in Acts 10:38:

> **...how God anointed Jesus of Nazareth with the Holy Spirit and power, and how he went around doing good and healing all who were under the power of** [or oppressed by] **the devil, because God was with him.**

This verse and the understanding of the anointing became the cornerstone of the ministries of John Alexander Dowie and John G. Lake. It was after the revelation of Acts 10:38 that their ministries of miracles were begun and were enhanced.

While I was meditating on this verse, I began to realize that the whole middle part of the verse was a parenthetical thought. It could read simply, **how God anointed Jesus...because God was with him.** In fact, the anointing can be summarized by **...God was with him.** Miracles took place in the ministry of Jesus of Nazareth because "God was with Him." In the same way, deliverance will take place in our lives and ministries because God (Emmanuel) is with us.

The Anointing Brings Boldness

Let me show you something about this concept in the tenth chapter of the Book of 1 Samuel.

> **Then Samuel took a flask of oil and poured it on Saul's head and kissed him, saying, "Has not the Lord anointed you leader over his inheritance?...**
>
> **The Spirit of the Lord will come upon you in power, and you will prophesy with them** [other prophets]**; and you will be changed into a different person. Once these signs are fulfilled, do whatever your hand finds to do,** *for God is with you.*
>
> **— 1 Samuel 10:1,6,7**

In this passage describing Saul's anointing, we find an amazing delineation of the meaning of this event. First the prophet of God says, "The Spirit of the Lord will come upon you in power..." Here is the key to true power in the life of believers everywhere. The true power we seek is in submission to the anointing of the Holy Ghost.

Next he says, "...you will prophesy..." I believe that when true anointing comes, we will see a resurgence of true prophecy. I'm not simply talking about lining up all the believers in a service and speaking into their lives. I'm talking about prophesying again to our nation. This anointing will restore our credibility and allow us to speak into the highest offices in the land.

Next he says, "...you will be changed into a different person..." So many times I meet people who say, "I'm just not the kind of person who can be used of the Lord." The good news is, the anointing changes us into different people. Whatever God calls us to do, He will equip us to do it.

Lastly he notes, "Once these signs are fulfilled...." What signs? Power coming in our lives, prophecy restored to us as believers, and the Body of Christ truly being changed into different people. Once those things occur, he says, "...do whatever your hand finds to do, for God is with you."

Once we understand that the anointing is God with us to accomplish His tasks, it changes the way we view things. Think what it means in reference to Luke 1:37: **"For nothing is impossible with God."** If nothing is impossible with God and we are with God, then nothing shall be impossible for His servants under the anointing. (Look at the context of passages like 1 Samuel 16:3; Judges 6:16;1 Samuel 17:37, for examples.) That's why we so often say, "The anointing breaks the yoke."

Many people believe that Jesus exercised His ministry based on His "Godness," but Philippians 2:5-7 tells us:

Your attitude should be the same as that of Christ Jesus:

Who, being in very nature God, did not consider equality with God something to be grasped,

but made himself nothing [emptied Himself], **taking the very nature of a servant....**

Jesus divested Himself of His divine privileges. All the miracles done in Jesus' life were the result of the anointing on His humanity, not of His being divine. In Luke 4:18, Jesus said:

"The Spirit of the Lord is on me, because he has anointed me to preach good news to the poor.

He has sent me to proclaim freedom for the prisoners and recovery of sight for the blind, to release the oppressed...."

In the life and ministry of our Lord, it was the anointing that set the captive free.

Isaiah best describes the anointing of the Spirit. He sets the stage with a brief history lesson and in 10:24 he speaks the word of the Lord to the people of his day: **"...do not be afraid of the Assyrians, who beat you with a rod and lift up a club against you, as Egypt did."** He was saying, "Do not be afraid of the Assyrians any more than you were of the Egyptians before them." In other words, do not be intimidated by the world.

Once, while I was still serving a pastorate in East Texas, my wife, Judy, and I took a second honeymoon to Padre Island, Texas. We walked the moonlit beaches at night hand in hand and had a wonderfully refreshing time. At the end of three days, we boarded the airplane to go home. We sat down next to an obviously very successful man. He was dressed in expensive clothing and carried himself confidently.

I often get on planes, and people ask me, "What do you do for a living?"

I usually answer, "I'm a minister."

Then a response follows along the order of, "Oh, I'm a Christian, and I was in church just last week."

For whatever reason, I wanted to avoid any such replay on this occasion.

Thus, I initiated the conversation by asking, "What do you do for a living?"

My remark was like an open door for an "eighteen-wheeler"! He proceeded to expound on his profession and reenact everything about his business. He flaunted his names and big accounts around in such a way that the more he talked the more intimidated I became. Subtly, I began to slouch down in my seat.

Finally, the inevitable moment arrived, my important fellow traveler turned to me and said, "What do you do for a living?"

When he asked the question, something went through my being. Remembering Mario Murillo's classic line, I sat up in my seat, squared my shoulders, and proudly proclaimed, "I work for the richest Jew in the world!"

Suddenly, my new-found friend's nonchalant attitude perked up. He looked at me curiously and said, "What did you say?"

I repeated my comment, and with a very interested look on his face, he asked, "What does the richest Jew in the world do?"

I replied, "He takes old things and makes them new!"

It did not take long for him to figure out the "Jew" I was talking about was the greatest Jew of all time, Jesus.

Almost immediately God began speaking to me, "It's time My people learned not to be intimidated by the world."

Instead, it is time for the Body of Christ to be the intimidators.

In Isaiah 10:25 the Lord continues His word to His people about their enemies:

"Very soon my anger against you will end and my wrath will be directed to their destruction."

He uses the phrase "very soon." That phrase tells me that no matter what we face, it is temporary!

Someone might say, "Well, you do not know my husband."

My answer is, "No, you do not truly understand your God!"

"But, you don't understand my drug problem."

"No, you don't know the Deliverer. With God on your side, your problem is temporary."

I may not understand your problems, but Jesus does, and whatever those problems may be, they are temporary when submitted to Him. It is the same way with revival. Difficult times in the Church are temporary; they can be changed when the Anointed One comes on the scene. The point is simple: *Things do not always have to be this way.*

Then in verse 26 of Isaiah 10, the prophet says of the enemies of God's people:

The Lord Almighty will lash them with a whip, as when he struck down Midian at the rock of Oreb; and he will raise his rod over the waters, as he did in Egypt.

"Oreb" refers to the oppression of Israel during the time of Gideon. The people of God found themselves tired of fighting. No longer wanting to enter into conflict, they reverted to hiding in caves. They laid down their weapons for the shelter of a hiding place. It was time for fresh oil. The "waters" in this passage refer to the time when Moses lifted his staff over the Red Sea, which parted before him.

That reminds me of a story of a student in a liberal Bible class. His professor was attempting to explain away the miracle of the Red Sea.

He said, "First of all, it wasn't the Red Sea, it was the Reed Sea. Second, the children of Israel were able to cross it because this sea in many places was only a foot deep."

There was a moment of silence before this student suddenly shouted at the top of his voice, "Hallelujah! Praise the Lord!"

Somewhat offended, the professor indignantly asked, "Son, what seems to be your problem?"

Enthusiastically the student replied, "God drowned the entire Egyptian army in one foot of water!"

You see, either way you have a miracle. God is saying to His people, "The season of despair will give way to a miracle when you come under the anointing."

Isaiah lays all of this as a foundation to this message:

> **And it shall come to pass in that day** [of deliverance]**, that his** [the enemy's] **burden shall be taken away from off thy shoulder, and his yoke from off thy neck, and the yoke shall be destroyed because of the anointing.**
>
> — **Isaiah 10:27** KJV

Here Isaiah shares the concept of the anointing in a way that every Israelite would understand. Any passerby in Israel could observe two oxen yoked together. In the case of oxen of differing sizes, the smaller ox would simply have to go wherever the larger animal would lead.

That is precisely what happens to us. We somehow submit ourselves to the devil, and we yoke ourselves to him. Wherever he leads us, we follow. If he leads us in sin, we follow. If he leads us in low self-esteem, we follow. If he leads us in discouragement and doubt, we follow. If he leads us in the path of sickness, we follow.

It is the anointing, or the divine enablement of God manifesting Himself on our behalf, that breaks the yoke. Many people come into worship services relying upon the anointing of the one ministering to break such a yoke off their lives. Indeed, God does use such powerful ministry to set people at liberty. That is part of what revivals have been all about, the miraculous display of God among the masses.

Revival in its purest form, however, calls for the revived to be the anointed ones. We are delivered to become deliverers. The anointing was never meant to be confined to a select few people who stand on platforms to minister to the masses. While that will always remain a standard for God, revival was meant to revitalize a people who will operate in the anointing.

If the Church ever recognizes this concept, we will give the prince of darkness fits. In the past, if the devil could hinder a handful of people, he could halt a whole revival move. What would happen if the entire Body of Christ took on the anointing? All the ulcers, headaches, and back spasms would be on Satan's demonic force instead of on God's people. We need to divide the devil's power by multiplying the anointing.

Once I had grasped the importance of the anointing in revival, I set out to understand it better. I searched the bookstores for material, but I found very little written on the topic. Finally, I discovered a book on this subject. Quickly, I dissected the entire volume searching for sound advice on how to better appropriate and cultivate the anointing. Toward the end of the book I discovered what I was seeking. The author indicated that the key to cultivating the anointing in the life of the believer is yielding to the Holy Spirit.

I thought, "Oh great, all I have to do is yield to the Holy Spirit. That's wonderful, but how do I do that?"

Three Steps to Yielding

One day I was out driving, and the answer to how to yield to the Holy Spirit suddenly "hit" me. I came to a yield sign and noticed that I did three things: 1) I slowed down, 2) I stopped, and 3) I surrendered the right of way. Suddenly I realized that these were the same steps a person must follow in order to yield to the Holy Spirit.

1. *Slow Down.* We must learn what it means to wait on the Lord. We live in an instant, "microwave" society. If we cannot get it in forty-five seconds at the fast-food window, we do not want to wait for it. I am convinced I know what the next fast-food chain will be like. It will be a new chicken place to replace "the Colonel." You drive down the highway at sixty-five miles per hour, call in your order ahead on your car phone, and just roll down your window as you drive by — "Fling-a-Wing!"

The only problem is that miracles are not microwaveable. They are the product of waiting hours before Almighty God to develop a relationship with Him and a communion with the Holy Spirit.

Often people with whom I share such a concept will almost rebel in response, "You don't understand, I don't have time to wait on the Lord."

If you do not have time to wait on the Lord, you are too busy! If you do not have time to wait on God, you do not have time for the miraculous. I know what it means to be busy. I have served as pastor of congregations of several thousand people. I was alumni director of a university. I wrote for and edited a magazine. I write monthly letters to a constituency, and beyond all that, I have two active boys who play soccer, basketball, and baseball. I know what it is like to be busy like anyone else. Yet I have learned that my top priority must be to wait upon God.

Isaiah said it this way:

> **Hast thou not known? hast thou not heard, that the everlasting God, the Lord, the Creator of the ends of the earth, fainteth not, neither is weary?....**
>
> **He giveth power to the faint; and to them that have no might he increaseth strength....**
>
> **But they that wait upon the Lord shall renew their strength; they shall mount up with wings as eagles; they shall run, and not be weary; and they shall walk, and not faint.**
>
> **— Isaiah 40:28,29,31 KJV**

The word *wait* is important for us to understand in order to grasp this concept. The word means "to bind together" or to tarry in expectancy.[2] In America, we think to wait on God is to haphazardly twiddle our thumbs for a length of time hoping God will do something. This word is more like our concept of waiting on a table at a restaurant.

Let me see if I can put both of these concepts in one example. Suppose you are in a restaurant, and a waiter comes to your table. You give the person your order, and he simply stands there.

"What are you doing?" you ask, and he responds simply, "I am waiting on you!"

In confusion you say, "I've already given you my order. Now please wait on me!"

Again, the response is, "I *am* waiting on you. I am waiting for you to do something."

On and on the conversation goes, interweaving the confusion of two totally different aspects of what it means *to wait*. One aspect of the word means to remain in anticipation of something to happen. The other definition means to give personal attention to in service.

The second meaning is the one that applies here. While we give personal attention and expectant service (as worship — see Acts 13:2) to God, He binds us together with Himself and renews our strength. A derivative of the Hebrew word translated renew in Isaiah 40:31 is *cheleph* meaning *"exchange."*[3]

In other words, they that wait upon (those who minister with personal attention and service to) the Lord, He binds together with Himself and exchanges His strength for their weakness. What an incredible concept! If I wait on God, I get His strength for my weakness, His power for my impotence, His miracles in place of my frailties. *Waiting on the Lord* is the first step to appropriating the anointing.

2. *Stop*. I also saw that I had to stop. So I asked myself, "Stop what?" Stop sinning or anything that would grieve the Holy Spirit. In First Corinthians 15:34, the Apostle Paul wrote, **Come back to your senses as you ought, and stop sinning; for there are some who are ignorant of God — I say this to your shame.**

In other words, what Paul was saying to the believers in Corinth is, "If you had any sense and understood the things of God, you would not sin." Why? Because sin sears the heart, and grieves the Holy Spirit. It quenches the flow of God. The key understanding about sin is not that it makes an individual "a bad person," but rather that it quenches the Holy Spirit.

In the *King James Version* of 1 Thessalonians 5:19 we are warned: **Quench not the Spirit.** The *New International Version* translates this verse: **Do not put out the Spirit's fire.** *The Amplified Bible* further elaborates on this verse in its translation: **Do not quench (suppress or subdue) the (Holy) Spirit.**

Thus we see that the word *quench*, as used in the New Testament, means to extinguish, to suppress a divine influence, or to cause it to go out.

Here is an example of the dangers of quenching the Spirit of God. Suppose you are in an airplane and the Holy Spirit says to you, "Witness to the flight attendant!" If you are attentive to the voice of the Lord, you will do as He directs. The problem arises, however, when you've quenched the Spirit, suppressed His divine influence, and extinguished the fire of the Holy Spirit in such a way that it goes out; therefore, you don't even hear the words of the Lord to you.

Paul also uses the word *grieve* concerning the Holy Spirit in his letter to the Ephesians: **And do not grieve the Holy Spirit of God, with whom you were sealed for the day of redemption** (Eph. 4:30). This word means to offend, to make one uneasy, to sorrow.[4] It is possible to cause the Holy Spirit to sorrow because of our lifestyles. The result is that grief quenches or extinguishes the power, or fire, of His presence.

3. *Surrender the right of way.* Finally, I learned that in order to yield, we must surrender the right of way to God. John the Beloved Apostle tells us:

But you have an anointing from the Holy One, and all of you know the truth....

As for you, the anointing you received from him remains in you, and you do not need anyone to teach you. But as his anointing

**teaches you about all things and as that anointing is real, not coun-
terfeit — just as it has taught you, remain in him.**

— 1 John 2:20,27

There is an anointing, like faith, that has a dual role. One kind
is a supernatural gift from God. The other is a supernatural deposit
to which we must learn to submit — something to which we must
surrender the right of way. There is a presence of the Holy Spirit
that is resident in every believer. When we learn to rely upon Him,
He teaches us what we need to know in every situation.

Less of self means more of God. This is a release of a supernatural energy that allows God to manifest Himself through a
human vessel. It allows the human vessel to "remain" in Him, or
to "abide" in Him. The word *abide* means "to maintain unbroken
fellowship with."[5] As a person has unbroken fellowship with
God, he is led into truth, and such truth allows him to empty himself in order for the supernatural energy of God to manifest itself
on his behalf.

One of the problems with the Church is that it is a New
Covenant institution trying to operate under the principle of the
Old Covenant as far as the Holy Spirit is concerned. In Old
Testament days, the people of God had to wait for the Holy Spirit
to come upon a person for service. Since the New Covenant was
instituted, the Holy Spirit abides within the believer to teach him
what is right in every circumstance.

Now let's apply this principle to Isaiah 10:27. When a person
empties himself through divine energy by waiting upon God, not
grieving the Holy Spirit in sin, but instead calling upon the
deposit of anointing in himself, the yoke of bondage is broken.

Interestingly, the same Hebrew word translated *anointing* in
Isaiah 10:27 can also be translated *fatness*. The *New International*

Version translates the latter part of this verse: **"...the yoke will be broken because you have grown so fat."** The idea is once the yoke is broken off by the anointing, if Satan tries to bring the yoke back at another time, it won't fit due to the increased "fatness" or strength of the person's neck. Such an anointing will move believers to new levels of maturity. Instead of being yoked to Satan, we will become yoked to Jesus. (Matt. 11:29.)

Jesus Himself operated under the anointing. Out of His own mouth He quoted Isaiah:

> **"The Spirit of the Lord is on me, because he has anointed me to preach good news to the poor** [the destitute].
>
> **He has sent me to proclaim freedom for the prisoners** [those in bondage] **and recovery of sight for the blind** [both physical and spiritual]**, to release the oppressed** [the abused]**, to proclaim the year of the Lord's favor** [the Year of Jubilee]**."**
>
> **— Luke 4:18,19**

The anointing is the key to breaking bondage and releasing the presence of God. The 1940s and 1950s were truly an "Age of Anointing." The revivalists understood the anointing. Some came to rely on the anointing at the expense of character, however. That leads us to a study of this vital quality. A person's inward character must match his outward anointing, if he is to turn revival into a move of the Spirit.

Chapter 15

Public Success, Private Failure

As time went on.... it became more and more apparent that Dowie was not the same man he had been in the beginning of his ministry.

Now these things occurred as examples, to keep us from setting our hearts on evil things as they did.

— 1 Corinthians 10:6

The end of the decade of the Eighties left a Church marred by an ominous cloud of scandal that threatened to destroy the impact of her ministry. The lingering echoes of infidelity, financial treachery, scandal, avarice, and even incarceration of key leaders have sought to follow us into "prime time" disclosure even today. The Church has languished in a nebulous state between destiny and failure.

This presented an opportunity for discouragement on one hand, but also was a tremendous sign that God was preparing the Church for the next move of the Spirit. Above all, this season was a call to understand past shortcomings in order that we not subject ourselves to similar future pitfalls. That seemed to be Paul's heartbeat when he wrote that the things of the past were examples to keep us from making the same mistakes as a previous generation.

History is filled with examples of the discovery of new (restored) principles that launched revivals. History also is full of patterns of the things that destroyed the move of God which some revival had initiated.

I quote the adage over and over again, "Those who do not learn from history are doomed to repeat it."

Many sincere men and women, whom God greatly used, ultimately gave way to carnal desires and left the move of God limping at best, but often destroyed, lying "in a rubble heap." Many of the giants of the faith were public successes on the outside, while private failures slowly destroyed what God had developed.

The Healing Revival of the 1940s and 1950s was truly an age of anointing. Several of its key figures, however, never changed in character to measure up to the anointing.

A person ministers in anointing, but lives out of his or her character.

There may even be some who would dispute such a statement. They might point out that the Scripture says that we live by the Spirit. (Gal. 5:16.) However, if we examine Paul's explanation in Galatians 5:16-26, we will find that life in the Spirit is the fruit of the Spirit, or the character of God. Without character, there is no catalyst to the move of God, and likewise, there is no anointing to perpetuate that move.

The very passion and heartbeat God placed within my being for writing this manuscript is to sound a warning so that the next generation will not repeat the mistakes of the past. The patterns are clear and most repetitious. It behooves us to learn of their examples in order that we may keep the flame of God burning in our generation. My earnest prayer is that this chapter will serve as a clarion call to respect the boundaries of God's parameters.

Many of the spiritual leaders of the past experienced that invincible feeling that comes from the anointing. Their mistake was in assuming that the anointing placed a seal of approval on the way they acted in their personal lives. The feeling of the anointing that comes upon a person to speak and act as Jesus is given for the sake of ministry. The person's everyday life, however, is lived out of his or her innate character.

The revivalists who failed to understand this distinction found themselves teetering on the brink of destruction, oftentimes proportionate to the anointing that launched their ministries.

Character refers to the conspicuous traits and dispositions of Jesus reflected in us that bring God's approval.

Character is the moral excellence and firmness in trying times that promote God's affirmation.

To be of good *character* is to be of good reputation, of tried worth, trustworthy, or approved of.[1]

Character is the sometimes imperceptible quality of godliness that makes a way for the Lord's blessing. A person of "good character" is someone who practices what he preaches.

Time and time again, God's reputation has been slandered by people who say one thing, but live another. That is why Paul insisted on certain qualifications for an elder. (Titus 1:5-3:11.) He knew that, no matter how spiritually gifted people might be, God ultimately would be shortchanged by those who had no roots in the character of Jesus from which to bring forth the fruit of the Spirit. (Gal. 5:22,23.)

Qualities such as love, integrity, faithfulness, truthfulness, trustworthiness, peace with oneself, goodness, accountability, and self-control make up the cornerstone of a foundation for God's approval. As hunger is the key to initiating God's move,

His character is the key to perpetuating it. A lack of character will inevitably interrupt the flow of God's Spirit.

No man or woman of God (of past or present moves) ever deliberately set out — or even desired — to have a lack of character. However, so many have unwittingly failed to deal with key issues in their lives that those things have finally led to their downfall. Perhaps no one better exemplified this problem than John Alexander Dowie. He was raised up by the anointing, but lived by integrity of character — and it was by the disintegration of character that he fell.

At the turn of the twentieth century, Dowie began to change almost imperceptibly. People who had been most intimately associated with him in his early years in America became vaguely conscious that something was happening to their leader. At first, they found it difficult to lay hold of tangible evidence of some change. As time went on, however, it became more and more apparent that Dowie was not the same man he had been in the beginning of his ministry.

In his earlier days, Dowie would make the statement about worldly ambition and power from which I previously quoted a portion:

I think some of you have a false conception of power in the Church of God. Power in the Church is not like power in the government of the United States, where a man climbs to the top of a pyramid of his fellows to the acme of his ambition, and there makes it fulfill his personal pride and purpose. Power in the Church is shown [rather] in this, that a man gets lower and lower, and lower, and lower until he can put his very spirit, soul, and body underneath the miseries and at the feet of a sin-cursed and disease-smitten humanity and live and die for it and for Him who lived and died for it.[2]

In his early days, Dowie was a man who clearly understood the dangers of self-exaltation and wanted no part of it. Gordon Lindsay pointed out that the man who spoke those words in 1896 was not the same man in the year 1900.

In those five years of success, something in Dowie's nature surfaced that had been inoperative as long as he remained humble. Around 1900, there was a peculiar erosion of key character traits that altered his perspective on life.[3] This strange metamorphosis led to an alarming declaration that shocked even those closest to him.

Almost without warning, in June of 1901, Dowie declared himself to be "Elijah, the restorer," whose return had been prophesied centuries earlier in the pages of Scripture. Dowie was an incredible restorer in this era. There can be little doubt that this man restored to the Church the concepts of miracles, healings, and the authority and power of God, but somehow an apparently sudden, strange infusion of deluded pride pushed this champion of God to an unscriptural conclusion.

John Alexander Dowie, 1904. In June 1901, Dowie declared himself to be "Elijah the restorer." His life (1847-1907) is one of the greatest object lessons in all history.

Solemn Object Lessons

How could a man so mightily used of God make such a mistake as to impair his obviously very important ministry? The answer is in human character not yet transformed to the image of Christ. The Scriptures abound with illustrations of men who were greatly used of God, but who afterward failed because of human weakness. Balaam was a prophet to nations, yet ended as a classic example of one who prostitutes spiritual gifts and offices for profit. (Rev. 2:14.)

When Saul was anointed king of Israel, he was so unassuming and humble that it required the insight of a prophet to locate him hiding among the baggage. (1 Sam. 10:17-24.) He was a man who led God's nation to great victory, yet pride and jealousy eventually brought him to disgrace and suicide. Later, David his successor, lamented his predecessor by proclaiming, **"...How the mighty have fallen!"** (2 Sam. 1:19).

Then there is David himself, a man after God's own heart. In my mind, he is perhaps the greatest hero in the Old Testament; yet through spiritual neglect, he sinned grievously to the point of adultery and murder. (2 Sam. 11.) The story of the failure of outstanding and good kings such as Solomon and Asa are warnings ignored by only the most foolish.[4]

Gordon Lindsay later would say of Dowie's life:

...John Dowie affords perhaps the most solemn object lesson of any character in church history....If studied dispassionately for the purpose of learning the secret of his success, and again the cause of his failure, one will perhaps have learned that the life of one man can teach another.[5]

As noted and anecdoted previously in this manuscript, Dowie was a man who learned to rely heavily on God in times of persecution and adversity. Time and time again, God's grace would carry him past seemingly impossible odds to victory in Jesus' name. However, Dowie, as many others before and after him, was finally brought down by a surprising nemesis: success.

Once he reached a pinnacle of success where people idolized him, Dowie lost that sense of desperation for God. He involved himself in a fatal error: He became too busy to seek the God of redemption. Dowie had been a man of intense prayer. As long as he spent time in "the secret place" of the Most High, the gates of hell were at his mercy. However, with the inception of Zion City, Dowie found himself engaged in a multitude of secular endeavors demanding time, attention, effort, and expense. Like Joshua before him, he became susceptible to deception when he became so preoccupied with other matters that he **...did not inquire of the Lord** (Josh. 9:14).

One of the greatest historical pitfalls for the halting of revival has been success. Men will pray and fast, seek God, and wait on His favor in trying moments, but once the breakthrough comes, they strangely become self-sufficient. Somehow, they begin to believe the adulation of men and become "doers" for God instead of "receivers" from God.

Another contributing factor to Dowie's downfall was his inability to receive counsel from anyone but his own hand-picked subordinates. Dowie became a man who, in his own eyes, had no peers. Men who pay such a great price to launch controversial, yet godly ministries learn to stand against the rejection of men. Historically, that kind of dogged self-reliance also seems to propagate a mentality of independence in the time of established ministry.

The apostles and elders knew to consult one another in decisions of vital importance (see Acts 15). Dowie, as well as others, removed himself from valuable counsel that might have checked unwitting abuses. There is a serious need for a fraternal fellowship of love and submission among the Charismatic leaders of the day to avoid future excesses and delusions.

Dowie's progression was typical of so many others who fall: Success gave way to pride, pride led to self-sufficiency, and that made him "too big" for consultation with his peers. Lack of a fraternal fellowship left him open to criticism, and his reaction to criticism in the later years was bitterness.

It is certainly no surprise that Dowie's proclamation of himself as "Elijah" gave way to a flood of criticism. Yet being attacked was not new to Dowie. He had experienced criticism throughout his entire ministry. However, the way he responded to attacks after 1900 was entirely different from the way he had reacted in the past.

Previously, Dowie honestly evaluated all criticism, but failed to compromise God's call. He would openly hold his ground against those who opposed God's standard. He denounced the enemies of God from time to time, but never with bitterness or antagonism. However, after the Elijah declaration, when criticism came in "bushels," Dowie's response was uncharacteristic of his earlier years. He spent more and more time denouncing and castigating his enemies in open bitterness. He also no longer simply proclaimed the Gospel, but spent an inordinate amount of time defending himself.

My observation has been that ministries great or small begin to disintegrate when "passing judgment" on others becomes a preoccupation. Bitterness begins to dominate, and the flow of

God's Spirit is quenched. For Dowie, the wonderful blessing of that revelation which had been a result of God's message was now reduced to defending his own projects.

How a person responds to criticism is a tremendous key to the perpetuation of God's move of the Spirit. The initial response of a person of God to criticism must always be to seek God before responding. The first question should be, "Is there any truth to the allegation?" A Christian has a responsibility to respond in humility and repentance to any aspect of truth in criticism.

Second, the accused should seek the counsel of those for whom he has respect in the Lord. Church history is full of ministers who seek only to "steamroll" subordinates (or who choose only subordinates who will acquiesce to any decision the leaders make). There always has been a tremendous need for those in ministry to seek the advice of peers with whom they are fraternally linked in Christ.

The end of the 1980s was haunted by the declaration of one of our greatest spiritual leaders who proclaimed, "Who was I supposed to get advice from?"

Such pride is the cornerstone of the crumbling revival. Dowie's progression in his fall ultimately led him to a "fixation."[6] His fixation, or delusion (2 Thess. 2:11-17), led him to excess in understanding. Such excess led to his delusion and downfall. The only antidote for such delusion is *humility of soul*. A person in a position of great responsibility must seek humility at all costs until it permeates the deepest recesses of his spirit and nature. Then the delusion of personal exaltation will find no proper soil in which to take root.[7]

Traits of Fallen Ministries:
Pride and Glory-Seeking

When so much of Dowie's energy was invested in secular enterprises — erecting buildings, tending to business projects, defending his claims, fending off accusation — rather than in preaching the Gospel of deliverance, he fell. That is not to say in any way that building a ministry is wrong, but when it becomes the major preoccupation, the fall is inevitable.

In his later years, the memory of his great healing ministry was marred when he died in a wheelchair devastated by a stroke but still proclaiming that he was "Elijah." The man who had humbled even great city newspapers by the anointing of the Spirit lived to see multitudes walk out of his crusades mocking him. The devil's subtle treachery and deceit interrupted his incredible message of power.

Crippled, humbled, and devastated in his later years, Dowie seemingly hung on to his "Elijah revelation." He signed all documents and correspondence, "Elijah, the First Apostle." However, his last article was simply signed, "John Alexander Dowie." I believe that act showed a subtle repentance and acknowledgement of wrongdoing.

No outward enemy conquered Dowie, only the enemy within. Unfortunately, although Dowie was certainly the most classic modern example of the consequences of violation of character, he is by no means the last.

The Healing Revival of the period 1947-1958 was perhaps the most noted time of healing miracles in our day; however, that move was mixed with excesses that brought it to an untimely end.

Gordon Lindsay, a noted historian of the era, was in the best position to head off those excesses. He was more than simply an advisor to the many ministries of the time, he was like the conductor of a discordant symphony. Indeed, David Harrell once described Lindsay as a "director of an unruly orchestra."[8]

Lindsay did his best to bring respect to the revival. He advised the evangelists, "It is better for one to go slow. Get your ministry on a solid foundation....By all means avoid this Hollywood press agent stuff."[9]

He was particularly leery of evangelists who seemed to have an inordinate ambition to glorify their own ministries and to "amass money for personal comfort."[10] Lindsay and others became deeply concerned about certain excesses, and time proved they were right. Those excesses became "killers" of the impetus of God.

In 1958, after eleven years of a marvelous and miraculous era, the Healing Revival came to an end. Many of the principal "players" died early, were scandalized, or victimized by their own excesses. In 1962, the troubled conscience of the move was expressed in a series of articles published by Juanita Coe in *International Healing* magazine.

Mrs. Coe was the wife of Jack Coe, a prominent healing evangelist during this revival. Oral Roberts once confided in me that he knew no man who demonstrated greater faith than Jack Coe. However, a brutal schedule and carelessness with his health led to Coe's untimely death in 1957. Mrs. Coe took up the banner of the ministry with the continuation of the magazine.

In 1962, she employed G. H. Montgomery (1893-1966), a prominent writer and controversial figure of the movement, to publish a series of articles concerning the excesses of the period that brought the revival to its knees. The series was entitled "Enemies of the Cross."

I have had the opportunity of carefully examining these articles, and it is my opinion that they were flavored with a mixture of truth and Montgomery's own hurts and prejudices. There were at the time even some allegations of personal indiscretion made against Montgomery himself. The articles, nonetheless, carry certain "documented" truths that should sound a warning signal to the new bearers of the next move of God.

I have included several noteworthy abuses from those articles:

In Montgomery's words, as the crowds got bigger, the offerings grew larger, and the reports got higher, "The inevitable happened. Pride and glory-seeking entered the revival." Bigger and better became banner headlines in many newsletters of the evangelists, he wrote.

Jack Coe, on one occasion, visited an Oral Roberts meeting, measured his tent, and promptly ordered a larger one. In that way, Coe could publicize the fact that he had the largest meetings in the revival. This was one of many such unfortunate incidents of the era.

Montgomery seemed to paint "the lot" of evangelists as glory-seeking men. There is little doubt that some were, but the movement was not of "con men," but sincere God-fearing men. Some went astray. Some were bitten by the bug of success that breeds arrogance. However, in my opinion, the movement was not dominated by the unrighteous.

Like Dowie before them, these men found that success can be a cruel taskmaster. A close observer of the movement has said that, for many revivalists, success came too quickly. They received too much money and recognition too soon. Success became commonplace; it was easy for many of the evangelists to rely more upon atmosphere and routine than to continually seek God.

God has not called His people primarily to be successful, but to be obedient. I believe that is the heartbeat of God as evidenced in His word spoken through the prophet Zechariah: **"...'Not by might nor by power, but by my Spirit,' says the Lord Almighty"** (Zech. 4:6).

Success and adulation tend to lead toward self-sufficiency. Obedience directs toward "God-sufficiency."

The word *might* used in Zechariah 4:6 means force, personal virtue, or wealth, resources of the individual, or of a band of men.[11] Similarly, *power* describes personal hardiness or ability.[12] The word of warning spoken through Zechariah is to understand that no personal resources or hardiness can sustain God's move. Only His Spirit can maintain His purpose.

"Lone Rangers" Usually Get Into Trouble

Montgomery asserted that independence had been the path to excesses within the revival. He alleged that many of the revivalists became "a law unto themselves," thereby leaving them susceptible to their own frailties. There was little oversight to check **...the lust of the flesh, and the lust of the eyes, and the pride of life...** (1 John 2:16 KJV). Montgomery accused many ministries of having "hirelings" who could be "steamrolled" into agreeing with controversial decisions.

This lack of "checks" by peers, Montgomery felt, led to a multitude of other wrong ideas, such as a casual view of sins including, for example, drugs and alcohol abuse, wife abuse, and prostitution. Such charges have surrounded every revival era. At the turn of the century, Dowie's shortcomings were well documented. Another of the most prominent men of that era was arrested in Texas on charges of homosexuality, although the charges ultimately were dropped.

The Healing Revival was marred by charges of drunkenness, with one evangelist even being charged with assault and battery. Many others had problems with avarice and materialism. Similar charges have turned up at the door of our present era. All of us have heard the recent allegations of involvement with prostitutes, misappropriation of funds, exaggeration of numbers, and the use of gimmicks, manipulation, and otherwise improper methods of fund-raising.

Montgomery also claimed that many of the healing evangelists exaggerated their results. He noted one such incident in two years of recorded results in Jamaica. Evangelists reported a total of more than three million converts there during the revival. The only problem was that Jamaica only had a total population of one million six hundred thousand people. Nearly everyone would have had to be saved twice!

I believe two things happened: there was a certain exaggeration that took place, and many times the same people went to the altar in several crusades. However, it is highly unlikely that the whole country of Jamaica responded to a salvation call. It is a natural human desire to want to publicize the best results possible, but we should never forget that God can bless only in proportion to our truthfulness and integrity.

Today, we tend to laugh off such incidents as the Jamaica report as examples of what some would call "evangelistically speaking." It is sad to think that the word *evangelistic* would come to be associated with gross exaggeration.

Smith Wigglesworth was a man who loved the truth. His personal adherence to scriptural principles would never allow him to exaggerate on any issue. He was often aware of inflated claims of the numbers of converts and healings, and he refused to be a party to such misrepresentation. That attitude is the call of God for us today: honesty and integrity.

International Healing magazine continued to blast abuses and accused many of the evangelists of the use of *gimmicks and manipulation* in an attempt to stimulate the interest and contributions of their constituents. Montgomery listed twenty-three "interest catchers" which he had considered manipulative.

He said that for many, manipulation had become a substitute for anointing. He also wrote there had been widespread diversion of funds to purposes other than those for which they had been solicited. He reported that one ministry collected a million dollars for a certain project, but less than fifty thousand dollars was actually distributed for that cause.

The last few years of the Eighties also brought a concern for integrity as in few times this century. Many questions have risen concerning financial integrity and accountability. I have heard people say that ministers should be publicly and officially accountable, and others say that the Church cannot demand such accountability because the Bible does not.

My conviction, however, is that the Bible *does* address this volatile issue. In 2 Corinthians 8, Paul openly dealt with the issue of accountability of funds. The Corinthian church had raised an offering for the poor in Jerusalem. (vv. 16-21.) Paul wrote giving directions as to how the finances should be handled.

In verse 17, he stated that he would send Titus with the funds; then, in verse 18, he added that he also would send another along with Titus. In verses 19 through 21, Paul elaborated on the concept, stating that he wanted to avoid criticism in the way the "liberal gift" was administered:

> **And not that only, but who was also chosen of the churches to travel with us with this grace, which is administered by us to the glory of the same Lord, and declaration of your ready mind.**
>
> **— 2 Corinthians 8:19 KJV**

In verse 21 he goes on to point out:

> **For we are taking pains to do what is right, not only in the eyes of the Lord but also in the eyes of men.**

Paul was saying that the churches had elected an officer (the word *chosen* in verse 19 means voted on in the Greek[13]) to travel with the disciples and help be responsible for what was obviously a large sum of money. Paul organized the collection to honor God and to help those in need. To that end, he took scrupulous pains to avoid bringing any disrepute on the Lord's name because of mismanagement or avarice — not just to preserve integrity in the eyes of God, but also in the eyes of men.

Accountability demands and results in integrity. The word *integrity* comes from the root word *integer,* which means completeness, or a whole number.[14] Part of our understanding of this issue is that our integrity is made "complete" by being rightly related to the "whole" of those who are mature leaders in Christ.

Real or even perceived manipulation brings reproach on the Body of Christ. Recently, Evangelist Kenneth Copeland said to me, "Whenever I write a letter to my partners, I make sure I am writing to meet their needs and not mine. If I am God's servant, He will make sure His needs are met in me."

Brother Copeland stated a priority that it behooves all ministers to keep in mind: the needs of the people and the purposes of God.

I believe that God is calling us to a fraternal fellowship. The pressures of ministry demand that we find other ministers with whom we can develop relationships open enough to confess our faults and shortcomings. This "fellowship" does not have to form a bond of submission that attempts to curtail one's vision, but should constitute an open door to share honestly, to help promote God's highest and best in our lives.

A Call to Fraternal Fellowship

No longer can Christians afford a lack of accountability in lifestyle or a lack of fellowship so that we cannot be totally truthful to a group of committed leaders. I honestly believe that we could have avoided recent scandals if such a commitment to one another existed. If we could "let our hair down" and not be condemned, gossiped about, or judged, many of our public dealings could be corrected in private.

I believe the Holy Spirit is going to divinely orchestrate the cooperation of Christian leadership of men and women who will be committed to one another in relationship — not to prove their spirituality, but to help one another grow in Christ and in integrity.

Several years ago in East Texas, another pastor asked to come to my office and meet with me. We exchanged pleasantries, and he spent much time expressing his personal encouragement concerning my ministry. I felt, however, that there was something else on his mind. When I asked him if there was anything God was dealing with him about, he became flustered, stammered a little without really saying anything, and then left.

Later, I learned that he had been having a problem with pornography. That obsession led to an affair and, today, he is out of the ministry. His ministry could have been spared if either of us had understood or been willing to submit to a bond of fraternal fellowship.

Other shortcomings in many revivals have been the inordinate craving for materialism and the failure to allow personality flaws to be healed, the failure to completely put off the "old self" (KJV, "the old man") and to "put on the new self." (Eph. 4:22-24.) In the next chapter, let's take a look at these things.

∽

Chapter 16

Fewer Heroes, More Leaders

In the Twenties, Aimee Semple McPherson's love for "things" had led to much persecution.

What a failure to think that people have their eyes on me. God will never give His glory to another. He will take me from this scene.

— Smith Wigglesworth

One morning recently, God awakened me with these words, "We need fewer heroes and more leaders!"

At first, I was confused by His words, then I began to realize the far-reaching implication of that statement. The fact is that *heroes* promote vicarious living and adulation of man.

If I cannot play baseball, I do so vicariously through Barry Bonds. If I cannot play basketball, I do so through Michael Jordan. I spend my time praising others and *observing* rather than *doing*.

Such actions in the Body of Christ are disastrous for two reasons:

1. If we live our lives vicariously through those ministering on the platform, we absolve ourselves from any real ministry.

2. If we spend our time praising a man rather than God, we set the man up for a fall. A man often praised may feel invincible under the anointing. He may never feel the need to deal with his own shortcomings and hurts. That often leaves him subject to downfall.

Leaders, on the other hand, not only do the works of God and are respected for it, but teach others to do the same. The next move of the Spirit must have more leaders and fewer heroes.

The role of "hero" set many of the revivalists up for criticism. As I mentioned earlier, one intimate observer of the Healing Revival noted that many of the revivalists accumulated too much personal property too quickly. Many of them simply did not know how to handle the newfound blessing. Montgomery continued to write about the healing revivalists in Mrs. Coe's magazine, detailing that an undue emphasis on wealth had caused many of that era to lose a proper perspective on ministry.

Biblical prosperity certainly carries with it the connotation of wealth. There are, however, a number of words that can be translated *prosperity*. These words also mean to give skillfully; to be well, happy, friendly, or peaceable; to have favor; or to succeed in reaching a journey's end.[1]

That last definition, "reaching a journey's end," is clearly delineated in Scripture: **But thou shalt remember the Lord thy God: for it is he that giveth thee power to get wealth, that he may establish his covenant...**(Deut. 8:18 KJV.) Paul elaborated on Moses' words by saying, **You will be made rich in every way so that you can be generous on every occasion...**(2 Cor 9:11.)

Materialism, on the other hand, has a connotation of an undue regard for the things of this world — possessions and wealth. *Prosperity* in the Bible does not imply an unhealthy penchant for spending money on the lusts of the flesh or the eyes. Wealth is a blessing given us for God's purpose: to establish His Kingdom in the earth.

Many struggling evangelists, who paid a tremendous price in past revivals, were rewarded with incredible material prosperity, only to be corrupted by it. As Christians, it is not wrong for us to have money, it is wrong when money has us. We are to seek God, not money. (1 Tim. 6:10.)

Part of the decline in John Alexander Dowie's life came from material well-being. Many felt that the blessing of prosperity proved corruptive for the entire Dowie family. Mrs. Dowie was said to have lost her former simplicity of lifestyle. She became infatuated with Parisian gowns and extravagant living.[2] Observers noted that, having sudden access to large sums of money from her husband's ministry after his success in Chicago, she developed an incredible penchant for finery and fashion. Some believe that she influenced her husband to spend extravagantly in the building and appointing of Shiloh Tabernacle, the eight-thousand-seat church erected in Zion City.[3]

Mrs. Dowie ultimately encouraged her husband to construct a very costly executive mansion in which he could entertain important visitors. The large house was elaborately appointed with expensive furnishings. The more Dowie lost himself in lavish living, the more he lost sympathetic contact with and understanding of ordinary people. In his later years, his financial irresponsibility and taste for personal luxury raised considerable obstacles to his credibility.

Prosperity Can Bless or Corrupt

Such wealth demands incredible responsibility from its recipients. Riches can provide an atmosphere of security and invincibility. In that atmosphere, leaders will often take on projects not in God's plan or timetable. Not satisfied with Zion, Illinois, Dowie fell into a mood of euphoria and planned to establish such towns all over the world.

Toward the end of his ministry, a "Zion" was planned in Mexico, but by that time, the ministry was experiencing a precarious financial stability. Zion itself was failing financially, and Dowie refused to acknowledge it. He continued to tour the world traveling in the most expensive ways, "taking the highest-priced suites at the finest hotels, entertaining lavishly at various places and purchasing considerable costly clothing and other merchandise."[4] By such thoughtless extravagances, Dowie eventually bankrupted Zion and his ministry.

Even the humblest of men is susceptible to financial faltering. By 1955, William Branham's ministry came into financial difficulties for the first time, and through naivety and carelessness, Branham shattered his own ministry. His problems, however, were not like Dowie's. Branham kept a simple lifestyle and did not use funds for his own benefit.

David Harrell wrote, "It seemed ironic that financial troubles should have fallen on the evangelist who had shunned the expensive lifestyle....Branham shunned personal gain, but proved unable to protect himself from bad managers."[5]

By 1956, the Internal Revenue Service launched an investigation of Branham. His business manager had filed personal income tax reports on eighty thousand dollars, while Branham claimed only to have received seven thousand. The unsophisticated Branham had no systematic effort to account for the thousands of dollars that flowed into his ministry. The government penalties levied against the ministry were so crippling that it never recovered.

By 1958, Branham found himself in desperate need and deeply reassessing his ministry. At the turn of the new decade, his problems intensified. Strapped for money, exhausted, competing with a multiplicity of new ministries, and with the anointing waning, he pressed on, seeking for "deeper truths."

By 1960, he began to stray doctrinally, fully embracing the oneness doctrine of the Trinity which he had believed since his early days. However, in the Forties and Fifties, he had avoided controversial subjects in his campaigns and had been able to minister across a broad range of Pentecostal sects, evangelicals, and mainstream denominations.[6]

Other doctrinal misleadings seemed to be given full reign in his life after the late Fifties, and by 1963, he fell into the same delusion as Dowie. He declared he was "the Elijah of God."[7]

Finally, one of the era's strongest evangelists approached Gordon Lindsay and declared prophetically that a great leader of the movement was to be taken home before he lost his relationship to Christ. Lindsay has said that he recognized in his spirit that the prophecy was about Branham.

On December 18, 1965, while driving to Arizona, William Branham was killed in a head-on collision with a drunk driver. I am not intimating that financial mismanagement was the only cause of Branham's downfall, but it was certainly a main cog in the wheel.

At the end of the Healing Era, many established ministries changed for one main reason: the loss of financial support.[8] Jack

Coe moved into television to compete with other ministries, which strained his already shaky finances. In the Twenties, Aimee Semple McPherson's love for "things" had led to much persecution. The same proved to be true in the ministries of many during the Forties, Fifties, and Sixties.

My advice to young ministers is to decide ahead of time how much is enough. Then when that amount is reached, put the rest back into the Kingdom. Money tied up in things not ordained by God is a scheme of the enemy to destroy ministries. Money poured into ministry is for influence not affluence.

This whole area of finances can ultimately be the make or break arena of a ministry. There are indeed Kingdom laws of reciprocity, but character is the key to whether or not laws work for our good or contribute to our destruction.

One of those laws is: **"Give, and it will be given to you..."** (Luke 6:38). Oral Roberts calls the act of giving in accordance with this principle "Seed Faith." Over the years, he has expounded many times on the three tenets of this spiritual law:

1. Recognize that God is your Source. (You look to Him rather than to men.)

2. Plant your seed. (You give to God.)

3. Expect a miracle. (God, in covenant relationship, prospers you).

Kingdom laws work. However, revival history is full of examples of ministries destroyed by greed, pride, and corruption, all stemming from "blessings," without character.

Unhealed Personality Wounds and Flaws

One area I would like to add to Montgomery's list is unresolved personality flaws. The majority of key leaders came out of haunting poverty and crippling backgrounds. They had to overcome a mountain of obstacles to reach a pinnacle of success. Many of them, however, had residues of past problems that remained unresolved in their lives and ultimately surfaced under pressure. Others let present hurts cripple them with bitterness that altered their ministry and message.

John Alexander Dowie is in this last group. After his "Elijah declaration," criticism of his ministry became rampant. Dowie turned from proclaiming the gospel of deliverance to spending time in the pulpit defending his name and his projects.

In a final attempt to "show the world" and reestablish his credibility, he organized a magnificent crusade in New York City to validate his claims. Motivated by the need for personal vindication rather than the direction of the Holy Spirit, he took eight trainloads of Zion citizens to "attack New York in the name of Jesus." The venture cost a quarter of a million dollars, but he felt it to be a minor consideration compared to the objective he hoped to accomplish.

The first afternoon, Madison Square Garden was packed with people. When Dowie stood in the pulpit, according to a pre-arranged plan by his critics, thousands of people conspicuously vacated their seats and the building as a protest. Dowie in his earlier years would have been unmoved and remained in faith. This time, he desperately tried to stop them, became confused, and ended up humiliated. The meeting "flopped," and Dowie never recovered.

This generation of leaders must learn to live in forgiveness and not be moved by their hurts. When the root of bitterness sets in, it causes people to say and do things not in keeping with the Spirit. As the author of the Book of Hebrews warns, we must always be on guard against being defiled by what the *King James Version* calls a "root of bitterness":

> **See to it that no one misses the grace of God and that no bitter root grows up to cause trouble and *defile many.***
>
> **— Hebrews 12:15**

We must be willing to die to anything that is not like Jesus. We must learn to deal with wounds, hurts, unforgiveness, and other failings rather than suppress them under a "Band-Aid" of pride. *Ego has no place in a leader of God.* To truly understand that concept is liberating, not simply an exposure of weakness. We must understand that everyone has frailties, even Christians. Ignoring them or covering them with pride will only allow them to become destructive.

Many of the leaders of the Healing Movement struggled because of earlier hurts in their lives. Jack Coe had a difficult and rugged past. Before being saved, he developed a heavy drinking problem and had a fierce anger toward life. Because he suffered from rejection in his childhood, his love for the brethren was never as deep as it might have been.[9]

His ministry reflected his personality. During his prayers for healing, he would strike the person at the point of the disease, often with brilliant results. One time, he went down a line of wheelchairs, picked them up, and threw them across the platform. Sixteen of the twenty people in them were healed. Many people, however, felt that his demonstrations were not aimed at the devil as Wigglesworth's had been, but resulted from unresolved anger out of his past. Once while on trial for practicing medicine without a license, Coe struck one of his accusers outside the courtroom.

Coe would say that God spoke to him to stay humble, yet his humble upbringing often moved him to defensive pride. In

December 1956, while preaching in Hot Springs, Arkansas, Coe became critically ill. He had been working a brutal schedule, was extremely careless about his health, and was badly overweight. He was diagnosed with polio and, at thirty-eight years of age, went home to be with the Lord.

In my opinion, he died early because of unresolved character traits that promoted disease. Coe was an example of how one of the greatest men of faith of the era could allow God's plan for him and for God's people to be shortchanged.

A. A. Allen was another man with unresolved personality traits. He too came from a rough background. His parents had been alcoholics, and he inherited that tendency. His ministry was powerful. He was the "bold of the bold." Yet, in 1955, when the stress of his schedule stretched him to his limit, Allen was arrested in Knoxville, Tennessee, for driving while intoxicated.

A. A. Allen, c. 1950s. Allen, like Coe, came from a rough background. His ministry was powerful. He was the "bold of the bold."

He, like Coe, was asked to withdraw from his denomination. Allen died in 1970 from sclerosis of the liver. Many felt that his condition had been caused by a drinking problem.[10]

Some of these leaders failed to deal with their own spiritual needs, and the oversight ultimately destroyed them and the move of God. Others forgot this basic principle: What it takes to get it, it takes to keep it. They paid the price until success and breakthrough were achieved and invincibility was felt, only to ultimately fail and fall.

"Heroes" Are Like Samson

Samson is a classic example of one who was a public success and a private failure. Let's look at his life more closely to gain insight into the kind of character that invites a fall and the kind of character men and women of God need in any era.

Four times in two chapters, the Bible tells of how God came upon Samson in great power: Judges 13:25, 14:6, 14:19, and 15:14. Under the power of the Spirit, he tore a lion apart, single-handedly killed thirty men at one time, and broke open ropes binding him as if they were "flax." Then, grabbing the jawbone of a donkey, he killed a thousand men.

All Israel looked up to him as their hero and defender against the Philistines. However, Judges 16:1 records, **One day Samson went to Gaza, where he saw a prostitute. He went in to spend the night with her.** Obviously, moral weakness was unresolved in this incredible man. Word spread through the town that Samson was inside the city walls. Guards positioned themselves to kill him during his exit from the city at dawn.

When Samson arose, he became aware of his attackers. He walked over to the city gate, promptly ripped it off the hinges along with two posts, and walked away with it, bar and all.

If you are a guard lying in wait in a situation like that, what do you do now? Somehow, an attack would not seem as expedient as it did some hours earlier while you were discussing it, would it? Samson just looked at them and said, "Say what?" — and walked off.

The problem, however, is that Samson had been set up for a fall by the devil. Obviously his physical and spiritual strength was only surpassed by his moral weakness. Samson must have thought to himself, "No matter what I do, the Holy Spirit comes upon me."

He felt what so many leaders have felt throughout history — the invincibility of the anointing of the Spirit. The devil rarely tries to "take us down" with the first indiscretion. It is far more important to his ultimate plans to get the attitude that "no matter what I do, the power of God is still on me," planted in a person's mind as an operating truth for behavior.

Texas Evangelist James Robison's well-documented testimony of his own vulnerability points out this truth in a very dramatic way. In his autobiography, he admits that he battled lustful thoughts, even during his services, but that the devil was not able to tempt him into indulging in illicit acts.[11]

Once when Robison was on the campus of Oral Roberts University, I heard him relate this story. One night before a crusade meeting, he was struggling with lust. He had spotted a young woman in the audience and had been overcome with sinful feelings toward her. He struggled through his message captivated by unhealthy emotions, but when he gave the altar call, more people than usual responded. He went back to his hotel room seeking some kind of rationale for how he could be filled with sinful thoughts — yet people were still drawn by the anointing.

Then God in His graciousness revealed it to him. The devil was setting him up for a bigger fall. If he thought he could violate purity, be invincible from the enemy, and still have the anointing, the devil would be set to "take him out." A loss of character is ultimately the loss of the favor of God.

Fortunately, James Robison's story is one of redemption and victory. God sent a man to him to bring understanding of his problem and deliverance. His experience reinforces my conviction that men and women of God *must* come into a fraternal fellowship to help one another overcome the human frailties to which we are all susceptible.

Samson's story is a warning to all Christian leaders. He grew to feel that he had license to do anything, and the power of God would still be upon him. Then Satan moved into phase two and sent in the "heavy artillery." Her name was Delilah, and I am sure you know the story well. She used her feminine charms on several occasions to lure Samson into sharing the secret of his power.

Judges 16:16 shares these words of Satan's most productive tactic — persistence: **With such nagging she prodded him day after day until he was tired to death.** (She must have had some incredible feminine charms for any man to put up with "such nagging.") Verse 17 reveals the sad end of the scenario: **So he told her everything....** Now Samson's doom was sealed. He had betrayed God, broken covenant, and fallen headlong into the trap.

Delilah shared his secret with her companions before lulling Samson into falling asleep on her lap, allowing her an opportunity to cut his hair and thus rob him of his supernatural strength. Verse 20 contains some of the saddest words in all of scripture:

> **...He awoke from his sleep and thought, "I'll go out as before and shake myself free." But** *he did not know that the Lord had left him.*

How many times have those words been repeated in history? How many times has the man of God gotten up to "go out as before," and suddenly realized (or perhaps did not realize) "that

God had left him." The Holy Spirit had left, because the minister had never learned that *an individual ministers in anointing, but must live out of character.*

Character is one of the great keys to perpetuating the move of God. The lack of it is a slow, but sure, killer of revival.

Many people are confused about why the anointing goes on for a season, even when sin persists. Paul tells us that **...God's gifts and his call are irrevocable** (Rom. 11:29.) Once God bestows a gift upon a person, He never takes it back. That individual can misuse God's gift or nullify its operation in his or her life, but God never revokes it.

Even if stewardship of the gift has been violated, if the person is repentant, God will restore the gift in full operation and anointing. Thus, for a season, the gift will manifest itself.

In this chapter I have tried to isolate some of the character flaws that postpone or destroy revival. I will close with a review of them along with God's antidote for each one. God gives us grace to overcome and thus be His people so that He can truly be our God.

Antidotes for the Poison of Personality Flaws

1) Success   Victory/Obedience
2) Pride (self-sufficiency)   Humility/God-sufficiency
3) Secular enterprise   Prayer/Relationship to God
4) Bitterness   Forgiveness
5) Independence   Fellowship/Accountability
6) Exaggeration   Honesty
7) Gimmicks   Faith/Integrity
8) Materialism   Prosperity for God's will
9) Background problems and hurt   Healing and the Cross
10) Sin   Holiness

Perhaps, this whole issue is best summed up in the words of the person who said, "Character is revealed by how we act when we think no one is looking."

God's approval comes in the form of the anointing and is not simply the result of faith on the platform. It is also the result of the character that makes up the private area of our lives. That is what causes the momentary flow of God's Spirit to become perpetual.

Smith Wigglesworth said that, on one occasion, God spoke to him and said, "Wigglesworth, I'm going to burn you up till there's no Wigglesworth left; only Jesus will be seen."[12]

On another occasion Wigglesworth said, "...What a failure to think that people have their eyes on me. God will never give His glory to another. He will take me from this scene."[13] The purpose of fulfilling our calling is not for us to build a big ministry, but to cause people to see Jesus. If we will do that, then the Lord will take care of building His own ministry. (Acts 2:42-47 KJV.)

Wigglesworth always believed that, without holiness, no one had the right to expect to see the miraculous.

John G. Lake said without hesitation that holiness is the key to the perpetual moving of God's power.[14]

The goals and purposes of our lives are best summed up in the words of the late great Bible teacher, Henryetta Mears: "to know Him [Christ], and to make Him known." Anything less is off-center.

The final question that rings in my mind is, what kind of atmosphere produces a climate, or provides an opening, for these failures and shortcomings to manifest and cause such tragic downfalls? That question brings us to consider what I call "the number-one killer of revival."

The Number One Killer of Revival

Similarly, *Aimee Semple McPherson* allowed increasing exhaustion, recurring bouts of loneliness, and mounting levels of stress to provoke ill-timed decisions....

Come unto me, all ye that labour and are heavy laden, and I will give you rest.

— Matthew 11:28 KJV

People who know my fascination with revival often ask me what I think is the "number-one killer of revival." I never hesitate with my answer, and they are almost always shocked. In my opinion, the number-one killer of revival is *lack of rest*.

I believe that answer surprises most people because we are used to expecting a high-energy, high-intensity ministry that makes things happen. Unfortunately, often we are more accustomed to "might" and "power," than we are to " 'by My Spirit' says the Lord." (Zech. 4:6.)

Some ministries today have totally dedicated themselves to the "burn out" syndrome. Because of the unbelievable attrition rate in the ministry, we now have "burn out" camps and seminars strung across America. Ministers are exhausted in their own efforts instead of flowing in the Spirit. Ministry people often try to live up to a false standard of what ministry is, rather than relying upon God.

Several years ago, my wife and I moved back to Oklahoma in order for me to assume the position of campus pastor at Oral Roberts University. Our house in Texas was up for sale and, in the meantime, we looked for a place to lease in Tulsa. We found lodging suitable for us owned by a beautiful Korean couple. They had been members of Dr. Cho's church in South Korea.

When the lady learned that we wanted to rent from them, she was thrilled. She had heard about our ministry and was excited to have us in her house. When we met to sign the agreements for the lease, this precious woman saw me for the first time.

In her humble Korean manner and broken English, she said, "Oh Brother Ron, I hear about you. You very powerful man. God use you mightily."

Right in the middle of her high-sounding praise, she suddenly stopped, looked at me, and asked — "You him?"

It was one of those moments of great exhilaration and humility at the same time, if you know what I mean. Evidently she did not think my five-foot-ten-inch, one-hundred-and-fifty five-pound body and baby face measured up to her precon- ceived estimation of who I was supposed to be.

That is what happens to many ministers. They think their con- gregation is going to take a good look at them and ask, "You him?" They overwork in a misguided attempt to reach some level of acceptance with the congregation, with God, or even within themselves.

Many of the great revivalists took on more of a burden than God ever intended and literally pushed themselves until they were completely expended. This exhaustion prepared the ground for a fall in many cases. For some it led to pride in works, others slipped into sin, and some burned themselves out so completely they were never heard from again.

Charles Finney once said:

Revival will stop when the church grows exhausted through its labor. Multitudes of Christians make a mistake here in times of revival. They are so thoughtless and have so little judgment that they break up all their habits of living, neglect to eat and sleep at proper hours, and let the excitement run away with them. By doing this they overwork their bodies, and they soon become exhausted. It becomes impossible for them to continue in work. Revivals often cease, because of negligence and imprudence in the area on the part of those in charge of revival. Whenever Christians believe they are strong in their strength, God curses their blessings. In many instances, they sin against their own mercies because they become proud of their own success, take credit themselves, and do not give the glory to God.[1]

What an incredible description of the root cause of revival's downfall. Finney has provided for us a tremendous summation of Satan's plan to destroy God's move: Overwork leads to exhaustion, exhaustion leads to impropriety, and impropriety leads to a fall.

Long before Finney shared his evaluation, the prophet Isaiah sent forth similar warning signals: **Even youths grow tired and weary, and young men stumble and fall** (Is. 40:30). The *King James Version* says young men faint, become weary, and utterly fall.

Isaiah described a threefold process by which the fall of a man and a ministry are set up. First, he says a man grows tired and weary. This word *tired* or *faint* means to be fatigued.[2] When a man gets tired, his strength begins to leave him; he grows *weary*.

That leads to a *stumble*. This word refers to exhaustion, deprivation of strength or energy, too little strength to maintain focus or direction. Stumbling leads to an utter fall. This word *fall* means to: totter, waver, be in utter weariness, be totally faint, cast down, or decayed.[3]

Isaiah portrays the same decaying process that Finney would observe years later. Once a man becomes fatigued, he loses his ability to maintain strength or energy. He begins to lose his footing or direction and finally becomes cast down and falls away from God.

The Fall of Great Ministries

Even in his earliest years of ministry in Australia, John Alexander Dowie labored hard, often to the point of physical exhaustion. His intentions were noble. He made many painful sacrifices and tried to do what was right, often at the expense of his own interests. While his efforts were laudable, they also set a dangerous precedent for his later years.

In his towering moments, Dowie would have unusual stamina in ministry by the Spirit. He often operated in supernatural strength, discerning the deepest, most secret thoughts of a people. During those days, however, he slept only four hours out of a twenty-four-hour period. He was strong during this era, but like Samson before him, he was being set up for a fall.[4]

Dowie's activities showed him to be a man of ceaseless toil, for on behalf of the Kingdom he would often work all night to finish a task. Gordon Lindsay said this about the seeming virtue of ceaseless toil in God's work:

Continuous toil without interruption can cease to be a virtue, and may even be a sin against the body. Jesus taught the need of physical relaxation. On one occasion He called His disciples to Him, and together they went apart to a secret place where they could be alone and rest. By this Jesus taught that a certain amount of relaxation is necessary for the human body. Not only will the body break and nerves suffer if not given proper care, but the mind also becomes weary and as a result the faculties for exercising balanced judgment may become impaired.[5]

Dowie remains known as one of the most persistent toilers in the Kingdom who ever lived. One of his devoted friends, Judge v. v. Burns, said of him:

Dr. Dowie knew no rest, not even one day in seven.... Speaking many a time from four, five, and up to six, eight or nine hours in a single day. It was this that caused him to break, and when we began to remonstrate with and tell him he ought to be more temperate in his labors, he considered the matter and oftentimes made promises to reform — I have known him to work steadily forty-three hours in succession.[6]

Judge Burns later related that Dowie went through periods in his life when he could not sleep. He would ultimately begin to feel a sense of weariness and pain. Burns wrote, "There came a time when it could truly be said of him, 'He saved others, but he could not save himself.'"[7]

There is unquestionably a unanimity of belief that Dowie's habit of pushing himself beyond his human constitution undermined his physical strength, subjected him to his own human frailties, and finally resulted in impairment of his faculties of judgment and discrimination.[8]

True to Isaiah's forecast, Dowie's fatigue ultimately gave way to stumbling. His diverse enterprises led some to believe he had less quality time to spend with God. Finally, with the inception of Zion and other projects, he assumed personal control of the smallest and minutest of details. He delegated to no one, but retained responsibility for everything. Those who understood human limitations wondered whether a flesh-and-blood creature could long endure while attempting to accomplish so formidable a task.

Dowie's natural buoyancy of spirit made him believe that he had an inexhaustible supply of energy, and throughout his ministry, he "burned the candle at both ends." Success made him supremely confident that he should exercise no caution toward his own well-being.

The rest is history. Finally came his progressive fall. First came "the Elijah declaration," then bitterness, a stroke, and his ruin; he utterly fell. The strategy of Satan has not changed one iota in all of history: If he cannot coax a man to do too little, he will try to get him to do too much. A "burned-out" man is as worthless to himself and the Kingdom of God as is a lethargic one.

Perhaps, the strangest example of violation of the "rest" principle, and the most unexpected one, is that of Evan Roberts of the Welsh Revival. Roberts was a man of joy and prayer. It was said of Evan Roberts that he "smiled when he prayed, laughed, 'Ah, it is a grand life.'"

He would cry, "I am so happy I could walk on air. Tired? Never! God has made me strong. He has given me courage."[9]

Roberts was truly a man of great joy and apparently an exhaustible supply of energy. However, the seeming invincibility of the moment ultimately gave way to exhaustion and extinction. He never dealt with his nervous temperament and, finally, the weight of the revival began to put a strain on him.

Roberts began to assume a false responsibility for all misconceptions or misconduct of the young converts of the revival. Some members of the Body of Christ had criticized the revival as shallow and not genuinely of the Spirit. The physical strain and growing disunity led to a shocking ending to Evan Robert's ministry. He yielded to the compulsion to vindicate himself and validate his work instead of continuing the simple proclamation of the Gospel that had brought him such joy in the beginning.

When Roberts' exhaustion and strain reached a high point, holiness writer Jesse Penn-Lewis and her husband offered him a place of retreat in their home. He accepted the "respite," but ultimately became a complete recluse, never to be seen in society again. A lack of rest had once more killed a move of God.

Similarly, Aimee Semple McPherson allowed increasing exhaustion, recurring bouts of loneliness, and mounting levels of stress to provoke ill-timed decisions and bring periodic reproach upon her ministry from the public.

In regard to the rigors of full-time ministry of this type, David Harrell offered this assessment of some others who were engaged in it:

> It was an exhausting, grinding, draining way of life. William Branham was a broken man after little more than a year; Jack Coe was physically exhausted at the time of his death; A. A. Allen, an incredibly tough campaigner, tottered constantly on the brink of psychological collapse; the resilience of Oral Roberts became a legend among his peers.[10]

We have already seen that Mrs. John G. Lake died because of exhaustion and malnutrition.[11] Lake himself grew so tired in

South Africa, he often had to withdraw from ministry to recuperate. He frequently ministered six nights per week and twice on Sunday. He worked at such an accelerated pace that, coupled with the loneliness that followed his wife's passing, he finally had to leave the mission field.

He said, "When I got on a ship to return to the United States after being in South Africa, my eyes turned blind, and I was a tottering wreck," but God brought him through that perilous ordeal.[12]

William Branham, 1962. Just as he was beginning to attract world-wide attention, Branham announced he was ill forcing his withdrawal from the evangelistic field.

Time and time again, men and women of God in the midst of victory were snatched from their pursuits by exhaustion, illness, or even death. In May of 1948, just as he was beginning to attract world-wide attention, William Branham announced that he was ill and had to leave the evangelistic field. The long, grueling nights ministering to the sick had begun to take their toll.

In his last meeting, it was said that Branham was tottering and staggering from intense fatigue. He later told his constituents that he was suffering from nervous exhaustion because of the pressure of his work. It was later reported that the Mayo Clinic had rendered a verdict that he would never totally recover from "nerves" and stomach problems brought on by his father's drinking.[13]

Later fatigue, coupled with the need for affirmation, caused his stumble to become a fall. Branham too declared himself to be the "Elijah" prophesied in Scripture.

I have already documented how Jack Coe's brutal schedule and carelessness in health led to an untimely death. Similarly, A. A. Allen's marvelous ministry fell when "tireless dedication" took an apparent toll on his health. Once Allen spread himself too thin between crusades, television, a ministry center in Arizona, and a Bible school, apparently his human resources gave way, precipitating the craving for chemical help.

In America, for some unknown reason, we often act and feel as though it is spiritual to be overly busy for the Lord. However, it is my conclusion after studying revival history that once a person becomes too busy working for the Lord, he has little time to be with the Lord. Unless that situation is altered, the inevitable result is failure and defeat.

The "Rest" of the Story

The dangerous combinations of excessive fatigue, spending time on the wrong things, and increased temptation spelled disaster for many a revivalist. Kathryn Kuhlman, as much as anyone, became a model for us in this area.

She often warned her listeners, "Be careful, the greater the yieldedness, the greater will be the temptation."[14] She explained it this way:

Sometimes that responsibility is almost overwhelming. It isn't hard work. I can stand on a platform, the stage of some auditorium, for four and a half hours and never feel the weariness because I am so yielded to the Holy Spirit. But the burden of the responsibility drains the physical body....Not only do I walk off a platform fully refreshed after a very long service, but I feel as if I could turn around and do it all over again. The secret of it is this: Kathryn Kuhlman has nothing to do with it — it is the Holy Spirit....There is infinite renewal for my own body as He fills this body with Himself and His own Spirit.[15]

The question becomes, how do we appropriate such "rest" in the Lord? The answer to that question is what Jesus was trying to communicate when He said:

Come unto me, all ye that labour and are heavy laden, and I will give you rest.

Take my yoke upon you, and learn of me; for I am meek [gentle] **and lowly in heart: and ye shall find rest unto your souls.**

For my yoke is easy, and my burden is light.

— Matthew 11:28-30 KJV

Sometimes I hear people smugly say things like, "I'd rather burn out than rust out any day."

I would rather do neither. It is not spiritual to be too busy. God never called us to be overly occupied, only ordinately obedient. There is what Tulsa pastor and author Richard Exley calls a divine "rhythm of life."[16] It is in my mind like a spiritual isometric. We exert, and then relax; exert, then relax; exert, then relax.

In physical exercise, if we do nothing but exert, we will become exhausted and our muscles will be damaged. If we do nothing but relax, we will become useless and our muscles will atrophy. However, if we establish a pattern and rhythm of alternate exertion and relaxation, we will build up our muscles, increase our strength and stamina, improve our overall health, and be able to accomplish much more for ourselves and others. Similarly, that is how we build ourselves up in the Lord for service in His Kingdom. It is this principle that Jesus speaks of in Matthew 11.

If we are to be involved in spiritual "labour," we need to make sure that Jesus remains our primary focus. The word *labour* in this context has the connotation of someone underneath a burden or carrying a load. A laborer is one who toils, works hard, or is wearied.[17]

Some people fall prey to an attitude that causes them to think God could not possibly go on without their help. Yes, we were meant to work hard in joint-participation with God, but we are not the only ones dedicated to and involved in His pursuits. He can work through others without our partnership for a season. It is arrogant to think that the Creator of the Universe cannot fulfill His plan for it without our personal advice and assistance. If you have unwittingly fallen into that kind of thinking, you need to repent, or you may join the long list of the fallen in history.

Jesus said that when we labor or become weary, we should come to Him. For what purpose? In order for Him to give us rest. The word *rest* comes from two Greek words: 1) *ana,* which means "repetition" or "reversal," and 2) *pausis,* which has the connotation of a pause, intermission, refreshing, recreation, repose, or the taking of one's ease.[18]

Thus, the word *rest* refers to a repetitive pause, or an intermission from action, labor, or motion that brings a refreshing or a recreation. America is big on recreation. In God's mind, however, this word is spelled and pronounced "re-creation." We are re-created to do His work. We can re-create away from God's presence and simply postpone the stress, but if we come to Him, His rest will re-create us and refresh us to carry on His work and fulfill His divine purpose for our lives.

The point is this: Labor does not have to be laborious — if you know how to rest. Take a break so that God can re-create you, renew you, and restore you. This was no minor theme in the Jewish culture. The whole concept of *sabbath* involved rest. The word *sabbath* means "interruption," "cessation," or "intermission"[19] — in other words, a "stop-rest." But rest is what Americans call "wasted time." True rest is not wasted time, it is "re-created time."

God mandated the concept of rest in the ten commandments:

"Six days you shall labor and do all your work, but the seventh day is a Sabbath [a "stop-rest"] **to the Lord your God. On it you shall not do any work, neither you, nor your son or daughter, nor your manservant or maidservant, nor your animals, nor the alien within your gates. For in six days the Lord made the heavens and the earth, the sea, and all that is in them, but he rested on the seventh day. Therefore the Lord blessed the Sabbath day and made it holy."**

— Exodus 20:9-11

The Lord did not create the sabbath to make sure preachers would have a job. He created it as a day of re-creation and refreshing of the soul of man. I can hear the echoes of a multiplicity of objections: "That's an old-covenant promise, and I am not under the Law."

Neither was God! He did not stop to rest after six days of creation because He was exhausted, but because He wanted to show us the way. This principle is not simply lodged in the old covenant, however; the writer of the Book of Hebrews alluded to it. Hebrews 4:1 says, **Therefore, since the promise of entering his** [God's] **rest still stands....**

Undoubtedly, the primary exegesis of this passage is to help us understand *rest* as being the fulfillment of God's promises.

This concept of rest, however, cannot be divorced from its Old Testament roots. Rest has to do both with the fulfillment of God's inheritance (in this case the Promised Land) and with the fact that Israel's unbelief did not allow them to cease from toil for forty years in the wilderness. God's rest is a message that His promise will be fulfilled, and that you and I can remain refreshed at the same time. The fact is, "His rest still remains."

True rest always brings me back to the understanding that I do not have to *make* anything happen. I only have to be obedient to Christ. After all, it is He Who really brings things to pass. That is an important principle, one which the Church inevitably will have to learn sometime in history.

One day I asked God to help me understand this vital concept of His rest. His words to me were simple: "It is the difference between Isaac and Ishmael."

You already know the story. "Ishmael" was a shadow or type or symbol of man's substitute for God's plan. "Isaac" stands for the plan of God that must be received through patience and faith. A person who has God's understanding will not have to create his own plan and use his own energy to fulfill it.

In Matthew 11:29 our Lord offers us an invitation to come to Him for rest, adding: **...for I am gentle and humble in heart...** We have already rehearsed how pride is a subtle killer. It is only important to note here that simple humility is a liberator of the soul. It is easy to be swayed by the accolades of the crowd, but every man and woman of God should understand this simple but profound truth — apart from Him we can do nothing. (John 15:5.)

One of the most freeing aspects of any person's ministry is to be released from having to live up to another's expectations — or even his own expectations. Our only real responsibility is to obey God and to believe Him for the results.

In Matthew 11:29 Jesus concludes His invitation for us to come to Him with this promise, **...and you will find rest for your souls.** The "soul" can be thought of as the mind (the thinking faculty), the will, and the emotions. A refreshed soul is a refreshed ministry. However, when a person's soul is affected, when he becomes stressed, exhausted, and emotionally drained, that individual is liable to make failing decisions or faltering mistakes.

One important factor sustained Kathryn Kuhlman in her ministry. She knew how to "wait on the Lord" and never allowed herself to become separated from His presence. Rest is not so much circumstances as it is communion with God. It is communion between us and our Creator based on what He has said in His Word. Rest is more a matter of His flow than our function.

When God called Moses to lead the children of Israel out of bondage in Egypt, He told him, **"...My Presence will go with you, and I will give you rest"** (Ex. 33:14). True rest comes upon those who minister out of God's presence, more than by their own "noble efforts."

King Solomon said it this way:

"Praise be to the Lord, who has given rest to his people Israel just as he promised. Not one word has failed of all the good promises he gave through his servant Moses. May the Lord our God be with us as he was with our fathers; may he never leave or forsake us. May he turn our hearts to him, to walk in all his ways and to keep the commands...he gave our fathers."

— 1 Kings 8:56-58

The wise king gave us three keys to maintaining rest:

1. Remember that no word of God has ever failed. With this thought firmly fixed in our minds, we can relax and trust Him with our situation, whatever it may be.

2. Recall that God's Word has worked for generations before us. We can be at ease knowing that what He has done for others in the past, He will do for us in our day.

3. Recognize that if we will simply walk in His ways, we will find Him there. His presence will take care of us.

In the next chapter, I would like to discuss five areas that will enable us to walk in rest — if we can get them aligned with the principles of God.

How To Walk in Rest

Evidently, there is a walk in God that is not wearisome or burdensome and does not end in "burnout."

"In repentance and rest is your salvation, in quietness and trust is your strength...."

— Isaiah 30:15

I know from personal experience how easy it is to slip into overwork. Even as I wrote this manuscript, I had been through a grueling three-month schedule that culminated in a very intense week of ministry. The final night of that week unfolded in a stunning six-hour service on the campus of Oral Roberts University.

We were conducting our regular Sunday night campus church service. In the midst of the worship, a spirit of dance broke out. As I looked down at the front of the auditorium, one of our students was doing a beautiful interpretive dance to a worship chorus.

The Spirit of God said to me, "If you bring her to the platform and let her dance, the glory of God will fall on the people."

At first I thought that was silly and could not be the Holy Spirit. Then, I thought to myself, "What if it does not happen that way after you announce it?" Lastly, I thought, "What if it does happen?"

I opted for "Answer C," and did as I felt led. At my request the young woman came up and began to dance gracefully before the Lord. Remarkably, the power of God fell over the auditorium. I knew at once that the presence of God was there to heal. Dozens of students and guests came forward who needed a miracle touch from God. The power of the Lord started to move. In one case, glaucoma was instantly healed, and the young man who had suffered from it for years could suddenly see perfectly. In another instance, a twisted, broken ankle was instantly straightened and mended.

A young woman made her way through the line and, in a desperate plea, cried out, "I want to be healed. I have had a heart condition since I was a little child. I have never been able to do aerobics or even dance before the Lord in my short life. Please ask God to heal me."

I laid my hands on her, and she was instantly "slain in the Spirit." A few minutes later, she regained consciousness to discover that she had been healed. The place exploded with joy as she testified how God had breathed into her the breath of life. Then she ran and danced before the Lord for the first time in her life.

This kind of activity went on for a total of almost six hours. Unusual manifestations of joy and laughter came upon the congregation as God moved in a virtually unhindered freedom.

I was gloriously filled with the energy of God — until the anointing lifted. Suddenly, I found myself exhausted. The next week, my administrative schedule "kicked in" again. Months of little sleep, morning and evening duties, and, yes, even the joy of ministry began to take their toll on my body.

I found myself short in disposition and plagued by discouragement for no apparent reason. Everything was going wonderfully, yet I was susceptible to discouragement. I found myself unreplenished and apprehensive about certain ministry possibilities. My mind became filled with "what if's" instead of seizing opportunities for God.

In a Holy Spirit rescue effort, God started to show me in the clearest way possible the effects upon the believer of little or no rest. He revealed to me five "S's" that are the cornerstone of the "rest" message:

1. *Schedule*. If a person is to remain at rest, he must be in control of his schedule. Most Christians are good-hearted, well-intentioned, and diligent in their desire to follow God. Thus they are susceptible to schedule abuses. Every schedule must contain a balance of work, worship, recreation, and rest. All too many ministers zero in on work and effort in worship, and it becomes the formula for "burnout."

2. *Stress*. Stress in ministry is commonly a negative emotion that causes distress in the "soulish" realm. The mind, the will, and the emotions are stretched to their limit and, as a result, tension causes an overload and a breakdown. Such negative feelings place an unusual demand upon the body's vital energy and can often leave a person listless and drained. Energy that could be used for the creativity of the Spirit is tied up in dealing with unresolved negative emotions.

Perhaps the most common factor that causes stress in ministry is the assuming of unassigned responsibilities. Most men and women of God let burdens turn into a need "to make things happen." Unwittingly, hundreds of ministers of the Gospel have found themselves taking on in their own flesh the responsibility to do what God desires. Using human capabilities in an attempt to carry out divine duty always ends in futility. As servants of the Lord, our area of responsibility is one of obedience, not results. The results lie in His hands.

This simple distinction is a vital key to avoiding spiritual burnout. Countless ministers have found themselves emotionally, mentally, and physically drained as a result of trying to do the will of God in their own strength.

That is why Jesus said, **"Come to me, all you who are weary and burdened, and I will give you rest"** (Matt. 11:28). The idea is this, "Come to Me if you have spent your resources, and I will recreate them with Mine."

That is why Isaiah said:

Even ["vigorous"[1]] **youths** [AMP, "selected young men"] **grow tired and weary....**

[But] **He** [God] **gives strength to the weary and increases the power of the weak** [those weakened].

— Isaiah 40:30,29

He finished this passage with this incredible thought:

...they will run and not grow weary, they will walk and not be faint.

— Isaiah 40:31

Evidently, there is a walk in God that is not wearisome or burdensome and does not end in "burnout." If we can discover the secret to that walk, then we can be continually on the go and not wear out.

The key to this discovery is found in the first part of verse 31:

but those who hope [Hebrew, "in expectancy"[2]] **in the Lord will renew** [Hebrew, "change or exchange"[3]] **their strength....**

This simple but incredible revelation is the key to avoiding spiritual burnout. As God's ambassadors, we must learn to minister out of His strength by exchanging His strength for ours, and not out of our human faculties. It is not our responsibility to produce results. It is our responsibility "to wait on Him" (KJV) for instruction and simply to obey, trust, and believe Him.

I spent years hearing the revelation and promise of God and trying to do everything I could to make it come to fulfillment in my life. I would always see some results, but ultimately I would be disappointed that the promise was not fulfilled to the level of my expectation. The result was energy-sapping frustration, periodic discouragement, and lingering disappointment. Sometimes I was almost disheartened.

When I came to the point where I realized that I was simply a vehicle of obedience, and the results were not mine but God's — it opened a floodgate of joy for my life. To my surprise, not only was I relaxed, but His power increased. I found myself often surprised at the Lord's incredible manifestations. What a relief to realize that my job was not to produce results, but simply to obey and follow in the flow of His Spirit.

There is a place in God where Paul's prayer in Ephesians can be fulfilled:

...that you may be filled (through all your being) unto all the fullness of God — [that is] may have the richest measure of the divine Presence, and become a body wholly filled and flooded with God Himself!

Now to Him Who, by (in consequence of) the [action of His] power that is at work within us, is able to [carry out His purpose and] do superabundantly, far over and above all that we [dare] ask or think — infinitely beyond our highest prayers, desires, thoughts, hopes or dreams —

To Him be glory in the church and in Christ Jesus throughout all generations, for ever and ever. Amen — and so be it.
— Ephesians 3:19-21 AMP

As disciples of Jesus Christ, it is not our responsibility to produce results, but simply to be filled with His power, purpose, and direction, and then to let Him do the work. This concept, of course, grates against the human ego. We want the results to be a consequence of our faith or our actions.

While it is true that those factors of faith, works, and effort are necessary, it is also true that it is far more important to live in a joy-filled relationship with Jesus. That allows us to follow His direction and trust Him to produce what He promises.

3. *Sleep*. The third factor is God's restorative agency — sleep.

Many of us have heard stories of how Benjamin Franklin went with only four hours of sleep a night, and so we think we can. One of my fellow students at ORU heard that Kathryn Kuhlman slept only four hours per night. His conclusion was: The closer a person gets to God, the less sleep he or she needs.

He went on long fasts and began to do with less and less sleep. As I said before, one of the devil's oldest tricks is to get us to do too much, if he cannot get us to do too little.

I tried to convince this young man to listen to reason, but he would not pay any attention. After he had followed this lifestyle for a couple of months, I found him one day curled up in a fetal position on the floor of his room. He was almost totally irrational. Fortunately I discovered him in time to get help.

As human beings, we were created by God with the need to restore and recreate the energy of our physical bodies. People, like John Alexander Dowie, who abuse this process, ultimately pay the price.

4. *Sin.* I do not know any man or woman of God who deliberately sets out to sin. In fact, many have felt that under the anointing they were impervious to sin. Often, whatever is causing spiritual exhaustion leaves a believer with little fortitude to face temptation.

The end of the 1980s was marked by leaders of the Body of Christ who desired to do God's will, but who got caught up in sin and fatigue, and thus fell.

That is why we must take heed to Isaiah's declaration: **But the wicked** [those caught up in ungodliness] **are like the tossing sea, which cannot rest....**(Is. 57:20).

Sin is the greatest fatigue factor because it grates against the will of God that His people so desire.

Perhaps the greatest sin of spiritual leaders in history was the desire to do the right thing the wrong way. Many of the leaders of the last revival attempted to do God's will by their own strength. Listen to the words of warning echoed from the prophet Isaiah:

"Woe to the obstinate children," declares the Lord, "to those who carry out plans that are not mine, forming an alliance, but not by my Spirit, heaping sin upon sin; who go down to Egypt without consulting me; who look for help to Pharaoh's protection, to Egypt's shade for refuge."

— Isaiah 30:1,2

Revival history is filled with men and women who began in the Spirit and ended in the flesh. Floundering to secure themselves, many of them formulated plans that were not God's plans. Some even sought alliances that were not godly. Their plans became sinful because God did not breathe His life into them.

Isaiah finished his declaration with this astounding statement in verse 15:

> **This is what the Sovereign Lord, the Holy One of Israel says, "In repentance and rest is your salvation, in quietness and trust is your strength...."**

Israel and its leaders rejected such advice, but in this passage we find four major keys to the perpetuation of revival to a move of God.

First, we must first *repent of any sin* — especially of any attempt to carry out God's plan by our own efforts.

Second, we must *rest*. We must draw our lives from the One Who authored the plan to begin with. It is not our ability, but our availability, that makes the difference to God.

Third, we must *wait on the Lord in quietness*. This word *quietness* means idleness, rest, repose, or being settled.[4] It carries the connotation of being in contact with oneself. It also implies placing something for management or control in the keeping of another.

In the past we Christians have been guilty of creating programs and then trying to keep them afloat by our own efforts. The time has come that we must inquire of the Lord for His plans and then place ourselves under His management in order to accomplish them. There is a considerable difference between having a plan and asking God to bless it, and finding His plan. His plan is already blessed.

Finally, according to Isaiah 30:15, we must *trust* the Lord. *Trust* is a word that means to rely upon or adhere to, to place reliance on the ability of another, or to have faith in another person.[5]

Trust is something committed to the care of another person. All the worry, extra effort or work in the world cannot activate God's will, only trusting and adhering to His presence can bring it to pass.

Isaiah's proclamation can be summed up this way: "Turning away from your own effort and allowing God to breathe His recreated life into you will be your answer and salvation. Trusting in and submitting to His managing steps, coupled with relying upon His ability to get the job done through you, will be your sustained strength in the effort."

These are difficult words to grasp, particularly in the modern "pull-yourself-up-by-your-own-bootstraps" society in which we live.

Sin, however, in its simplest form is best expressed in the words of James: **Anyone, then, who knows the good he ought to do and doesn't do it, sins** (James 4:17).

That simple "definition" certainly has the latitude to include knowing the difference between doing God's will by our own effort and learning to rely upon Him in rest.

5. *Spirit.* It seems almost foolish to say that what takes place must be done by the Spirit, because nearly every Christian already knows that fact. Yet, somehow, it seems that we forget. It is true that in the Kingdom of God, there are no great people, only humble people whom God has chosen to use greatly.

Some Final Thoughts on Rest

The rest we seek is not simply a rejuvenation of energy. It is an *exchange* of energy — our lives for God's, through which our "vessel" is filled with a divine presence and the all-sufficiency of Christ Himself.

God asks for nothing but ourselves. Our beautiful buildings and slick programs are virtually useless to God. He does not want *what we have;* He wants *who we are.* Our rest is not in the Sabbath, but in the Lord of the Sabbath.

This rest is a call to life in union with our Divine Creator. That is why Jesus said, "Come to Me." We cannot produce it by our own efforts, but we must come to Him.

Many leaders work themselves to exhaustion, when what they really need to do is to learn to rest in the Lord. Francis Frangipane says it best, "If they spent half their time with Him in prayer and waiting before Him, they would find His supernatural accompaniment working mightily in their efforts."[6]

God's rest requires that we abide in surrender to His will. Frangipane adds, "Turmoil caused by unbelief is brought to rest by faith. Fear is arrested by trust. Questions are answered by His wisdom."[7]

We must learn to truly commune with the Holy Spirit. That is God's way to enter into His rest. (Heb. 3:7-12.)

Once I was approached by a woman who said to me, "Why do you preachers always talk about being harassed by the devil? He never bothers me!"

I replied with a statement I have often heard, "The devil does not bother those who are not bothering him."

As long as we are making progress for the Kingdom, the devil will try to deceive, discourage, kill, rob, and destroy us. There is, however, a flow of God that allows us to stay at rest in Him.

This process of flowing in harmony with the Spirit is much like swimming. When we first learn to swim, we discover that fighting the water tires us and makes forward progress more difficult.

Ezekiel saw a vision of a river flowing from under the temple altar and said that it **...was deep enough to swim in — a river that no one could cross** (Ezek. 47:5).

If an individual tries to swim it, he will only be fatigued. But if a person learns to "go with the flow," as a kind of "white-water rafting" with God at the helm, he will soon discover that the thing which fatigued him is now a source of strength. No amount of human effort can accomplish God's purpose in the earth, but an individual who knows his strength in God has no bounds.

The last issue to be examined concerning revival is: Can God do it again? In order to answer that vital question, let's look at what is involved in a return to divine destiny.

A Return to Destiny

God has ordained a destiny upon this generation.... The frightening thing, however, is that destiny can be lost.

The American church seems all dressed up with nowhere to go, drowning in "what" for lack of "why."
— Mario Murillo

T. L. Osborn was perhaps the greatest modern missionary evangelist in the world today. It is likely that he spoke face to face to more people than any other individual in the history of the Church. His initiation into ministry, however, is humble at best. He had a limited education and began ministering as a young man in a small Pentecostal Church of God.

In 1946, at age twenty-one, he and his wife, Daisy, a dynamic evangelist in her own right, spent a discouraging year as missionaries in India. They returned from overseas, sick and disappointed, and settled into a local ministry in Oregon, seemingly forever doomed to obscurity.

Then, in 1947, destiny invaded their lives. William Branham came to Portland that summer. Daisy Osborn witnessed the meeting's first night and persuaded her husband to attend the next evening. After viewing what transpired in that incredible service, T. L. Osborn recorded his own reflection:

As I watched Brother Branham minister to the sick, I was especially captivated by the deliverance of a little deaf-mute girl over whom he prayed thus: "Thou deaf and dumb spirit, I adjure thee in Jesus' name, leave the child." When he snapped his fingers, the girl heard and spoke perfectly. When I witnessed this, there seemed to be a thousand voices speaking to me at once, all in one accord saying over and over, "You can do that."[1]

In time, T. L. Osborn would not only do "that," but greater miracles as he and Mrs. Osborn ministered for decades around the world to crowds in excess of several hundred thousand.

My prayer for this book is that, as you read these pages, something will jump up inside of *you,* and you will hear God say to you, "You can do that."

The problem with a "Judges 2:10 generation," or a generation in transition, is that a sense of divine destiny is lost. That generation loses the sense of ordination that God has given to them to change their world. Instead, they settle into what I call the "yuppie syndrome."

Beginning in the 1990s, we have evolved into a society where young upper-class people no longer believe they can change the world. They are obsessed with changing themselves. They no longer believe they can make an impact in their world, so their only real concern is to make an impact on their own lives. Christians no longer feel called, commissioned, and compelled to "turn the world upside down" (Acts 17:6 KJV) for the Kingdom of God.

That is why materialism and humanism have had such a profound influence on this century. These philosophies are man's attempts to take care of himself.

Yet, God is calling His Church back to an increased sense of divine destiny. It is His covenant understanding that man's needs will be met, but His heartbeat does not end there. God meets a person's needs so that individual can in turn become a needmeeter. Jesus heals His Body in order for it to become a vessel to heal. He delivers an individual to become a deliverer. He touches humanity with a destiny to transform the world in accordance to His Kingdom.

What is destiny? *Destiny* is a design or appointment to a distinct purpose or end. It is the understanding of a preordained plan of God for a person's life. No one will ever do anything truly great without a sense of destiny. That feeling is a realization of a call that God has placed squarely and distinctly upon him or her as an individual. No two people's destiny is quite alike.

The trigger to destiny is *revelation*. I like to define *revelation* as something always known, but never realized. The awareness of destiny gives way to a realization of God's purpose in an individual's life.

Many people, however, steer clear of words like destiny because of their association with controversial religious terms such as "predestination." The theology of predestination has become a complex debate that frightens them away from the securing of destiny in their own personal lives.

The prefix *pre* means before. *Destination* refers to a journey's desired end. Therefore the word *predestination* simply expresses the idea that God knows the desired end of a journey — mine, yours, the Church's, and the entire world's — before its beginning.

God Does Not Start Until He Finishes

Bahamian evangelist Myles Munroe suggested that the real meaning here is that *God never begins a thing until He finishes it*. When it is finished in His mind, He looks back and says, "Now we can begin." That is why the Scriptures can say:

> **For he chose us in him** [Christ] **before the creation of the world to be holy and blameless in his sight. In love he predestined us to be adopted as his sons through Jesus Christ, in accordance with his pleasure and will....**
>
> **In him we were also chosen, having been predestined according to the plan of him who works out everything in conformity with the purpose of his will.**
>
> **— Ephesians 1:4,5,11**

In other words, the Council of Heaven got together and planned out creation, the progression of humankind, the possibility of the fall of mankind, and their redemption in Christ. Once heaven finished the work in the mind of God, He said, "Okay, now We can begin."

God said to Isaiah:

> **"Remember this, fix it in mind, take it to heart...**[Evidently, what is about to follow is of imminent importance, for three times and in three different ways He says, "Pay attention."]
>
> **Remember the former things, those of long ago; I am God, and there is no other; I am God, and there is none like me.**
>
> **I make known the end from the beginning, from ancient times, what is still to come. I say: My purpose will stand, and I will do all that I please."**
>
> **— Isaiah 46:8-10**

God did not start until He finished. Scripturally speaking, Jesus did not die two thousand years ago, He **...was slain from the creation of the world** (Rev. 13:8).

Jesus said, "No man takes my life, I give it." (John 10:18.) When He came to earth, it was a "done deal." He knew His purpose, His destiny on the earth. As His disciples, the same should be true of us. We do not have to be surprised, and we do not have to experiment. God has a plan for us. If we ask Him, He will make that plan clear to us so that we can cooperate with Him in fulfilling it. It is time we stopped being busy and started being effective.[2]

Destiny is the awareness of God's purpose or intent in a person's life. Destiny gives birth to revelation, which is a realization of what is known. Destiny is the defining of the awareness that God has placed in the heart of each one of His children.

God has ordained a destiny upon this generation. That destiny is the raising up of a new generation to make known His ways and power. As ambassadors for Christ, we are called to establish God's Kingdom on the earth. This is a generation of revival that is destined to become an irresistible move of the Almighty.

The frightening thing, however, is that destiny can be lost. People can forfeit their purpose in God through disobedience, neglect, or apathy, or by viewing their God-given destiny too lightly. God will accomplish His purpose in the earth, but if not through us, He will wait for a new generation.

God never panics. He has eternity on His side, and He will find Himself a group of human beings who will be His people. He will establish His will and purpose in His time.

The Bible is filled with examples of people who lost their destinies. One of the most fascinating accounts is found in Genesis 11:31,32:

> **Terah took his son Abram, his grandson Lot son of Haran, and his daughter-in-law Sarai, the wife of his son Abram, and together they set out from Ur of the Chaldeans to go to Canaan. But when they came to Haran, they settled there.**
>
> **Terah lived 205 years, and he died in Haran.**

At first perusal of this passage, it seems like an insignificant event: "Abram's father died in Haran at two hundred and five years of age." The significance is found in the fact that *it was Terah*, Abraham's father, who was called to lead his family to Canaan, not Abraham. (v. 31.)

Notice two key words in verse 31 — *came* and *settled*. The word *came* could be translated to cause to come in,[3] by implication here referring to a stopping place. In other words, Terah came to Haran where he "stopped" and "settled." He stopped half-way to his destination (his ultimate destiny) and thereby settled for less than God's best.[4]

A certain mentality has arisen in the Church that would hold that part way is better than no way. Part way, however, is forfeiting of God's best. We have healing services and get excited about healing hangnails — while walking right by those poor people confined to wheelchairs. We compare ourselves to others in the Body of Christ and say that we are better, thinking we have something they do not have.

It is easy to compare ourselves to others, if they are still back at Ur of the Chaldeans, and we at least are in Haran. However, what good is Haran if our destiny is Canaan? That would be like me comparing myself to Pee-Wee Herman and, thus, feeling that I was Arnold Schwartzenegger.

We can never compare ourselves to anyone or anything but God's destinies for *our* lives. The destiny of this generation of believers *is the revival of all that God has for the Church.* We cannot stop and settle for anything less. As noted, the Bible is, however, filled with examples of people who lost their destiny.

Adam and Eve lost their destiny because they deliberately disobeyed God by partaking of the one fruit that was expressly forbidden to them by their loving Creator. There is always at least one thing in our lives that can be a roadblock to God's destiny for us. If, like Adam and Eve, we do not heed God's warning, we too will forfeit our divine destiny in this life.

Esau lost his destiny. He should have had the Hebrew birthright of a double portion of his father's inheritance, but he sold it for a pot of stew. (Gen. 25.) The writer of the Book of Hebrews later tells us that Esau looked for a place of repentance and restoration, but he could find none. (Heb.12:16,17.)

Moses was destined to lead the people of God out of Egypt and into the Promised Land, but because of his disobedience to God, he was never allowed to set foot in that blessed place.

Eli, the high priest in Samuel's day, lost his destiny because of his failure to bring up his two sons "in the way they should go." Their subsequent unfaithfulness even cost his life and theirs. (1 Sam. 4.)

Aaron's sons, Nadab and Abihu, lost their places and their lives, because they offered improper sacrifices. (Num. 3:2,3.)

Because he acted improperly and in disobedience to the word of the Lord, Saul, king of Israel, lost his destiny:

> **"You acted foolishly,"** Samuel said [to Saul]. **"You have not kept**
> **the command the Lord your God gave you; if you had, he would**
> **have established your kingdom over Israel for all time. But now**
> **your kingdom will not endure...."**
> — 1 Samuel 13:13,14

Even Jerusalem, the city of God, missed her purpose
"...because [she] **did not recognize the time of God's coming to** [her]"
(Luke 19:44).

It is possible for God's planned destiny to be thwarted, but it
never frustrates God. He simply waits for a generation who will
believe Him to establish His purpose on the earth.

Is America Losing Her Destiny?

I believe that the United States of America is a nation that was
established by God to promote (Christian) liberty in the world.
However, I also believe that America is in jeopardy of losing her
destiny. The *Almanac of the Christian World* printed these star-
tling statistics concerning our nation:

Every day in the United States:

- 2,975 teenage girls get pregnant.
- 372 teenage girls have miscarriages.
- 689 babies are born to women who have had inadequate
  prenatal care.
- 67 babies die before one month of life.
- 105 babies die before their first birthday.
- 27 children die from poverty.
- 10 children are killed by guns.
- 30 children are wounded by guns.
- 6 teenagers commit suicide.

- 135,000 children take a gun to school.
- 7,742 teenagers become sexually active.
- 623 teenagers get syphilis or gonorrhea.
- 211 children are arrested for drug abuse.
- 437 children are arrested for drunken driving or drinking.
- 1,512 teenagers drop out of school.
- 1,849 children are abused or neglected.
- 3,228 children run away from home.
- 1,629 children are in adult jails.
- 2,556 children are born out of wedlock.
- 2,986 children see their parents divorced.[5]

In a similar survey, the almanac reported the seven major problems in schools in 1940 as compared to today.[6]

1940	Today
1) Talking	1) Drug Abuse
2) Chewing gum	2) Alcohol Abuse
3) Making noise	3) Pregnancy
4) Running in the hall	4) Suicide
5) Getting out of line	5) Rape
6) Wearing improper clothes	6) Robbery
7) Not putting paper in the wastebasket	7) Assault

The moral and spiritual disintegration in America is astounding. How can we call ourselves a Christian nation when forty-four hundred babies are killed daily in abortuaries, only five percent of our teenagers attend church, ten percent of Americans are addicted to cocaine, child abuse is the number one killer in children under five, the number of AIDS cases is projected to rise to ten million in ten years, one million teens run away from home every year, suicide is the second leading killer among college students, eating disorders are rampant, and still one out of every two new marriages ends in divorce?

Teenagers are adopting a wrong set of role models. America and the world desperately need for the Church of Jesus Christ to wake up and realize her destiny. Unless America repents, she is in jeopardy of losing her destiny, and the negative impact on us and our children will be incalculable, to say nothing of the devastating effect on the Church and the world.

We seem to be stalled in what I call "the Terah principle." We can "stop" and "settle" here, or press on to a revival that will give birth to the next move of God. During the last five years of the Eighties, the number of born-again believers in the United States increased from thirty-three to thirty-eight percent. Yet, today the influence of Christianity on our nation as a whole is less than it was in the past.

We are turning out high-maintenance, low-impact Christians. The fire and destiny of God needs to be reinvested in the Body of Christ.

Why did Terah stop and settle short of his destination? The passage does not say.

Perhaps, to put it in modern-day terms, he had a nice riverside condo, all his bills paid, and box seats at all the Giants and Forty-Niners games. Maybe it was something more than mere apathy. The point is not *why* he stopped, but the fact *that* he stopped.

The Lord has shown me some elements that destroy destiny in a person, and the same things would be true in a corporate body — the local church or the Universal Church. In the next and final chapter of this book, let's look at these things to see if we can determine what can be done about them.

Chapter 20

Overcoming the Terah Principle

Several attempts were made on his life and also on the life of Maria Woodworth-Etter, but all of them failed.

Several years ago in my ministry, while I was still serving a pastorate in East Texas, I encountered a situation whose fate became its destiny.

A member in my church asked me if I would witness to a local judge who was dying with cancer. He was unsure of this judge's eternal condition and hoped that I could lead him to Christ.

Later that day I arrived at the judge's home. What I witnessed was almost shocking. What had formerly been a tall, strapping robust specimen of manhood was now reduced to an emaciated shell of humanity in the last stages of malignant cancer.

After the shock of his condition wore off, I got to know this delightful man. As the conversation progressed, I finally asked him, if he died, was he certain that he would go to heaven? Graciously, in the moments that followed, it was my privilege to lead this judge to Jesus Christ.

After some rejoicing following our prayer, I got ready to go. As I was leaving his bedroom, I was arrested by the Holy Spirit. I turned to him and said, "Judge, do you know that Jesus can heal your body as well?"

His shocked look told me he had never heard of a healing Jesus. I proceeded to tell him the wonderful story from the Bible of how Jesus still heals today.

He was utterly fascinated as I unfolded the Scriptures to him. He asked me if I had any materials about this newfound discovery of the healing virtue of Christ.

Later that week, I took my new friend a series of six tapes containing healing messages I had recently preached in the church. He listened to all of them the first day.

The next time I saw him, he looked at me and said, "Ron, God's going to heal me, because He's got a destiny for my life."

That was the first time I realized that God does not want to heal an individual simply so he will be well, but because He has a wonderful plan for his life, a destiny to destroy the works of the devil.

The judge looked at me and said, "The next time you see me, I'll be sitting on my bed. The next time, I'll stand. The next time, I'll walk to my bedroom door. Our next visit will be in my living room. I'm going to get better, Ron, until I can stand in your pulpit and tell the world that the healing power of God has touched a man in East Texas."

To my delight, this faith-filled judge prophesied his own fate. My biweekly visits were almost the literal progression he spoke to me about.

One day I arrived for my normal visit, and to my surprise, my new friend was not home. Later that week, I got a call from the judge. He had been to M. D. Anderson Hospital in Houston where the medical staff happily reported that they could not find a single trace of cancer anywhere in his body. Within two weeks, the judge fulfilled his own words as he stood in my pulpit to tell the congregation of a healing Jesus Who had encountered and forever altered his life.

That was the beginning of my discovery that God does not want us well simply because of His great love for us, but that He also wants us well for a purpose — to fulfill a destiny.

The Seven-Fold Cycle That Kills Destiny

I have seen a seven-fold cycle that kills destiny in a person.

The first cycle is *fear.* Destiny calls a person to the cutting edge and demands the willingness to pay a price. The appropriation of God's destiny for you and me is not without cost. In the beginnings of their ministries, every great revivalist paid the price not to settle for less than God's best, even if they had great falls in later years.

John Alexander Dowie was arrested one hundred times in one year for practicing medicine without a license as he prayed for the sick. Several attempts were made on his life and also on the life of Maria Woodworth-Etter, but all of them failed. In Dowie's earliest years of revelation, his friends failed and rejected him, but God was there to shore him up and to lead him step by step. Perhaps the greatest lesson to be learned from Dowie is that *paying the price to overcome persecution is the key to success.*

Oral Roberts once told me the things he considered prerequisites for a great world-shaking ministry.

• *A person must know God.* That should go without saying, but it is essential to know Him, not about Him.

• *He must have an "entrepreneurial spirit."* He must be disciplined about his schedule and able to organize business details. Also, the mark of a good administrator is his ability to delegate. William Branham paid a tremendous price at the end of his ministry for his lack of administrative skills.

• *He must take care of his body.* Oral Roberts' resiliency from stress or criticism and the longevity of his ministry are legendary among his peers.

• *He must be able to take the heat if God gives him a plan.* It stands to reason that the devil will challenge the implementation of the plan of God. Only those who can tolerate the heat will reach their full destiny.

Many past leaders learned to pay the price. Winkie Pratney wrote about the persecution that often came against those in the early days of the Pentecostal move:

> Some were hated, spat on, even shot at. Religious leaders named them in derision at first, "holy rollers" and "tongue talkers." Eventually, seeing they were here to stay, they called them "Pentecostals."[1]

Those people fasted, prayed, and paid a price in order to usher in what they knew was an incredible sense of destiny for their time.

Yet many a person's destiny is derailed by fear. However, unlike many people I have heard speak on this subject, I do not believe it is wrong to experience fear, nor is it a sin to fear. It is whether an individual gets in agreement with it or gives way to it that makes the difference. Initial fear in a crises does not negate or invalidate a victory if one knows what to do with it. Paul said it this way:

> **Do not be anxious** [or fearful] **about anything, but in everything, by prayer and petition, with thanksgiving, present your requests to God. And the peace of God, which transcends all understanding, will guard your hearts and your minds in Christ Jesus.**
>
> — Philippians 4:6,7

The difference between those who reach their destinies and those who "stop and settle" is what they do with fear. Those who learn to inquire of the Lord will never be turned back. Those who submit to fear will always be defeated just short of the finish line.

Remember the example of Jehoshaphat in the chapter on worship? He inquired of the Lord, and God not only gave him peace, but victory.

Second, I have found that fear is often transformed into *fatigue*, or weariness. Fear is a negative emotion that will weary the person who does not know how to deal with it.

Third, fatigue leaves an individual prey to *disappointment*. Coming into the 1990s, that is all I heard: "This person fell, that one abused me." I say it is time for the Body of Christ "to get through what we are going through." A human being may disappoint you, but God never disappoints those who truly know Him. It is time to look at God and not people. We have a choice: We can "stop and settle" or we can inquire of the Lord.

Fourth, disappointment gives way to *deception*. We are now in and dealing with a generation that is struggling to understand whether they can really make a difference. It is the deception of the age. We are destined to be a "new generation of God" reaching our natural generation in the world. But that will not happen if we listen to the voice of despair, discouragement, depression. and disillusionment.

Fifth, deception leads to *lethargy*. Lethargy is "indifference," an attitude that the writer of Proverbs called casting off restraint (Prov. 29:18.)

Lethargic people say, "What's the use? It doesn't matter anyway.

Sixth, lethargy gives way to *sin,* and, seventh, sin leads to *destruction.*

How many destinies have been derailed by this cycle of deception? How many moves have been halted because a person's awareness of God's purpose has been darkened by the shadow of the enemy?

As we have seen, it is possible for God to be doing a "new thing," and His people be entirely unaware of it. There is a revival in the birth canal. Do you not realize it? Transition is coming to an end, and God is about to give birth to a new move of His Spirit. Are we ready to appropriate our destiny?

We Must Appropriate Our Destinies

The writer of the Book of 2 Kings records such a time of crisis and decision in Judah's history.[2] The nation was in a shambles following years of unbelief and idolatry. The temple had fallen into disrepair and even been desecrated by King Manasseh. On the throne in this time was an eight-year-old boy named Josiah. For almost twenty years of his reign, Josiah was a "do-nothing," a pathetic excuse for a king. His biggest concern was what kind of wallpaper should go into the restored temple of God.

Yet, something thoroughly transformed him from an apathetic do-nothing to a radical powerhouse for the kingdom. In a split second, he was transformed from a Peewee Herman to an Arnold Schwartzenegger for God.

In the eighteenth year of his reign, Josiah began to repair the temple and to restore it to its former condition. What transpired as a result of that renovation is told in 2 Kings:

> **Hilkiah the high priest said to Shaphan the secretary, "I have found the Book of the Law in the temple of the Lord." He gave it to Shaphan, who read it.**
>
> **— 2 Kings 22:8**

Evidently, Manasseh or Amon, who preceded Josiah, had attempted to destroy all copies of this book, or there had been years of priests who no longer operated righteously in their offices. For the sake of the destiny of Judah, this was an extremely important find.

The story continues:

> **Then Shaphan the secretary informed the king, "Hilkiah the priest has given me a book." And Shaphan read from it in the presence of the king.**
>
> **When the king heard the words of the Book of the Law, he tore his robes.**
>
> **— 2 Kings 22:10,11**

One night Shaphan, the secretary, took the boy-wonder king a bedtime snack and decided to read to him from the rediscovered book. Suddenly, in the middle of the reading, Josiah screamed at the top of his lungs. This is certainly not normal procedure by the standards of our day.

Knowing the young man as they did, the palace staff must have thought that something drastic had taken place, such as his copy of *Better Homes and Gardens* or *Wallpaper Digest* had run out. Without warning, God had suddenly invaded Josiah's lethargic state. As a result, the youthful king received a vivid revelation of how far he and his people had departed from God's declared will.

What did Shaphan read that day? No one knows for sure. Theologians and Bible scholars speculate that it might have been a copy of Deuteronomy or perhaps the entire Pentateuch (the first five books of the Old Testament). I like to imagine, however, that Shaphan read the account of Josiah's own pre-recorded history.

Three hundred and fifty years before that night in Josiah's palace, these words were recorded:

> **By the word of the Lord a man of God came from Judah to Bethel, as Jeroboam was standing by the altar to make an offering. He cried out against the altar by the word of the Lord: "O altar, altar! This is what the Lord says: 'A son named Josiah will be born to the house of David. On you he will sacrifice the priests of the high places who now make offerings here, and human bones will be burned on you." That same day the man of God gave a sign: "This is the sign the Lord has declared: The altar will be split apart and the ashes on it will be poured out."**
>
> **When King Jeroboam heard what the man of God cried out against the altar at Bethel** [which he had presumptuously erected], **he stretched out his hand from the altar and said, "Seize him!" But the hand he stretched out toward the man shriveled up, so that he could not pull it back. Also, the altar was split apart and its ashes poured out according to the sign given by the man of God by the word of the Lord.**
>
> **— 1 Kings 13:1-5**

What an absolutely incredible prophetic unfolding! Three hundred and fifty years before Josiah, an unnamed, seemingly insignificant prophet showed up before the man who was the first king of the northern kingdom of Israel after its division into two nations. And that prophet described the events that were to occur hundreds of years later concerning a king of Judah, the southern kingdom — including the exact name of that future king.

Our Names Are Written in the Book

The implication for us is simple: *Things don't always have to be this way.* There may be apathy, fear, and sin, but God intends to raise up a people who will change all that.

Outraged at the prophet's denunciation of his ways, King Jeroboam cried out for his accuser to be seized and punished. The Bible says that as he reached out to give the order to apprehend the prophet, his hand shriveled up. That's the kind of thing that will quench criticism in a real hurry!

I have no evidence that this passage is what was read to King Josiah, but, if it were, can you imagine the impact it would have had upon his life? Everything he was destined to accomplish for God was amazingly recorded three hundred and fifty years before the event. That would be like us finding a book written in 1645 describing what we were purposed to do in 1997. Suddenly, our whole sense of destiny would change!

Whether the king actually heard his own prophetic history read that night or not, the principle is still the same: *Josiah realized that his name was written in the Book.* Even if he never saw or heard the prophesy about himself, he was made to realize how far he and his people had strayed from God and that something had to be done about that perilous situation. Precisely as was recorded in the prophesy, Josiah fulfilled its tenets. Second Kings 23:24,25 records what happened.

> ...This he [Josiah] **did to fulfill the requirements of the law writ-
ten in the book that Hilkiah the priest had discovered in the temple
of the Lord. Neither before nor after Josiah was there a king like
him who turned to the Lord as he did — with all his heart and with
all his soul and with all his strength, in accordance with all the Law
of Moses.**

What happened to transform a "wimp" into a king so that
there was not another like him "neither before nor after" his
reign? *He realized that his name was in the Book.*

This is not an isolated scriptural principle. On the Day of
Pentecost, Peter stood and proclaimed to the masses who had
gathered together because of the outpouring of the Spirit of God,
"...this is what was spoken by the prophet Joel..." (Acts 2:16).

In other words, Peter said, "What Joel prophesied hundreds of
years ago is now taking place in our midst. Our names are written in the Book! That word spoken so long ago by the prophet
Joel was describing the destiny of our generation."

The Bible tells us in Daniel 9 that after years of Judah's captivity in Babylon, Persia conquered the Babylonian empire. Daniel,
now an old man, was reading what must have been Jeremiah
29:10 where the prophet had recorded the word he had received
from the Lord about the future destiny of captive Judah:

> **This is what the Lord says: "When seventy years are completed
for Babylon, I will come to you and fulfill my gracious promise to
bring you back to this place. For I know the plans I have for you,"
declares the Lord, "plans to prosper you and not to harm you, plans
to give you hope and a future. Then you will call upon me and come
and pray to me, and I will listen to you. You will seek me and find
me when you seek me with all your heart. I will be found by you,"
declares the Lord, "and will bring you back from captivity."**
> **— Jeremiah 29:10-14**

Daniel realized that *his name was written in the Book*. As a result, he began to pray, and thus secured the release of a nation.

Esther, in the midst of Persian bondage, was told by Mordecai, her cousin and guardian, that she had been elevated to royal position **...for such a time as this...**(Esther 4:14). She realized that she had been granted favor to save her people from destruction. Her name was in the Book.

Once we realize that our names are in the Book, we can fulfill our destinies. The power of God is released when destiny is realized. Long ago, in Old Testament days, the prophet Haggai foresaw and foretold a generation like ours:

> **"This is what the Lord Almighty says: 'In a little while I will once more shake the heavens and the earth, the sea and the dry land. I will shake all nations, and the desired of all nations will come, and I will fill this house with glory,' says the Lord Almighty. 'The silver is mine and the gold is mine,' declares the Lord Almighty. 'The glory of this present house will be greater than the glory of the former house,' says the Lord Almighty."**

> **— Haggai 2:6-9**

God will never be outdone by a previous generation. He is saving His best for last. The culminating move of His Spirit will be the most powerful ever unleashed. Not only can He do it again, but the "new thing" of God will be the best thing of God. The greatest churches are yet to be built. The greatest signs and wonders are yet to be performed. The greatest move is yet to be accomplished.

But in order for us to see all this come to pass in our day, in order for us to have a part in God's greatest revival of the ages we must realize that our names are written in the Book. Then our destinies will be brought to life through that revelation, and a new move will be birthed. Then the thing we have always known but never realized can be appropriated.

I have heard people say, "The glory days of the Church are gone."

However, Paul said that the gifts and calling of God are "without repentance." (Rom. 11:29 KJV.) The *New International Version* translates this verse, **for God's gifts and his call are irrevocable.** Once God purposes a thing, He never falters in His resolve. Once He bestows a gift, He never takes it back. We can fail in His purpose for us, we can deny His gifts to us, invalidate them, or even lose them, but if we repent and are restored to God, the call is as valid as it was when He first gave it.

With the help of His Holy Spirit, we *will* fulfill the purposes of God — if we do not quit.

Conclusion:

God Will Not Be Defeated

God will accomplish His purpose in the earth no matter how negative the facts may appear. He is looking for a generation that will rise up and believe Him again. That generation will be a generation of a "new thing" that God will do in the earth.

In His Word, God has declared, "**...I say: My purpose will stand, and I will do all that I please**" (Is. 46:10).

I once heard Myles Munroe make this statement, "Whenever someone as rich as God invests His prize possession in a dying market, that means He knows something about the market no one else knows."

Revival is a divine attack on the world's system. Revival is fatal. It is fatal to the kingdom of darkness.

Winkie Pratney wrote that revivals are "like a temporary glimpse of heaven to humanity; a transient glimpse of what it is like living in the manifest glory of God."[1]

He also wrote that revival is similar to the famous military principle known as *force,* "A commander husbands his reserves, concentrates them at a strategic point for a vital blow at a crucial moment."[2]

We are at a crucial moment in history, one in which God is raising up a new generation of destiny. The "Jesus Movement" in the Sixties was based on radicalism and rebellion. The move of the Nineties was one of radicalism and redefinition. Today,

the coming move must not only recover past truths but also rede-
fine them in new relevance to this generation. Our destiny will
be given birth from redefinition to revelation. Then that which
we have known we will also realize.

Our heritage is great, our future is greater. I again hear the
writer of Hebrews bringing us back to where we began:

**Remember your leaders, who spoke the word of God to you.
Consider the outcome of their way of life and imitate their faith.**

— Hebrews 13:7

What we have seen reviewed in this book is an inspiring piece
of spiritual history. Indeed we are indebted to these men and
women of our past as a source of true inspiration. But the next
verse from the writer of Hebrews puts all of that glorious history
into context: **Jesus Christ is the same yesterday and today and forever** (Heb.13:8).

What He did then, He will do today, and yes, even greater
things.

What we have seen in people like John Alexander Dowie,
Maria Woodworth-Etter, Evan Roberts, Charles Parham,
William Seymour, John G. Lake, Smith Wigglesworth, Aimee
Semple McPherson, William Branham, Oral Roberts, A. A.
Allen, Jack Coe, Kathryn Kuhlman, and others too numerous to
mention, we will see again.

To those great saints who preceded them, such as Zwingli,
Luther, Calvin, Whitfield, the Wesleys, Edwards, Finney,
Moody, and many others, we are deeply indebted.

However, it is now time for a new generation to come forward. Truly, the Church has had great revivalists to get the fire
started. Now it is our job to keep the flame of revival burning!

Endnotes

᠙᠙᠙

for The Quest for Revival

by

Ron McIntosh

Introduction

1 Dale Carnegie, *How To Win Friends and Influence People,* rev. ed. (New York: Simon and Schuster, 1981 by Donna Dale and Dorothy Carnegie).

Chapter 1

[1] Lester Sumrall, "I Saw the Glory," cassette tape.

[2] *Ibid.*

[3] Gordon Lindsay, *John Alexander Dowie* (Dallas: Christ for the Nations, 1980), p. 22.

[4] *Ibid.,* p. 23.

[5] *Ibid.,* p. 26.

[6] *Ibid.,* p. 16.

[7] *Ibid.,* p. 107.

[8] *Ibid.,* pp. 120,125.

[9] Gordon Lindsay, *Maria Woodworth-Etter: Her Life and Ministry* (Dallas: Christ for the Nations Inc., 1976), p. 18; and Maria Woodworth-Etter, *Diary of Signs and Wonders* (Tulsa: Harrison House, Inc., 1916), p. 29.

[10] Junia or *Iounian* could have been a common female name or the shortened form of a less common male name. For more information, see: Mary Evans, *Women in the Bible* (Exeter: Paternoster, 1983), p. 124.

[11] Woodworth-Etter, p. 73.

[12] Recounted from Sister Edith Heflin from a service in the early 1900s.

[13] Lindsay, *Maria Woodworth-Etter.*

[14] Woodworth-Etter, pp. 181,182.

[15] Colin C. Whittaker, *Seven Pentecostal Pioneers* (Springfield: Gospel Publishing House, 1983), p. 45.

[16] *Ibid.,* p. 46.

[17] *Ibid.,* p. 58.

18 *Ibid.*, p. 60. (Stephen Jeffreys and his brother, George, later formed the Elim Pentecostal denomination in Great Britain.)

Chapter 2

1 *Dictionary of Pentecostal and Charismatic Movements* (Grand Rapids: Zondervan Publishing House, 1989), p. 660.

2 *Ibid.*, pp. 660,657.

3 Charles F. Parham, "The Latter Rain," included in *The Life of Charles F. Parham: Founder of the Apostolic Faith Movement* by Sarah F. Parham (Joplin: Hunter Printing, 1969), pp. 51,52; quoted from: Donald W. Dayton, *Theological Roots of Pentecostalism* (Grand Rapids: Francis Asbury Press, 1987), p. 20.

4 James F. Goff in his book, *Fields White Unto Harvest* (Fayetteville: University of Arkansas Press, 1988), disputes Parham's account. Goff cites Agnes Ozman as saying, "Before receiving the Comforter, I did not know I would speak in tongues when I received the Holy Spirit, for I did not know it was in the Bible." I fully acknowledge discrepancies in the two accounts, but will leave the dispute for the historians to settle. I do believe, however, that there is evidence that Parham was moving his students to the concept of tongues being an initial evidence of the baptism of the Holy Spirit. Goff's book also disputes the time when Miss Ozman received the baptism, quoting her as saying that the actual occurrence took place the following day, not at the turn-of-the-century hour.

5 Gordon Lindsay, *They Saw It Happen* (Dallas: Christ for the Nations Institute, 1986), pp. 5,6.

6 *Ibid.*, p. 6.

7 *Ibid.*, p. 7.

8 *Ibid.*, p. 9.

9 *Ibid.*

10 *Dictionary*, p. 780.

11 Frank Bartleman, *Azusa Street* (Plainfield: Logos International, 1980), p. 58.

12 *Ibid.*, p. 60.

[13] *Ibid.*, p. 59.

[14] *Ibid.*; taken from a television show by Mario Murillo.

[15] Wilford Reidt, *John G. Lake: A Man Without Compromise* (Tulsa: Harrison House, 1989), p. 17.

[16] Gordon Lindsay, *John G. Lake: Apostle to Africa* (Dallas: Christ for the Nations Inc., 1987), p. 18.

[17] *Ibid.*

[18] *Ibid.*, p. 19.

[19] *Dictionary*, p. 532.

[20] Lindsay, *John G. Lake: Apostle to Africa*, p. 29.

[21] *Ibid.*, p. 4.

[22] *Ibid.*, pp. 53,54.

[23] Reidt, pp. 77,78.

[24] *Dictionary*, p. 531.

[25] Jack H. Davies, *The Life of Smith Wigglesworth* (Ann Arbor: Servant Publications, 1987), pp. 70,71.

[26] Lester Sumrall, "I Saw the Glory," cassette tape (South Bend: LeSea Ministries).

[27] Davies, p. 18.

[28] Albert Hibbert, *Smith Wigglesworth: The Secret of His Power* (Tulsa: Harrison House, 1982), p. 19.

[29] *Ibid.*, p. 27.

[30] *Dictionary*, pp. 568,569. Much of the story of Mrs. McPherson is taken from C. M. Robeck, Jr.'s article on her in this volume.

[31] Roberts Liardon, "The Healing Evangelists," tape series, tape 4 (P. O. Box 30710, Laguna Hills, California: Roberts Liardon Ministries).

[32] David Edwin Harrell, Jr., *All Things Are Possible* (Bloomington: Indiana University Press, 1975), p. 18.

[33] Gordon Lindsay, *William Branham: A Man Sent From God* Jeffersonville: William Branham, 1950), p. 30.

[34] *Dictionary*, p. 95.

[35] Douglas C. Weaver, *The Healer-Prophet: William Marrion Branham* (Macon: Mercer University Press, 1987), p. 33.

[36] *Ibid.*, p. 81.

[37] Lindsay, *Branham*, p. 77.

[38] *Ibid.*, p. 171.

[39] *Ibid.*, pp. 172,173.

[40] Weaver, p. 57.

Chapter 3

[1] Winkle Pratney, *Revival* (Springdale: Whitaker House, 1984), p. 17.

[2] Charles Finney, *How To Experience Revival* (Springdale: Whitaker House, 1984), p. 10.

[3] *The Amplified Bible*; James Strong, *Strong's Exhaustive Concordance of the Bible* (Nashville: Abingdon, 1890), "Greek Dictionary of the New Testament," p. 12, entry #403; Joseph Henry Thayer, *Thayer's Greek-English Lexicon of the New Testament* (Grand Rapids: Baker Book House, 1977), p. 43, entries #403, 404.

Chapter 4

[1] Lindsay, *They Saw It Happen*, p. 12.

[2] Pratney, p. 15.

[3] *Ibid.*

[4] Finney, p. 11.

[5] Ralph Mahoney, *Is a New Wave of Revival Coming?* (Burbank: World Missionary Alliance Plan, 1982), pp. 47,48.

[6] George T. B. Davis, *When the Fire Fell* (Salem: Schmul Publishing Company, 1983), p. 15.

[7] Pratney, pp. 125,126.

[8] Lindsay, *Dowie*, p. 195.

[9] Pratney, p. 191.

[10] *Ibid.*, p. 166

[11] *Ibid.*, p. 186.

[12] Bartleman, p. 15.

[13] *Ibid.*, p. 17.

[14] Oswald J. Smith, *Passion for Souls* (Burlington, Ontario: Welch Publishing Company, 1986), p. 26.

[15] *Ibid.*

[16] Mario Murillo, *Critical Mass* (Chatsworth: Anthony Douglas Publishing Company, 1985), p. 25.

[17] *Ibid.*, p. 26.

[18] Bartleman, p. 34

[19] *Ibid.*

[20] *Ibid.*

[21] *Ibid.*

[22] Hibbert, p. 41.

[23] Reidt, p. 49.

[24] *Ibid.*, p. 51.

[25] George Lamsa, *The Holy Bible from the Ancient Eastern Translators* (San Francisco: Harper & Row Publishers, 1933), as quoted in Mahoney, p. 76.

[26] Mahoney, p. 76

[27] Reidt, p. 80.

Chapter 5

[1] Thoughts adapted from a message delivered by Jerry Savelle, "Where Are the Elijahs of God?" (Fort Worth: Jerry Savelle Ministries.)

[2] James Strong, *The New Strong's Exhaustive Concordance of the Bible* (Nashville: Thomas Nelson Publishers, 1984), "Greek Dictionary of the New Testament," p. 76, entry #5426.

[3] *Webster's 7th Collegiate Dictionary* (Springfield, Massachusetts: G. & C. Merriam Co., 1963), s.v. "muse," "amuse."

4   James Strong, *Strong's Exhaustive Concordance of the Bible* (Nashville: Abingdon, 1890), "Greek Dictionary of the New Testament," based on definition of "fervently," p. 34, entry #2204.

5   H. W. F. Gesenius, *Gesenius' Hebrew-Chaldee Lexicon to the Old Testament Scriptures* (Grand Rapids: Baker Book House, 1979), p. 427, entries #3820, 3824.

6   Lindsay, *Branham*, p. 179.

7   *Ibid.*, p. 173.

8   Hibbert, p. 80.

9   Lindsay, *Dowie,* p. 186.

10 Interpretation of Strong, p. 66, entries #4726, 4727 as derived from entry #9727.

11 Personal interview with Charles F. Parham's granddaughter, Pauline Parham, conducted at Christ for the Nations Institute, Dallas, Texas, February 1992.

12 Harrell, p. 81.

13 *Ibid.*

Chapter 6

1   Reidt, p. 24.

2   *Ibid.*, p. 25.

3   Lindsay, *They Saw It Happen*, pp. 14,15.

4   Pratney, pp. 132,133.

5   Hibbert, p. 53.

6   Lindsay, *They Saw It Happen*, p. 17.

7   *Ibid.*

8   *Ibid.*, p. 18.

9   Roberts Liardon, *Kathryn Kuhlman* (Tulsa: Harrison House, 1990), p. 77. Quotes are taken from one of Kathryn Kuhlman's messages, "Jesus Christ Is All in All."

10 *Ibid.*, p. 78.

11 *Ibid.*

[12]   *Ibid.*

[13]   *Ibid.*, p. 79.

Chapter 7

[1]   Thayer, pp. 214,215, entries #1744, 1745, 1746.

[2]   *Ibid.*, pp. 351,352, entries #2841, 2842.

[3]   Hibbert, p. 50.

[4]   Thayer, p. 572, entry #4570.

[5]   *Ibid.*, p. 399, entry #3306.

[6]   Strong, p. 69, entry #4893.

[7]   *Ibid.*, p. 41, entry #2743 and Webster, s.v. "sear."

Chapter 8

[1]   Liardon, p. 66.

[2]   *Ibid.*, pp. 67,68.

[3]   Harrell, p. 6.

[4]   Lindsay, *Dowie*, p. 273.

[5]   *Ibid.*, p. 74.

[6]   *Ibid.*, p. 75.

[7]   *Ibid.*, p. 93.

[8]   Lindsay, *They Saw It Happen,* p. 45.

[9]   *Ibid.*

[10]   Hibbert, p. 103.

[11]   Roberts Liardon, *Smith Wigglesworth*, vol. 5, *God's Generals,* Infinity Video, 1988.

[12]   Hibbert, p. 90.

[13]   Lindsay, *Branham*, pp. 92-94.

Chapter 9

1 Some of these thoughts were derived from Mario Murillo.

2 Liardon, *Kathryn Kuhlman,* p. 66.

3 Hibbert, p. 91.

4 *Ibid.,* p. 19.

5 *Ibid.,* p. 40.

6 Gesenius, p. 293, entry #2617, p. 765, entry #7355.

7 Webster, s.v. "compassion."

8 Smith, *Passion for Souls*, p. 59.

Chapter 10

1 Webster, s.v. "momentum."

2 Murillo, p. 62.

3 Webster, s.v. "hunger"; Strong, p. 45, entry #3042, and p. 56, entry #3983; and a sermon by Larry Stockstill

4 Roberts Liardon, *The Quest for Spiritual Hunger* (Tulsa: Harrison House, 1987), p. 9.

5 Liardon, *Kuhlman*, p. 63.

6 Lindsay, *Dowie*, p. 45.

7 *Ibid.,* p. 86.

8 Hibbert, pp. 58,59.

9 W. Hacking, *Wigglesworth Remembered* (Tulsa: Harrison House, Inc., 1972), p. 17.

10 *Ibid.,* p. 18.

11 Reidt, p. 24.

12 Webster, s.v. "righteousness"; Thayer, pp. 148,149, entry #1342.

Chapter 11

1 Paul Prather, "Asbury's Sweet, Sweet Spirit," Lexington (Kentucky) *Herald-Leader*, December 23, 1990, p. H1.

2 *Ibid.*

3   Liardon, *Kathryn Kuhlman,* pp. 17,18.

4   *Look* Magazine.

5   Lindsay, *They Saw It Happen*, p. 21.

6   Bartleman, p. 33.

7   *Ibid.*, pp. 35,36.

8   *Ibid.*, pp. 55-57.

9   Reidt, p. 53.

10 *Dictionary*, p. 570

11 Gesenius, p. 371,372, entry #3427. Jay P. Green, sr. ed., *The Interlinear Bible* (Grand Rapids: Baker Book House, 1976-1983), p. 470.

Chapter 12

1   *Holy Bible: New International Version*, footnote to 2 Chronicles 20:26.

2   *The Amplified Bible*, translation of Joshua 6:20.

3   John F. Walford and Roy P. Zuck, *The Bible Knowledge Commentary* (Wheaton: Victor Books, a Division of Scripture Press, 1987), p. 640.

4   R. C. H. Lenski, *Interpretations of St. Paul's Epistles to Galatians, Ephesians and Philippians* (Minneapolis, Minnesota: Augsburg Publishers, 1961), p. 619. Spiritual songs interpreted as *"oide"* means, "Even as the mouth speaks from the abundance of the heart. . . with the richness and abundance of spiritual life 'in' our own 'spirit,' our life is to be so filled that it overflows with spiritual expressions." In other words, that expression is the overflow of our spirit at the moment.

5   Strong, "Hebrew and Chaldee Dictionary," p. 118, entry #8055.

Chapter 13

1   Strong, p. 101, entry #6869; Webster, s.v. "distress"; *King James Version* of Isaiah 37:3.

2   Strong, p. 123, entry #8433.

3   Strong, p. 75, entries #5006, 5007; Gesenius, p. 525.

4 Strong, "Greek Dictionary of the New Testament," p. 35, entry #2227; Thayer, p. 274, entry #2227.

5 Pratney, pp. 191,192.

6 Hacking, p. 18.

7 Based on Strong, p. 36, entry #2293; W. E. Vine, *Vine's Expository Dictionary of New Testament Words* (Old Tappan: Fleming H. Revell, 1940) Vol. I, p. 184; Jerry Savelle, "Shout It Out!" sermon.

8 Savelle.

Chapter 14

1 Lindsay, *Branham*, p. 12.

2 Strong, "Hebrew and Chaldee Dictionary," p. 102, entry #6960.

3 Strong, p. 40, entry #2500.

4 Thayer, p. 383, entry #3076.

5 Thayer, p. 399, entry #3306.

Chapter 15

1 Strong, "Greek Dictionary of the New Testament," p. 24, entry #1382 (KJV "experience," NIV "character").

2 Lindsay, *Dowie*, pp. 186,187.

3 *Ibid.*

4 *Ibid.*, pp. 193,194.

5 *Ibid.*, p. 194.

6 *Ibid.*, p. 205.

7 *Ibid.*, p. 208.

8 Harrell, p. 57.

9 *Ibid.*

10 *Ibid.*, p. 58.

11 Strong, "Hebrew and Chaldee Dictionary," p. 39, entry #2428.

12 Strong, p. 55, #3581.

13 Strong, "Greek Dictionary of the New Testament," p. 77, entry #5500; Thayer, p. 668, entry #5500.

14 *Webster's New Twentieth Century Dictionary Unabridged,* 2d ed. s.v. "integrity."

Chapter 16

1 Strong, "Hebrew and Chaldee Dictionary," p. 45, entry #2896, p. 99, entry #6743, p. 116, entries #7961, 7962, 7965; "Greek Dictionary of the New Testament," p. 33, entry #2137.

2 Lindsay, *Dowie*, p. 200.

3 *Ibid.*, p. 207.

4 *Ibid.*, pp. 243,244.

5 Weaver, pp. 93,94.

6 Weaver, pp. 16,17; *Dictionary*, p. 95; and Harrell, p. 163. Sources say that Branham believed the "Oneness doctrine" (which came out of a 1913 Los Angeles campmeeting), but his unorthodox doctrinal beliefs were not readily apparent until the late Fifties and early Sixties, when he "moved out on the fringes of orthodoxy" (*Dictionary*, p. 96).

7 Harrell, pp. 163,164.

8 *Ibid.*, p. 7.

9 *Ibid.*, pp. 58,237.

10 *Ibid.*, pp. 66,70,71.

11 James Robison, *Thank God I'm Free* (Nashville: Thomas Nelson Publishers, 1988).

12 Hibbert, p. 14.

13 *Ibid.*, p. 15.

14 Reidt, p. 31.

Chapter 17

1 Finney, pp. 73,74.

2 Gesenius, p. 357, entry #3286.

3 Strong, "Hebrew and Chaldee Dictionary," p. 57, entry #3782.

[4]   Lindsay, *Dowie*, p. 84.

[5]   *Ibid.*, pp. 195,196.

[6]   *Ibid.*, p. 196.

[7]   *Ibid.*

[8]   *Ibid.*, p. 197.

[9]   Pratney, pp. 191,192.

[10] Harrell, p. 6.

[11] Reidt, p. 54; *Dictionary*, p. 531.

[12] Reidt, p. 68.

[13] Harrell, pp. 32,33.

[14] Liardon, *Kathryn Kuhlman*, p. 60.

[15] *Ibid.*, p. 73.

[16] Richard Exley, *The Rhythm of Life* (Tulsa: Honor Books, 1987).

[17] Strong, "Greek Dictionary of the New Testament," p. 42, entry #2872.

[18] Strong, p. 11, entries #372, 373 from entries #303 and 3973; Thayer, pp. 496,497, entry #3973.

[19] Strong, p. 112, entries #7673, 7674, 7676, 7677.

Chapter 18

[1]   Albert Barnes, *Barnes' Notes: Vol. 1, Isaiah* (Grand Rapids: Baker Book House, 1951), p. 76.

[2]   Strong, "Hebrew and Chaldee Dictionary," p. 102, entry #6960.

[3]   Strong, p. 40, entries #2498, 2500; Gesenius, p. 282, entry #2498.

[4]   Strong, p. 120, entry #8252.

[5]   Based on *Webster's 7th Collegiate Dictionary*, s.v. "trust."

[6]   Francis Frangipane, *Holiness Truth and the Presence of God*, rev. ed. (Cedar Rapids: Advancing Church Publications, 1991), pp. 101,102.

[7]   *Ibid.*

Chapter 19

[1] Harrell, pp. 63,64.

[2] Ideas for these thoughts were triggered by a conversation with Myles Munroe, Nassau, Bahamas.

[3] Gesenius, entry #935.

[4] Thoughts based on a message delivered by Larry Lea.

[5] *The Almanac of the Christian World* (Wheaton: Tyndale House, 1992), p. 779.

[6] *Ibid.*, p. 788.

Chapter 20

[1] Pratney, p. 217.

[2] Some of these ideas were taken from Mario Murillo's thoughts on Joshua.

Conclusion

[1] Pratney, p. 287.

[2] *Ibid.*, p. 288.

About the Author

Ron McIntosh and his wife, Judy, live in Tulsa, Oklahoma with their three sons — David, Daniel and Jonathan. He holds his highest call to be to his family.

Ron has pastored for 13 years: six years in east Texas and seven years as the campus pastor at Oral Roberts University, where his ministry influenced thousands of young leaders. He has been blessed with an excellent teaching gift and an ability to flow in the Holy Spirit to touch the people.

Ron's ministry has taken him from coast to coast and to several countries of the world. He has also appeared on several television programs, including TBN's "Praise The Lord" show.

With a Master of Divinity degree, he has done extensive study on the principles of revival, from a historical, scriptural and practical basis. Ron's book, *The Quest for Revival,* is an in-depth examination of the key principles to igniting revival in today's believers.

Ron has the ability to teach complicated issues in a simple way to help the people of God grow. Through the years Ron's compassion, integrity and giftings have made him a man genuinely interested in seeing the Spirit of God bring revival to our churches.

To contact the author:

connect@ronmcintoshministries

Harrison House Living Classics

The Quest for Revival
By Ron McIntosh

Questions & Answers on Spiritual Gifts
By Howard Carter

A Diary of Signs and Wonders
By Maria Woodworth-Etter

Holy Ghost Sermons
By Maria Woodworth-Etter

Smith Wigglesworth — A Life Ablaze With the Power of God
By W. Hacking

Smith Wigglesworth — The Secret of His Power
By Albert Hibbert

The Living Classics Gift Series — Heroes of Faith

The Living Classics Gift Series — John G. Lake

Adventures in God (Revised)
By John G. Lake

John G. Lake — A Man Without Compromise
By Wilford Reidt

Smith Wigglesworth — A Man Who Walked With God
By George Stormont

Available from your local bookstore.

HARRISON HOUSE
Tulsa, Oklahoma 74153

In Canada books are available from:
Word Alive
P. O. Box 670
Niverville, Manitoba
CANADA R0A 1E0

The Harrison House Vision

Proclaiming the truth and the power
Of the Gospel of Jesus Christ
With excellence;

Challenging Christians to
Live victoriously,
Grow spiritually,
Know God intimately.